Great

CRIME

More Murder, Mayhem, Booze & Broads

II

Frederick Stonehouse

Avery Color Studios, Inc.
Gwinn, Michigan

ISBN-13: 978-1-892384-40-9
ISBN-10: 1-892384-40-X

Library of Congress Control Number: 2006940489

First Edition–2007

10 9 8 7 6 5 4 3 2 1

Published by Avery Color Studios, Inc.
Gwinn, Michigan 49841

TABLE OF CONTENTS

INTRODUCTION

Great Lakes Crime, Murder, Mayhem, Booze and Broads was a very successful book. So much so began the demand for a "Son of" volume, *More Great Lakes Crime, Murder, Mayhem, Booze and Broads*. Clearly folks just enjoy reading about the seamy side of life, perhaps to experience vicariously activities they would never do themselves.

So it was back to the files for more Great Lakes connected crime. And there is no shortage of it! It's just human nature I guess. Every rock I turned over, keyhole I peeped through and file I opened, the old tales (and a few new ones) came tumbling out.

There are many more Chicago tales, especially during the hey day of Prohibition, certainly a national disaster foisted on America by "holier than thou" evangelical Christian groups desperate to bend honest hard working citizens to their twisted will. As the old saying goes, "The road to hell is paved with good intentions." These Christian groups didn't just pave the road, they built an eight lane Interstate! Bums like Al Capone, Machine Gun McGurn and Killer Burke plus legions of crooked cops, politicians, judges and lawyers used Prohibition to make fortunes, taking the easy money and turning the law into an international joke and corrupting the legal system. The forces of the law were often bought and sold by the various mobsters so commonly it should have been listed on the Stock Exchange! Money fixed any charge or crime. It is often forgotten today that the massive amount of illegal money made during Prohibition funded the great increase in organized crime plaguing America ever since. It was also during Prohibition organized crime wormed it's slimy way into various unions. Once in, you never get the union "de-wormed" either. We had crime and gangs before Prohibition but the great infusion of money allowed them to spawn corruption far wider than ever before.

The book delves into the old American tradition of lynching too. Stringing up a miscreant wasn't an easy as the movies usually made it out to be. Whether a "nice and proper-like" legal hanging or a spur of the moment "launching to eternity" by an angry crowd bent on administering rough justice immediately, there was a real art to doing the deed correctly. Set the noose and/or height drop wrong and the "hangee" slowly strangles to death. Or worse, his head flew off like a ripe coconut. Hanging was an easy concept but hard to do the right way!

Read about some of the great Prohibition era roadhouses around Detroit and Windsor. A few are still standing today, their colorful past sanitized for political correctness. "You mean grandma did WHAT here?"

Some stories will make you laugh, others maybe shutter with horror. All are part of our rich Great Lakes history.

I hope the stories interest you enough to want to learn about our past. I am only able to just skim the surface. Dig deeper and you will be rewarded with a better understanding of a topic often ignored.

Great Lakes MURDER

Was it Murder?

A lightkeeper's life was always assumed to be peaceful and quiet with perhaps a storm or two to break the monotony. But anything could happen. Sometimes there was even a dash of murder most foul!

The light at little Clapperton Island probably should have been named Baker Light considering three generations of the Baker family ended up tending it from 1875 to 1962. Clapperton Island is located off the north coast of Manitoulin Island, Lake Huron. It was built in 1866 to keep ships away from a dangerous shoal called Robertson Rock.

The second keeper was Benjamin Baker. By all accounts he was an excellent worker, intelligent and dependable. No one ever faulted Benjamin for a problem with the light. Reflective perhaps of the mortality of the times, or at least the mortality of marriage, Baker had three wives. He must have been hard on women… or the life of a lightkeeper's wife wasn't something they could endure!

All went along fine until one day in September 1894 when Benjamin's son, Henry, noticed his father's small sailboat drifting past the island. It looked empty of life except for his loyal dog. Alarmed, Henry quickly launched another rowboat and went out to investigate. Benjamin had earlier gone ashore to the small community of Gore Bay for an evening of card playing and an occasional snort of good drink'n whisky. Going to Gore Bay was a common activity for Benjamin. What could have happened to him? When he reached the sailboat Henry discovered a partially filled whisky bottle rolling around on the floor and his father's empty wallet. Since there wasn't a bank anywhere close, it was common for Benjamin to carry a pretty hefty wad of cash with him. What happened to it? He certainly wouldn't have gambled it all away! And more important, where was his father? Did he fall out of the boat and drown? If so, why was the wallet still aboard? He would have carried it in his pocket and not left it lying on the thwart. In spite of the obvious questions, the Canadian authorities never pursued the mystery. Benjamin's body was never found. Given it's potential lake demise, this wasn't unusual. Of course if a rock or a length of chain weighted it down, it wasn't coming up either!

Henry took over the lightkeeping job and just carried on as best he could. He kept the empty wallet and placed the whisky bottle on the shelf in the pantry. Neither he nor his wife drank very much so the bottle sat undisturbed for years. When his wife developed a toothache, Henry suggested she take a good shot of the whisky and swish it around her mouth to see if it would help deaden the throbbing ache. She did so but was struck by a fearsome pain. Was it the raw whisky reacting with the open nerve of an infected tooth or something else? Could the whisky have been poisoned?

Perhaps Benjamin was having a streak of luck at cards and really raking in the cash. Perhaps, too, one of the other players took exception to his uncommon luck and managed to slip some poison into Benjamin's bottle. After taking a healthy swig of the doctored hooch, the lightkeeper felt ill and decided to row back to the island. However on the way to the boat he was robbed and killed. The body was weighted and dumped into the lake and the boat cast adrift, never suspecting it would drift past the lighthouse and his vigilant son. To this day it remains mystery. Was it an accidental death or murder most foul?

Henry Baker was touched by another odd death nearly thirty years later. An Indian from a local reservation, working for him, disappeared in November 1923. The following July his headless body was discovered washed ashore on nearby Bedford Island. Not only was the head missing but also his hands were bound tightly with wire. At the behest of the police, Henry identified what was left. Subsequent police investigation concluded the Indian's wife and stepson killed the man during a domestic squabble. After due consideration it was also found to be in self-defense although the casual reader would conclude the wire bound arms and severed head would point to deliberate murder.[i]

Murder on the Milton D. Ward

Usually when sailors get into a fight it's a short-lived affair. Perhaps the brawl is fueled by booze, or competing for the attention of a "pretty waiter girl." Sharp words are exchanged, maybe even a few punches thrown, but then that's the end of it. A few drinks patch up the problem and everything is fine. It didn't work out that way on the sidewheel steamer *Milton D. Ward.*

For reasons that were never completely clear, two of her sailors, Andrew W. Williamson and David Solemund, were at odds. When the *Milton* moored at Detroit on September 10, 1871, the captain decided it was time to end the problem. He paid off Williamson and fired him, as was his choice.

The following night Williamson found Solemund in a local saloon and lit into him with his fists flying. Williamson had been drinking for some time and was fired with the courage only John Barleycorn can provide. Solemund would take none of Williamson's abuse and soon the pair was out on the dusty street. Since Solemund was sober and Williamson snockered, the former didn't take long to "clean" Williamson's "clock" leaving him lying bleeding and battered in the dusty street.

Williamson may have been beaten fair and square but he wasn't out. He swore he would get even with Solemund! It was a threat Solemund didn't take seriously enough.

Just before midnight Williamson was lurking in the shadows on the dock. The *Ward* was due to sail soon and her crew was busy preparing her for departure. Solemund was working on deck. Williamson quietly walked up the gangway and aboard the steamer, a large knife grasped in his right hand. Before Solemund knew what was happening, Williamson stabbed him twice in the chest and ran off. Solemund fell to the deck and a large puddle of blood stained the wood beneath him. Sticking out of his heart was the hilt of Williamson's knife!

Police later arrested Williamson at his boarding house. It was reported they found him lying in his bed with his eyes open staring vacantly upward. It was nothing short of cold-blooded murder. Since Michigan didn't have the death penalty, the murderer was just shipped to prison.[ii]

The Murdered Priest

When we think of the days of the French voyageurs and explorers, we have visions of birch bark canoes gliding effortlessly along placid waters as Indian guides show the magnificence of the New World to the citizens of the old. We don't think of murder or deadly love triangles with the lifeless body of a priest stuffed into a hollow tree the result.

The priest was called Frere Constantin but it wasn't always his name. He was born to a privileged family named Del Halle in Florence. By most standards his life was perfect. He had money, social status and was engaged to a beautiful young girl from an equally privileged family. His world was ideal. Until he awoke one morning to discover the infamous Black Death arrived during the night, killing his bride-to-be and both parents. In a single stroke his wonderful world collapsed.

With his world destroyed, he fled into the priesthood to search for the next. He fled reality into a world of the supernatural. After a decade of religious service and study, he was sent to Montreal for missionary work in the New World. There he met a young soldier named La Mothe Cadillac. The two became friends, and when Cadillac hatched a plan to establish a fort at Detroit, the priest now called Frere Constantin, joined his group. The small force, consisting of 50 soldiers with an equal number of civilians, left Montreal on June 5, 1701, arriving at Detroit on July 24.

All was peaceful at the new post for a while at least. Just outside the new Fort Pontchartrain was a Pottawatomie Indian camp. Unknown to all, it contained the seeds of the priest's murder.

It seems the keeper of the king's storehouse, Etienne Veron de Grandmensil, a young man of hot blood, fell in love with the beautiful daughter of the local Pottawatomie chief. He wanted desperately to marry her but the chief forbade it. The love struck Frenchman was of course a Christian, while she still worshiped the Indian Manitou. In spite of the priest's best efforts, the Pottawatomie refused conversion to the white man's god. A prophet had "seen" that if the tribe abandoned the old god, disaster would befall them. They would be scattered to the winds, their wigwams burned and the tribe destroyed. Regardless of Frere Constantin's endeavors, the Indians would not renounce the old gods.

This created a major problem for Veron. If his Indian princess would not become a Christian, allowing a marriage sanctioned by the church, then he must accept a native rite. To his view whoever sanctified the union was unimportant. He loved his Indian maid and she, him. What more could there be? He sought Frere Constantin's counsel but the priest was steadfast. If Veron went over to the Indians he would be excommunicated, thrown out of the Catholic Church! No slack was allowed. In today's parlance, it was the priest's way or the highway!

Meanwhile the Indian maiden was overwhelmed by the entire situation. Not only was the religious issue perplexing, but also her father was pressing her hard to marry a young Indian brave of her own tribe! She didn't love the brave. She loved Veron! What was she to do? After searching her heart she could fine no way out of her conundrum. Late one night, she slipped out of her wigwam and went down to the river. After stripping off her buckskin shift and piling it neatly on the beach, she swam far offshore and surrendered to the cold dark waters. Her lifeless body was discovered several days later. Her father and Veron were overcome with grief.

At this time Frere Constantin was called away to another mission. After conducting his business he left to return to Detroit overland. He never arrived. Parties of travelers who departed after he did made the trip without incident. They also saw no sign of the missing priest. What could have happened to him?

After a time, stories began to circulate about a haunted spot where the Savoyard stream crossed the northbound trail. It was claimed every morning the faint sound of a bell echoed in the trees and hushed sounds of mass could be heard whispering in the moving grass.

Soon after a brave came to the fort and asked Cadillac to come to the Indian camp. The old chief was dying and wanted to speak with him. A hunting party found the chief lying near death in the woods and carried him back to his wigwam. The chief confessed to Cadillac he murdered Frere Constantin in revenge for his daughter's death. The priest's constant preaching to the Indians about conversion, and refusal to allow Veron to marry the girl, was spiteful and evil. Does not the Bible say "an eye for and eye?" And did not the hated priest cause his daughter's death? Then the bastard deserved to die!

The chief also said he knew no peace since the killing. The spirit of the priest was haunting him. He heard the priest's voice in the forest and when he went to the place of the murder on moonlit nights, he saw his evil ghost standing silently on the path with his arms outstretched, beseeching the chief to have his bones buried in consecrated ground. Until this happened the chief would suffer his haunting. The priest's magic was strong. What could the old chief do but obey?

When Cadillac went to the spot the chief indicated, he found the priest's body hidden in a hollow tree trunk and covered with leaves. Once the body was properly laid to rest in holy ground, the haunting stopped.[iii]

The Disappearance of William Morgan

Private organizations are always subject to rumor; kind of a "if I don't know what they are doing, it must be bad" thought process. The Masons fall into this trap. For hundreds of years people have blamed them for every conceivable social ill from the crucifixion to the assassination of John F. Kennedy. Conspiracy theorists connected Masons with the Knights Templar, Priority of Zion, priests of ancient Egypt, Jack the Ripper and even the CIA. A fertile imagination fueled by a raving paranoia knows no bounds.

In reality Freemasons in North America contribute over two million dollars a day to charities such as children's hospitals, especially burn units, with the beneficiaries often having no affiliation with Freemasonry. The tenets of Freemasonry stress social responsibility and community involvement.

As a private organization the Masons do maintain "secret" rites and therein was a problem known as the "Morgan Affair." Determining what actually happened is impossible today so what follows is a reasonable version I believe to be generally accurate.

The incident sparked a wave of anti-Mason feeling and may well have been contrived solely for that purpose. The tale revolves around William Morgan, a resident of Batavia, New York. He immigrated to Batavia from Virginia in 1824 and claimed to have served with distinction in the War of 1812. He either joined, or attempted to join, the local Masonic Lodge. Regardless, he quarreled with its members and left, threatening to release a book he wrote describing the secret Masonic rites. Supposedly a local newspaper publisher, David C. Miller, smelling a bestseller, gave him a large advance and promised to publish the exposé.

Upset at his trickery, the Batavia Masonic Lodge published a newspaper advertisement denouncing Morgan. When he wasn't dissuaded from publishing the book, a group of lodge members claimed he owed them money and on September 11, 1826, had him arrested for debt in Batavia. Since the law required his jailing until the debt was paid, and Morgan in jail meant no book to publish, Miller, the newspaper owner, paid Morgan's way out. Morgan was quickly arrested and jailed again for other bad debts but this time in Canandaigua, New York. Again someone appeared at the jail with enough cash to satisfy his debt but since Morgan claimed he didn't know him, he was hesitant to accept his gratuity. But since getting out of jail is better than being behind bars, he reluctantly accepted the release. When Morgan walked out of jail the stranger was waiting for him in a closed carriage. Again Morgan was reluctant to get in but apparently was forced inside by other men. After a quick snap of the reins, the carriage quickly trotted away with Morgan calling loudly for help. His pleas were ignored by passersby.

The following day the carriage arrived at Fort Niagara, an abandoned fort on the U.S.-Canadian border. The caretaker left in charge of the post was a Freemason and he allowed the kidnappers to lock Morgan in the old powder magazine.

After a short time, perhaps a couple of days, Morgan was taken by boat to Canada and offered to a group of Canadian Masons who refused to take him. No one wanted to be involved with such a despicable character. He apparently was returned to the ad hoc magazine, jail and later disappeared between September 17-21.

Stories later circulated that the Batavia Masons wrapped Morgan in chains, took him to the middle of the river and dumped him into the swift current. Whether the body was ever recovered is unknown. A body did come ashore a few weeks later but a woman identified it as her husband and not Morgan. However conspiracy folks questioned her identification. No Morgan meant no crime. As long as his body didn't show up his death couldn't be proved. Therefore the body really was Morgan and the woman obviously paid off by the Masons to say it was her husband.

The Freemasons maintained Morgan certainly wasn't harmed but rather was paid a $500 bribe to just quit the country. Meanwhile Miller decided to publish Morgan's book, which became a best seller. Everyone likes a good "conspiracy" tale and Morgan's book spun a good one. Some folks in fact thought the whole "Morgan Murder" was just a publicity stunt rigged up by Miller and Morgan. One theory maintained Morgan moved to Albany, Canada or the Cayman Islands, an impressive array of possibilities. One variation claimed he was even eventually hung as a pirate! Some research has pointed toward his marrying a Cayman Island girl and raising a family in Honduras where he died in the 1860s. To help solve the mystery, DeWitt Clinton, the Governor of New York and a Mason, offered a reward of $2,000, a considerable amount of money for the time, to whoever could unravel the disappearance. No one ever claimed the reward.

The men involved in the kidnapping from the jail were sentenced to less than a year in prison. At the time kidnapping was not a felony but only a misdemeanor.

Regardless of the truth of the matter, Morgan's "kidnapping" produced a mass of protests against the evil of Masonic lodges. A large part was politically driven attacks against Andrew Jackson, who was a Mason and would be elected President in 1829. Attacking the Masons was a way of attacking Jackson.

Regardless of whatever happed to Morgan, his first wife eventually married Joseph Smith, becoming one of the Mormon's many, many wives. After a time the courts declared Morgan dead even without a body, allowing her to follow her dreams (or nightmares) and marry-up with old Joe. The cult couldn't let Morgan's soul rest in peace and reportedly he was one of the first official (and infamous) Mormon postmortem baptisms, likely at the requesting of his meddling wife. As with all of these bogus baptisms, no one ever asked whether the "baptisee" wanted the "honor."[iv]

More Murder

The conflict between Indian and European cultures not only was sometimes bloody, but depending on an individual's role, emotionally difficult. It wasn't uncommon for European women and children to be kidnapped during Indian raids and "adopted" into the tribe. After a time the "Stockholm Syndrome" took effect and they "became" Indian, identifying completely with their captors. Sometimes they developed a kind of split personality, moving easily between the two cultures.

John Tanner was kidnapped as a child and raised by the Ojibwa.

The case of John Tanner is a good example. He was kidnapped as a child and grew to manhood among the Ojibwa eventually marrying an Indian maiden and siring several children. In 1820 he moved his family to Mackinac Island. At this point he switched from being Indian back to European, changing his dress and mannerisms as did his wife. Neither however was happy in their new environment.

Tanner didn't stay at the Island but moved freely about the Midwest. Reportedly, he traveled to Kentucky and the Red River area before eventually becoming an interpreter for the government agency at the Sault.

When James Schoolcraft, the brother of Henry Schoolcraft the famous Indian Agent at the Sault, was murdered in an ambush on July 6, 1846, it was thought Tanner did the deed since he disappeared at the same time. Since Tanner reportedly burned his own house down the day before, the circumstances were confused at best. Did he torch his own home as a way of protesting against the Europeans? No motive for the murder was ever promulgated nor was Tanner definitely tied to it. Regardless of the facts, Tanner was considered the killer and never apprehended.

For many years commercial fishing was a very important business on the Great Lakes. It was intensely competitive between not only fishermen but governments too! U.S. fishermen sometimes "poached" on the Canadian side of the line and Canadian fishermen crossed to American waters too. Both nationalities felt the fish knew no border so why should the fishermen?

Government regulators often tangled with fishermen as they tried to enforce the law. Sometimes the outcome was deadly.

In 1863 the Canadian fisheries overseer for the Lakes Huron and Superior was at Manitoulin Island trying to resolve a leasing dispute between two fishermen when the emotional situation apparently boiled over. He ended up "disappearing" at night from the boat in which he was returning south to Collingwood. His body came ashore several days later. Although a coroner's jury ruled it was death by murder, the killer was never found.[v]

Accident or Murder?

Sometimes murder is suspected but not proven. Everything points that way. It all lines up – motive, opportunity and means but the final proof is missing. So was it really murder or just a remarkable coincidence? Without a "smoking gun" it is impossible to be certain and the truth will never be known. A good example is the Dodge Affair on Manitoulin Island in northern Lake Huron.

The Dodge family of automotive fame had a vacation lodge on the island for many years. It wasn't a mansion by any means, but was a comfortable family retreat far from the pressures of the Detroit business and social scene.

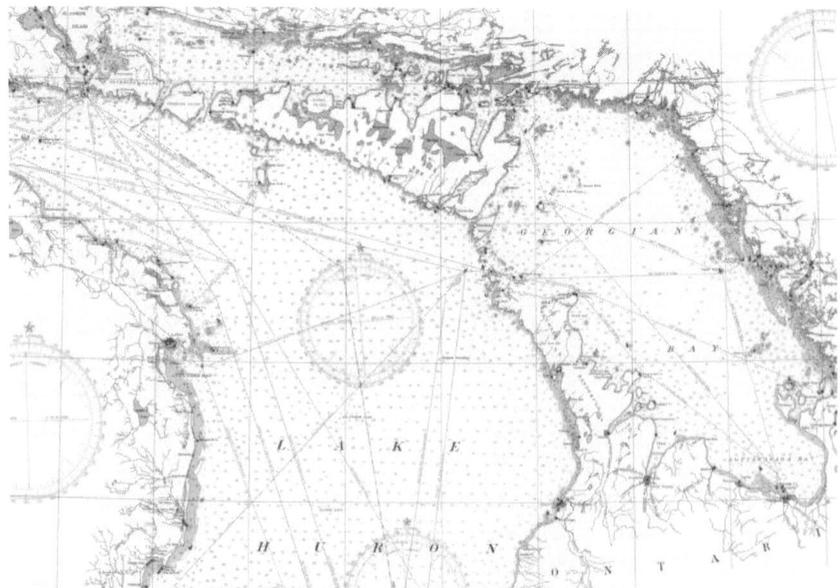

Manitoulin Island is in northern Lake Huron.

Danny and Annie Dodge

The victim of the murder or accident was Daniel George Dodge although everyone just called him Danny. He was the son of John Dodge, one of the founders of the company. John was deceased at the time of Danny's demise. Danny was known as a quiet youth, finding his chief pleasure in tinkering with his airplanes and boats. He was the youngest living child of John, and besides his sister had two half sisters and a half brother from his father's earlier marriage.

The lodge was at Maple Point, just down from the sleepy little village of Kagawong. Danny spent his summers at the island and in many regards, grew up there. He palled around with the local boys and since he had a fast red convertible and speedboat, was always available to give rides. The rich boy had all the toys.

Danny fell in love with an island girl, Annie Lorraine MacDonald, the local telephone operator and daughter of a retired tugboat captain. He knew her for three years and frequently flew his plane up from Detroit to just to visit. After a time he proposed and she accepted. She was 19 at the time of their marriage and he, 21. Neither family was happy with the match. Danny's side thought she was nothing but a gold digger, ready to latch on to a real "meal ticket." After all, Danny was the heir to a reputed $9 million share of the family fortune and a prime catch for any young woman. Annie's side believed she would be happier with someone in her own social set and background. On August 2, 1938 they were married at Meadowbrook Hall in Rochester Hills, Michigan, in metro Detroit. They returned to the lodge to honeymoon.

Their ceremony was in sharp contrast to that of Danny's sister Frances in the same mansion a month before. More than 800 guests crowded the mansion for her wedding. Danny and Annie had virtually none. A single bridesmaid, her sister, attended her. A mechanical organ provided the wedding march. Since her mother was reportedly ill, neither she nor her father attended. No advance warning was given or formal public announcement until after the fact. This was most unusual for a family as powerful and socially prominent as the Dodge clan.

Annie soon made changes at the lodge, firing the old caretaker and hiring three of her friends instead. Of course this was a new wife's prerogative but in retrospect, it also could be seen as a way to set up the subsequent "accident."

Whether accident or murder, it happened on August 15. There are two versions of the story. In the first, Danny was bored and went into the garage with his new pals to see what they could find for entertainment. Glory be, he finds a box of dynamite sticks complete with blasting caps and fuse! Being a red-blooded American boy he crimps a fuse to the cap, jams the cap into a stick, lights the fuse and throws it out the window to see what happens. The result is a very satisfactory "Boom." Soon everyone is joining in, tossing lit dynamite charges out the window and enjoying the "booms." His new wife is watching appreciatively from the doorway. She sure got a good one with Danny! As luck would have it, one of the charges Danny throws out the window, doesn't. It hits the frame and bounces back inside where it explodes, setting off the box of blasting caps for good measure.

A variation of the story claims Danny was in the garage alone when he discovered the dynamite. After setting up the charge and lighting the fuse he tossed it out the door. When the explosion startled the people in the lodge, they came running over to see what was going on. Meanwhile Danny had rigged a second charge and lit the fuse. As he started to toss it out the door, his wife and friends unexpectedly appeared in it. Since he can't throw it that way, and not thinking fast enough to simply pull the fuse out, he tries to pitch the charge out an open window but his aim is off and it hits the frame and bounces back inside the garage where it explodes. A third variation is that the trailing sparks from the fuse fell on the pile of seven or eight dynamite sticks, fuse and caps on the work bench resulting in an explosion.

Regardless Danny is terribly injured. Some reports suggested he was near death with his left arm hanging in shreds. One of his pals, Lloyd Bryant, is also badly injured. Two others are also wounded but not as seriously. The flying glass and splinters also struck Annie in her head, right arm and leg.

The reason is unclear but the decision was made to take the speedboat to Little Current, the nearest place with a doctor. Perhaps they thought the road was too rough for Danny and Lloyd to survive the trip.

Under good conditions the run to Little Current could be made in 40 minutes in the 250 horsepower boat but the lake was riled by four-foot waves. Regardless, the wounded were loaded into the boat and headed out. Annie took the wheel since she knew the waters and also seemed the most in control of the situation.

The going was very difficult. After two hours of smashing through the waves they were still 40 minutes from Little Current. Annie slowed to turn the wheel over to one of the men when Danny suddenly goes over the side. A witness in the boat later claimed Annie tried to go in after him. The boat quickly turned back to pick him up but he was already gone. They looked for Danny for ten minutes without success before turning and continuing on to Little Current and medical attention for the badly wounded Lloyd Bryant. Initially little hope was held out for Bryant, who suffered internal injury as well as wounds to his arms and legs, but he eventually made a full recovery. Annie's wounds eventually required plastic surgery.

When initial efforts failed to recover Danny's body, the Dodge family flew specialized equipment up to Manitoulin Island in their Sikorsky amphibian along with two Detroit police officers from the harbor patrol and a nurse. Dragooning police support was a prerogative of money and influence and the Dodges had plenty of both. The area where Danny sank is deep and currents swift, complicating the recovery regardless of the new equipment or police presence. Persistent work by local fishermen finally paid off, recovering Danny's body 23 days after his death.

Perhaps motivated by a tinge of suspicion but certainly by the high profile nature of the death, the Ontario Attorney General's office sent an inspector from their criminal investigation branch to attend the local inquest. In October the coroner's jury in Little Current ruled "accidental death by drowning." No official action was ever taken to dispute the ruling.

If Danny's death was ugly, it was nothing compared to the wild speculation concerning it. Some folks believed Annie had planned the whole thing. She was just a good for nothing gold-digger after his money. Maybe she planned the explosion. Or maybe she took advantage of the opportunity it offered? Only the people on the boat know whether Danny "accidentally" fell overboard or was "accidentally" pushed. Was Danny so desperate for relief from the terrible pain of his wounds he just jumped into the lake to end it all? A local doctor suggested the shock of the injuries, "...may have led to a temporary derangement and in delirium the unfortunate man leaped overboard." We will never know the true answers.

Annie eventually inherited $1.25 million but only after a long court fight by the Dodge family. The rich don't give up money easily, which after all is why they are rich. Danny would not have received the bulk of his inheritance, which was tied up in a trust until age 25.

So was it murder or accident? You be the judge.[vi]

Dr. Holmes I Presume?

Not only is Chicago given credit for the first "knockout drops", aka the "Mickey Finn," and the first large mirror mounted over a doxie's bed to enhance client visual effect, but also as the home of America's generally recognized first serial killer, Dr. H. H. Holmes.

When the police finally nabbed the fiend, some investigators estimated he murdered 200 men, women and children. The true total will never be known. He wrote not only a new chapter in Chicago crime, but American criminal behavior too!

Holmes was apparently spawned in Gilmantown, New Hampshire on May 16, 1860 and tagged with the moniker Herman Webster Mudgett. He would adopt his

Holmes is considered the first mass murderer in American history

Holmes alias later. Other names he used were numerous and there is no certainty all were ever identified. At a minimum he, at one time or another, went by: Henry Howard Holmes, H.M. Howard, Harry (Henry) Gordon, Edward Hatch, J.A. Judson, Alexander E. Cook, A.C. Hayes, George H. Howell, G.D. Hale and Mr. Hall. His tale of terror has numerous variations and the complete truth will never be fully determined. What follows is a reasonable adaptation of the truth, as least as we know it.

As a young man Mudgett was considered very bright and apparently fascinated with surgery. It also was claimed he captured stray animals and performed all sorts of vicious experiments on them. Certainly this was a disturbing trend and a clear indication of his demented personality. After high school he married Clara Loveringat, the daughter of a local farmer. She was one of the few women to come close to him and survive. It was claimed he attended the University of Michigan Medical School and made extra cash by stealing bodies from the dissecting laboratory, mutilating them and passing them off as the victims of terrible accidents after he insured them. Of course he was the beneficiary of the policies. The scam worked well until a night watchman caught him removing a female corpse, resulting in his expulsion. There was a suggestion he was doing more with the body than a simple insurance fraud but nothing was ever proved.

For unclear reasons, he sent Clara back to New Hampshire and went wandering about the country. Where he was is unknown but for a time he was in St. Paul, Minnesota and later taught school in Clinton, New York. While teaching he boarded with a local farmer. After seducing the farmer's wife he skipped town leaving her pregnant. To add insult to injury, he never even paid the farmer for his "rent" assuming, I suppose, his "deposit" was sufficient to cover arrears. He arrived in Wilmette, a north suburb of Chicago in 1885. There he married Myrta Belknap, the daughter of a wealthy businessman. Strangely she continued to live in Wilmette while he took rooms in Chicago. Perhaps feeling Holmes was continuing to chase other women, she divorced him in 1889. Prior to the divorce Holmes attempted a swindle on her father which doubtless soured family relations a bit.

While Holmes was undoubtedly insane, catching him was pure luck.

After failing at a downtown business, he showed up in Englewood, Illinois, just south of Chicago. Apparently he decided to seek work as a druggist. Finding a likely store, he walked in and introduced himself as Dr. Henry H. Holmes. As luck would have it, the pharmacist was dying and his elderly wife was trying to run the store alone. Desperately overworked, she thanked her guardian angel and hired Holmes on the spot.

Holmes was an instant success. He was very excellent with customers and his good looks went a long way to gaining new ones among the neighborhood ladies. With his stylish "walrus" mustache and dapper little derby he was the epitome of men's fashion. When Holmes offered to buy the store after the druggist's death, the widow was overjoyed but only with the condition she be allowed to live upstairs. She considered herself too set to move to a new apartment. Holmes agreed with her terms.

The only problem was he never paid her a plug nickel or thin dime or anything else. With no other recourse, she started legal action against him. Likely Holmes thought about his problem for a bit and then just as luck would have it, she disappeared. Folks who asked about her whereabouts were told she moved to California. Holmes of course just chalked up another victim.

It is likely the neighborhood gals who so frequented the store didn't realize Holmes was already married, twice in fact! They thought he would be a good catch for one of them. While the local beauties fluttered about trying to entice his wandering eye, he continued to prosper, selling a variety of his own "elixir cures" by mail order.

Doubtless bored with the opportunities offered by the lowly drug store, and certainly with a pile of cash made from it's successful operation, he began to dream of something bigger and better. After due consideration he bought the lot across the block and built a new building designed by him for his nefarious purposes. Work on his new structure began in 1888, the same year "Jack the Ripper" started stalking victims in the fog shrouded back alleys of White Chapel. Jack was just a minor league killer compared to Holmes!

The three story Holmes house of horror burned to destruction shortly after his arrest.

Finished in 1892, the three-story building was unique in the world. There certainly was nothing like it anywhere else. It was his private castle of horror. No one knew what secrets it hid since he kept changing workmen. After a week or so of their labor he would fire them, claiming they were doing poor work for him. And of course he never paid them for what they did since bad work didn't deserve pay!

Various descriptions of the villainous castle appeared in the press following his ultimate apprehension. What follows is a reasonable compilation of the tales. The lower floor was setup for retail shops and was standard in design, containing a restaurant, jewelry store and candy shop. The upper two floors were far different and much more sinister. There were 35 guest rooms, half fitted out normally for use by the people working for Holmes. The others were much different, each soundproofed with doors only locking from the outside; gas pipes leading into a special room with the controls in a closet in Holmes' private apartment. Human size greased chutes ran from the special room to the basement too.

Holmes' office on the third floor had a large walk in vault and oversized stove. The basement contained a huge tank filled with acid, perfect for destroying bodily tissue, a dissecting table and crematorium.

Throughout the upper floors were trap doors, secret passageways, stairs leading nowhere and doors opening to brick walls. It made no sense to anyone but Holmes.

With his castle ready to go, Holmes went to work. His first victim may have been Julia Conner, the wife of his jewelry store manager. Holmes managed to seduce Julia away from her husband who soon divorced her and left. When Julia became pregnant, Holmes convinced her to let him do an abortion; after all he was a "doctor." She showed up at the Hahnemann Medical School as a skeleton in a couple of months. The medical school paid Holmes $36 for the excellent specimen. Her three-year-old daughter, Pearl, who remained with Julia when her husband left, never showed up until much later but she was in no condition to ever testify.

About this time Holmes seduced beautiful young Emmaline Cigrand, a local stenographer. He soon sold another excellent skeleton, this time to LaSalle Medical School.

Holmes went into high gear for the 1893 Chicago World's Fair. The festival grounds were just a convenient train ride away from his castle. A little advertising of inexpensive lodging and his castle was filled with eager customers. Just go to his office, turn on the gas, wait a decent interval and walk down to their room. Dump the body and personal effects down the chute to the basement and the room was ready for another rental. In the basement he could either take his leisure with a slow dissection and disposal of the remains and personal effects in the crematorium or acid vat. If he was too tired to work, he just burned everything. Some experts suggest 50 fair goers never made it home, taking a permanent detour through Holmes' evil castle of deathly delights.

Holmes just didn't rely on the fair as a way to fill his empty guest rooms. He also advertised in small town newspapers offering lucrative jobs for young ladies. When he received a reply he suggested several positions were open but she would have to come and interview for them. He had a great "line" since he usually convinced them to empty their bank accounts and keep the name of the employer secret, even from their family. Once the victim arrived, she was all but dead.

In other instances he placed advertisements looking for a marriage partner. When potential wives came for a visit, he tortured them in his especially equipped basement to find out if they had any valuables, and then murdered them.

The fair didn't run forever and after it closed, Holmes decided he needed to raise some additional money. Running a murder castle wasn't cheap and neither was being the dapper dandy about town. Considering his previous success with insurance fraud, it seemed to be a good scam to run again. He convinced his assistant, Benjamin Pitezel, to give him a hand. He would insure Pitezel for $10,000, naming Mrs. Pitezel as the beneficiary. Pitezel would "die," his wife would collect and they would split the money. Since Pitezel had already "helped" in a number of murders, what was a little insurance scam? The three agreed to the plan and Holmes and Pitezel went off to Philadelphia to fake the death. Why Philadelphia was selected was never clear but it led to Holmes, eventual undoing.

Benjamin Pietzel was Holmes' partner until he murdered him as part of an insurance scam.

Holmes also changed the plan in one critical detail without telling Pitezel or his wife. Pitezel's death would not be faked. Pitezel was a loyal assistant. Why Holmes decided to "cash him in" is also unclear. Once the assistant turned up stiff, the "body" needed to be identified and since Mrs. Pitezel had a sick child at home, she sent her 15-year-old daughter, Alice, with Holmes to do it. It was a horrendously bad move. Holmes in turn killed Alice as well as her sister and brother, stashing the bodies in the basements of different houses he rented in the Philadelphia area.

Acting on a tip, the insurance company decided to investigate. Six weeks later the Pinkerton Agency nabbed Holmes, returning him to Philadelphia for trial. Luck was still on Holmes side however. All the local authorities knew anything about was the insurance fraud involving Pietzel. While it was a serious charge with a term in the state pen on conviction, it was nothing in comparison to his actual crimes. The authorities had no idea of the true horrors perpetrated by the mild mannered doctor.

A Philadelphia detective named Frank Geyer however was curious about the missing Pietzel children and started to investigate. Their mother had no idea the doctor had murdered them too! It didn't take long for him to find their remains and identify Holmes as the killer.

Chilled by the discoveries of the Philadelphia detective, authorities finally entered the Chicago castle and found a chamber of horrors beyond anything ever seen in America. They found part of a human body in his office stove. The skeleton of a young child, likely Pearl Conners, the daughter of his former jewelry manager, was found lying forlornly in a basement corner. The more the police looked, the more they found, and gradually all of the dreadful secrets of the house were discovered. Piles of human bones were literally heaped everywhere in the basement. There were also racks of surgical instruments and special torturing devices hanging from the walls. One instrument was identified as an "elasticity determinator," a contrivance designed according to Holmes, to stretch subjects to twice their natural length. Several quicklime pits were available to dispose of excess "tissue." On August 19, the castle burned to the ground. When a gas can was discovered in the debris, it was ruled arson, but whether by an accomplice afraid of evidence not yet found, an outraged neighbor or victims, family member is unknown.

Detective Frank Geyer nabbed Holmes for the Philadelphia area murders.

When the police carefully worked through their list of missing persons, they found name after name once associated with Holmes. Women who had an innocent lunch with him were murdered and disposed of forever. Men who worked for him disappeared in the crematorium too. The newspapers had a field day. There was nothing they could compare it to! Any description was far too mild to explain the hell of Holmes and his wicked castle.

Regardless of what the Englewood Police found, the Philadelphia authorities were going to try Holmes first. They had him cold for the murder of Benjamin Pitezel and justice would be served. During the trial Holmes admitted to 27 murders but since some of his admitted victims later showed up alive and well, his veracity is questionable. The trial lasted a mere five days but every day brought sensational headlines in the papers.

While held in Moyamensing Prison in downtown Philadelphia, he made a last minute conversion to Catholicism and claimed he was the devil reborn. No one could dispute the boast based on his vicious actions.

He did write a long, convoluted confession, which was later published. He showed no remorse for the women he murdered, but did mention, "There were two particularly sad deaths, both on account of the victims being exceptionally upright and virtuous women and because one woman, had she lived, would have soon become a mother."

He was hung on May 7, 1896; dancing the "Texas Two Step" as the old time rangers used to say. He was 35 years old. The huge crowd that showed up for the hanging had to be held back by police. There was nothing they could see since the execution proper was inside the prison walls. It was all morbid fascination, to be there when the devil was sent back to hell. As protocol a small number of tickets to the actual execution were provided to official witnesses, prison officials and members of the press. When the doors opened twice that number forced their way inside to see the devil swing.

Standing on the gallows Holmes made a short statement of innocence, claiming he did not kill Pitezel or his children. When the official executioner's hands trembled a bit, he gallantly told him to "Take your time old man."

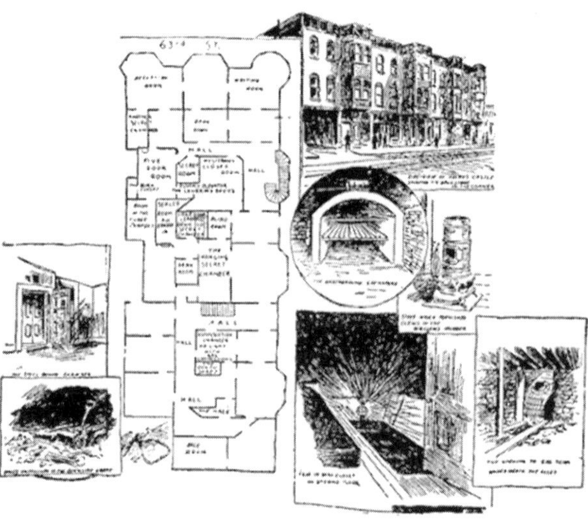

A diagram of horror castle shows a glimpse of its diabolical design.

His weirdness didn't stop with his death. In accordance with his wishes, the bottom of his casket was filled with cement and his remains dropped inside before another load of cement completely filled the container. After being nailed shut it was buried ten feet deep. Two more feet of cement were dumped into the grave before the hole was filled with dirt. Evidently Holmes was desperately afraid of having his body stolen by grave robbers. Burial was at a Holy Cross Cemetery. There is no headstone or marker of any kind. Only a patch of grass marks the spot where the fiend still lurks.

By any standard of humanity, Holmes was the devil reincarnate. And he did his worst work in Chicago![vii]

The Woman in Red

One of the most famous Chicago crime tales involves the infamous "woman in red." It is a love story (kind of anyway), treachery, murder and ultimately mystery. As with most tales of this kind, there are many differing versions favoring varying viewpoints of the incident. The following one is a reasonable variant.

John Dillinger was the "Number One" criminal of his time. In fact good old J. Edgar Hoover himself named John as "Public Enemy Number One." For a short time in the 1930s Dillinger and his gang of reprobates terrorized the forces of law and order as they cut a bloody swath through America's heartland. Since it was the depths of the Great Depression, and the Dillinger gang was stealing money from "rich" banks, (and only gunning down a comparatively few innocent people along the way) a considerable segment of the population lionized him. Reading about Dillinger leading Keystone Kops on chases over hill and dale was great entertainment. That Dillinger and his gang were nothing but a bunch of cheap thugs willing to murder innocent people for a few dollars didn't make any difference to many folks who saw him as a reincarnation of Robin Hood with a twist. Dillinger kept all the loot. He didn't give a nickel away to anyone. This was all heady stuff for the 1930s.

J. Edgar Hoover called Dillinger "Public Enemy No. 1."

Dillinger began his criminal career in 1925 when he held up a grocery store in his hometown of Mooresville, Indiana. Robbing a store in your own hometown wasn't the brightest move Dillinger ever made, but then again he would never be accused of being overly smart. The cops nailed him without much effort and an irritated judge shipped his sorry butt off to spend the next eight years in state prison. He wasn't released until May 1933. Dillinger must have found something worthwhile behind bars since he decided as soon as he hit the street it was off to play cops and robbers again.

A wild spree of bank robberies and murder followed his entry back into civil society. In a little over 14 months he and his vicious mob knocked off 11 banks, brutally murdered four law enforcement officers and another four totally innocent bystanders. The Dillinger gang cut a wide and bloody path throughout the Midwest. Along the way they shot their way out of half a dozen police ambushes and escaped twice from jail. Once when he was caught and thrown into the "escape proof" prison in Lima, Ohio, his gang quickly broke him out. Nabbed again, he "phonied" up a gun out of a bar of soap, using it to escape from the Crown Point, Indiana jail. Since 50 guards, armed citizens and a contingent of the National Guard were supposedly protecting the jail, the escape garnered national attention. He fed on the publicity like a shark on swimmers.

Dillinger was a flamboyant crook, which was part of the reason he became a public hero. He usually dressed in a stylish straw "boater" hat and often

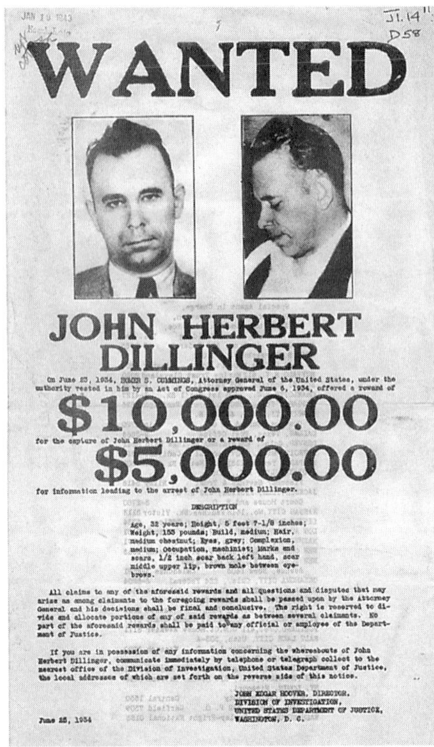

A reward poster for Dillinger.

leaped over the teller's bars to get to the cash stashed behind. Occasionally he wore a bulletproof vest, adding to his legend of invincibility when police bullets allegedly bounced off him.

His gang usually included a few girlfriends and other well known killers. For a time trigger-happy murderer, "Baby-Face Nelson," aka Lester Gillis, ran with Dillinger. The gang was innovative. Once, when chased by the police, they threw handfuls of nails on the road behind them to puncture tires of chasing police cars. When their car was too shot up to keep running, the gang calmly stole another one. It was said they preferred Packard's for their speed and handling, an endorsement the auto company likely looked at with mixed emotions. The gang wasn't above putting innocent hostages on the running boards to act as human shields. When they ran low on guns and ammo, they just knocked off a handy police station.

If pursuit by the cops got too hot, the gang went into hiding. Once Dillinger and his girlfriend (in popular gangland slang, a moll) hid out at his old Mooresville, Indiana home. Another time he and a gang member made the long run up to Sault Ste Marie, Michigan to hole up with the companion's sister. They weren't there long before the FBI was tipped off but by the time agents arrived, the pair had "blown" town.

The pressure was on the Dillinger gang. J. Edgar had thrown the full force of the FBI against his apprehension. Public Enemy Number One had to be brought to justice! Edgar said so!

In an effort to disguise his well-known appearance, Dillinger's mouthpiece (lawyer) found a disreputable plastic surgeon willing to do the job. On May 27 the doctor and an assistant operated on him with mixed results. They were supposed to eliminate the distinctive cleft in his chin, some moles and a scar. When the pair finished, he looked a little different but he wasn't a "new" man. A couple of days later they tried to alter his fingerprints with little effect.

On June 30 Dillinger and his gang tried to knock off a bank in South Bend, Indiana. The effort quickly went sour. One of the gang members was severely wounded and a local cop was killed in a shootout. The take was a mere $4,800, peanuts compared to the riches they hoped for.

Anna Sage, the infamous "lady in red," set up Dillinger for the FBI.

Dillinger quickly went underground in Chicago, holing up with a new girlfriend, Polly Hamilton, and using the alias Jimmy Lawrence. His new girl rented a room from a Rumanian immigrant named Anna Sage, who was facing deportation for running bordellos in Gary and East Chicago. Anna recognized Polly's new beau as Dillinger and went to a crooked East Chicago police sergeant she knew offering to make a deal. If the deportation charges were dropped she promised to deliver Dillinger. She also wanted the reward money.

The front of the Biograph Theater.

The cop in turn went to FBI special agent, Melvin Purvis, who was heading up the Dillinger manhunt with the offer. Purvis accepted the deal.

The ambush was set for July 22, 1934. Purvis and all available federal agents staked out Chicago's Biograph Theater on North Lincoln Avenue. The film "Manhattan Melodrama" starring Clark Gable was the feature. At 10:30 p.m. the movie ended and the crowd flowed out of the theater and into the street. In the throng were Dillinger, Polly and Anna. To make certain the agents recognized Dillinger after his botched surgery, Anna wore a red dress to "flag" him.

Once the agents identified Dillinger they moved fast. The stories of what happened next are numerous and conflicting. Apparently Purvis yelled for him to surrender but Dillinger reached into a pocket while running into the side alley leading to Halstead Street behind the theater. The FBI didn't bother with any warning shots or nonsense about "stop or I will shoot!" They just cut loose. Three FBI agents fired a total of five shots and Dillinger crumpled face down on the alley concrete. He had been hit three times and likely was dead before he thumped to the ground. The killing shot entered his neck exiting under his right eye.

Pandemonium erupted on the street. The unexpected gunfire scattered the crowd. Supposedly several innocent citizens were also wounded in the gunfire. Considering the shots were fired in a crowded street without apparent regard for bystanders, this would seem likely. What was truly grisly was the behavior of many in the crowd. Once Dillinger was down with a huge pool of his blood flowing out on the cold concrete, many folks, especially women, ran up soaking

The alley where Dillinger was killed.

their handkerchiefs as a macabre souvenir! Sopping up the blood of execution victims was an old European tradition especially popular during the French Terror. Some folks thought the blood had magical healing powers. But certainly soaking up Dillinger's blood was just ghoulish.

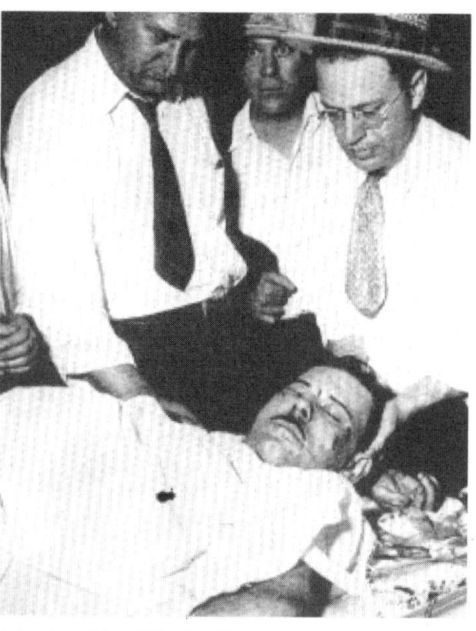

The FBI quickly bundled the body to a local hospital which refused to allow it inside since he was dead. Hospitals are for the living, not perforated mobster cadavers. With no other choice, the agents dumped it on the front lawn until transport was arranged to the Cook County Morgue where it was autopsied and positively identified. The FBI claimed the fingerprints positively proved it was Dillinger, even though the surgeons earlier tried to obliterate them. The next day the corpse was propped up on the slab and displayed for the thousands of people who trooped through the morgue to gawk at the famous gangster.

Eventually the remains were hauled down to his hometown and buried. As in the morgue, a crowd of thousands was on hand to see the macabre spectacle. To prevent any attempt at grave robbing, a couple of feet of concrete was poured on top of the coffin after it was lowered in the grave.[viii]

Of course no good story can end so cleanly. In this day and age we have to attach a wild conspiracy theory to everything. For example, remember the environmental lobby's claim President Bush caused hurricane Katrina to force Black people out of New Orleans? Or the nonsense about the government having "captured" several space aliens from a flying saucer crash near Area 51 in the 1950s?

In the decades following Dillinger's death there were claims the wrong man was killed by the FBI and that J. Edgar didn't want the bad publicity from admitting it, so if Dillinger wasn't going to say anything, Hoover wasn't either! Supporting claims included a supposed mismatch between Dillinger's Navy service record (he briefly served) and the corpse on the autopsy table. The tale continues Dillinger moved to Oregon and lived his day out as a peaceable citizen.

By the way, Anna Sages' agreement with the FBI was never honored. Apparently J. Edgar refused to support Purvis and she was deported to Rumania.[ix]

The Iroquois was considered the finest of Chicago's theaters.

Iroquois Fire

Some crimes are obvious, like sticking a gun in someone's ribs and saying, "Give me all your money or I will shoot!" Other crimes can be just as potentially deadly, but are often less evident.

Chicago's Iroquois Theater was considered the best of the many Chicago theaters when it opened in 1903. Located on Randolph between State and Dearborn, it was known as a palace of earthly delights. Stained glass and highly polished wood abounded. The ceiling in the ornate lobby soared fully 60 feet high. Gleaming white marble walls were fitted with huge mirrors to increase the spacious effect. Two huge grand staircases soared upward from the lobby floor to the balcony. The theater, described as an "absolute temple of beauty," awed the patron before the first actor strode on stage.

The nation had just suffered through a rash of deadly theater fires with deadly results and the architect wanted to make certain such a disaster would not befall the new Iroquois. His plans called for 27 exits and he claimed the entire building could empty in a mere five minutes. As an added precaution, a fireproof asbestos curtain was hung between the stage and audience. Should a fire breakout back stage, it would lower and seal the blaze off from the theatergoers. In recognition of the effort to make the theater as safe as possible, one newspaper advertisement declared it "absolutely fireproof."

Regardless of what the design called for and what the owners claimed, corners were cut and critical safety items not purchased or installed. The likelihood of a fire was too remote to really consider anyway. Talk of all this safety stuff was really just advertising. The Iroquois is a business and no business can afford to invest good money in material and devices that would most likely never be needed. Or at least this was the general reasoning of the theater owners.

On the afternoon of December 30, 1903, the theater was absolutely packed; reportedly it was standing room only. By the book the Iroquois could seat 1,724

The lobby of the theater was stunning.

people but since Chicago area schools were on Christmas vacation, it is thought upwards of 2,000 people, mostly women and children, crowded the house. Another 500 or so performers were backstage.

A group of eight men and eight women were on stage in full costume singing a piece called "Let Us Swear By The Pale Moonlight" when the conflagration started. The fire allegedly ignited high over the stage, in an area where various "flats" were suspended on ropes waiting to be dropped into position as needed for various set changes. The flats were made of painted canvas stretched tight over wooden frames. Reportedly about 3:15 p.m. a set brushed up against a hot spotlight causing the highly flammable heavily painted canvas to catch fire. A stagehand saw the fire start but he couldn't reach it from his catwalk. He was just a couple of inches too distant. What happened next is confusing. Either a piece

This was the act on stage when the blaze started.

of burning flat dropped among the singers causing them to flee, or it lit off the large velvet curtain. Doubtless some members of the audience thought it was part of the performance. It wasn't. Instead it was the beginning of a tragedy nearly beyond comprehension.

For a few moments no one did much of anything. Then a stage set collapsed in flames and the rush was on. This was not part of any act!

A fire wagon in the side street.

The fireproof curtain was lowered to seal the stage off from the audience but it jammed in its cheap wooden tracks, leaving a 20-foot gap. Bedlam reigned backstage. Chorus girls fainted and strong men panicked in fright. Those that could ran for the rear stage exits.

If bedlam was backstage, absolute chaos ruled the audience. People rushed madly for the exits. Unfortunately the doors were designed to swing inward not outward and the crush of theatergoers trying to flee jammed up against them, sealing them shut. The more people ran for the doors, the greater the jam up. Many folks were knocked down and run over, literally trampled to death in the blind panic.

Choking thick black smoke filled the theater and waves of heat roiled over the trapped audience like a huge oven. A rush of air from opened doors backstage as performers ran from the flames caused a blast of fire to flare deep into the audience, roasting people in the balconies to death as well as generally feeding the fire. It was a scene right out of Dante's Inferno.

Since the Iroquois was sealed so tightly it was perhaps 15 minutes before anyone outside realized it was on fire. When firefighters finally arrived they couldn't enter because of the crush of charred bodies piled up inside against the doors. Eventually the firemen had to haul them away like so much stacked wood. They found bodies piled ten deep around doors and windows.

When firemen penetrated deeper into the theater they discovered a horror nearly beyond words. Bodies were lying all over. In aisle seats, hallways, stage and stairs; the innocent victims were all over the place.

A fireman carrying the body of a dead child.

There were also numerous examples of criminal negligence of the theater owners. The stairway fire escape from the balcony down to street level was missing. There were no stairs. When the terrified audience opened the doors to flee, they fell 50 feet to the alley below, pushed from behind by people unaware of the missing staircase. Roughly 150 people perished in this manner, their broken bodies piled high like so many discarded store mannequins. After the pile got deep enough, people who jumped on top of them often survived, the one below cushioning the drop. Many victims were found still in their seats, suffocated from the blaze.

For a fire with such deadly consequences, damage to the theater was remarkably light. Within half hour of arrival the fire department had the last smoldering embers of the blaze out.

The eventual death count reached at least 602, with 212 being children. It took five hours to carry out the dead. A temporary morgue was set up at nearby Marshall Field's department store as well as other places.

Chicago went into deep shock over the disaster, Mayor Carter Harrison Jr. issuing a proclamation banning the public celebration of New Years. There would be no fireworks or blasting horns this year. Nightclubs were also closed and January 2 was made an official day of mourning.

Once the smoke cleared it was time for an investigation and the results were damning to the theater owners and city: For example,

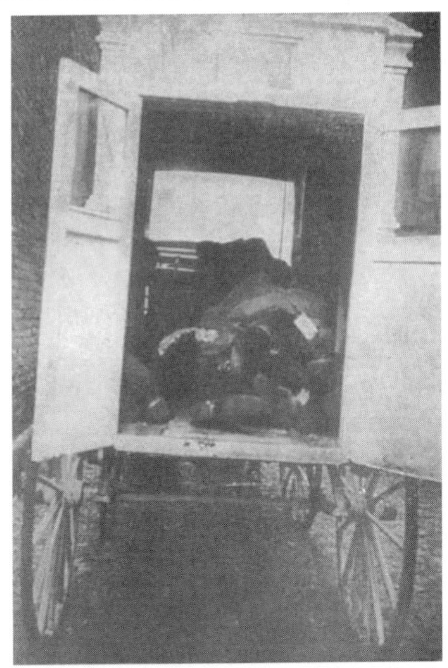

A delivery wagon is filled with the dead.

• Vents on the roof designed to let smoke and heat escape in the event of a fire were nailed shut, trapping the heat within.

• The "fireproof" asbestos curtain for the stage was made of cotton. Real asbestos was too expensive and the curtain wouldn't be used anyway since there would never be a fire.

• There were no fire alarms in the theater. Since there would never be a fire, alarms were clearly not needed.

• Water sprinklers were not installed. They were unsightly and too expensive anyway.

• To prevent people from sneaking into the theater without paying the admission, nine of the exit doors were padlocked shut preventing anyone from entering or leaving. Locked accordion style doors were installed in the stairways also.

• Because they considered them unsightly, exit lights were turned off during performances.

The investigation pointed clearly to the theater owners, city officials and fire department as the guilty parties. The last two groups played dumb, denying all knowledge of any violations, claiming individual fire inspectors must have been paid off with theater passes to ignore the problems.

A number of people were indicted by a grand jury, including the theater owners but none were charged with crimes. After a decent interval, the charges just faded away. After all, this was Chicago.

Relatives of the victims duly filed civil suits against the theater owners but never collected a dime. The Iroquois simply declared bankruptcy and faded away.

Driven by public opinion, Mayor Harrison closed 170 theaters, halls and churches until complete fire inspections were completed. A new fire code dictated doors must open outward, exits be clearly marked and steel fire curtains installed. Fire drills with ushers and management were also required.

The Iroquois fire was the deadliest in Chicago history, worse than the 1871 Great Chicago fire killing roughly 300 people. Even by national standards it was devastating. The Coconut Grove nightclub fire in Boston on November 28, 1942 killed 492 and the infamous Islamic attack on the World Trade Center in New York murdered 2,666.

The building reopened in 1904 as Hyde and Behmann's Music Hall and a year later as the Colonial Theater. The theater was demolished in 1924 to make way for the new Oriental Theater. It operated until the early 1980s and has since been remodeled into the Ford Center for the Performing Arts.

Perhaps only in Chicago in the 20s could a disaster like the Iroquois Theater fire happen, clearly the fault of the greedy owners and corrupt and compliant city officials, and have every single charge dismissed on legal technicalities. Only one person ever served jail time. A local saloonkeeper whose bar was used as a temporary morgue was convicted of robbing the dead.[x]

Murder on Mackinac

Mackinac Island is a very special place. To many visitors it is a fairyland from a time long past, almost Disneyesque in character. Certainly the tourists flocking to the island every day during the summer see it that way. During the height of the season 7,000 or more "fudgies" are on the island every day and with a 2,000-person work force, there is indeed a passel of people wandering around. But the island can be a dangerous place. A false sense of security can leave visitors open to danger, even murder!

Forty-nine-year old, Frances Lacey from Dearborn, Michigan found out the hard way just how death could strike from nowhere, even on Mackinac. On July 26, 1960 she reportedly became the first and only tourist murdered on the island.

Lacey came to the island with her daughter and son-in-law on a Saturday morning for a restful two-day vacation. She checked into the Murray Hotel right downtown while her daughter and son-in-law took a cottage with relatives at British Landing on the far side of the island. She was afraid the cottage would be too crowded, thus she decided to spend the night at the hotel. Lacey told them she would walk over to their place on Sunday, arriving around 11:00 a.m. Her husband died two years before and she was reputedly a wealthy woman.

After eating breakfast alone she checked out of her room, leaving a small suitcase at the desk. Since she was going to walk to British Landing, a distance of about three and a half miles, she wore a pair of comfortable shoes and slipped a pair of dressier shoes into a plastic bag. About 9:00 a.m. she started her hike, carrying the second pair of shoes in her bag as well as a purse.

She was hiking along Lake Shore Road that ran eight miles along the shore circling the island. Lacey reached the fieldstone gate leading to Stonecliffe Estate about 10:00 a.m. The estate was about half mile distant from the gate and at the time was hosting a Moral Rearmament retreat.

The organization originally arrived at the island in 1942, based in the old Island House Hotel, becoming a major force on the island in the 1950s and 60s. It started in 1938 when founder Frank Buchman – "called for program of moral and spiritual rearmament based on belief in God and adherence to four standards of honesty, purity, unselfishness and love." Between 1954-60 it built most of the present Mission Point complex, including a theater, residence buildings, conference rooms, dining halls, etc. In 1965 Buchman's successor, Peter Howard converted the complex into Mackinac College to better use the facilities and provide additional revenue. In 1970 the college financially failed and the relationship with Mackinac Island ended.

What happened to Lacey at this point is in part conjecture and in part reconstruction based on the evidence. Considering there were no witnesses, it is the best that can be done.

As Lacey sat on the low stone wall resting, a man came up behind her. She must have heard a footfall or sensed a presence. When she turned to look, her attacker smashed a fist into her face, knocking her partial dental plate onto the road. He then dragged her, conscious or unconscious, into the bushes and sexually assaulted her. When finished he strangled her with her panties. Returning to the road he stole her wallet from her purse that was lying in the open and threw her walking shoes into the water. Apparently she took them off while sitting on the wall. He dragged her body deeper into the woods and partially buried it under a fallen balsam tree. As he was doing so, a man and woman pedaled by on a tandem bike, saw the purse and took it with them. A horse and carriage followed and one of the hooves smashed the dental plate into the asphalt road surface. At this point the killer apparently fled. No one saw the man crouching low in the trees.

When Lacey failed to arrive at the British Landing cottage, her daughter notified the island police. A search was initiated including police, Mackinac Island Park personnel, the troop of Boy Scouts guarding Fort Mackinac, firemen, and tourists. Everyone was looking for Lacey. Even helicopters and fixed wing aircraft were used. Bloodhounds brought in from Niagara, Wisconsin and Norway, Michigan picked up her trail only to loose it.

Her empty wallet was discovered in a hedge near the Grand Hotel. Later this clue would lead police to conclude the killer had passed that way. Was he already heading for the ferry dock to flee the island or just blending in with the crowds arriving from the mainland?

The folks who picked up the purse found her name and address in it and since they were from the Detroit Metropolitan area too, thought it would be easier to just take it south rather than try to find her on the island. When they got home they called Lacey's telephone number but got no answer. When they heard the news on Wednesday of her disappearance, they contacted the police, telling them details of their discovery.

With the search area better defined, the police concentrated near the gate and soon found her smashed dental plate as well as one of the walking shoes in the shallow water near shore. Shortly after 7:00 p.m. Thursday they found the body.

They had the victim and the motive, but no suspect. A 25-man Michigan State Police task force worked hard on the investigation without success. Without some viable clue it was a hopeless case. There were thousands of people on the island that day and each male at least was a potential suspect. But who were they? Authorities knew who worked on the island and could run the hotel registers for people staying on the island over night but what about the thousands of day trippers? There was no way of accounting for the day trippers. The murder was committed early enough in the day, the killer could have taken an early ferry to the island and made an easy walk to the gate. What about the private boat owners? They were coming and going all the time. Could the killer have come to the island on one of them?

There was a train of thought suggesting it could have been one of the attendees at the Moral Rearmament retreat. They were just down the road from the crime scene. He could have murdered and taken the next ferry to the mainland, never to be seen again or just hiked back to the retreat with no one the wiser.

In spite of the best work of the investigators, Lacey's killer was never found. A hotel handyman was briefly detained and questioned when islanders remembered seeing red stains on his shirt but they turned out to be paint not the suspected blood. He was picked up again when a policeman remembered he had a cut over one eye, a wound that could have been inflicted by a desperate Lacey. But the man had an ironclad alibi and was released.

Whether he killed again or not, the murderer never repeated on the island. This does bring up an interesting point of speculation. Could not the perpetrator have been a serial killer, a man who gets his kicks out of raping and then strangling his victims and could not serial killers take vacations too? Could not he have taken a Mackinac Island vacation, been overcome by his demented "urge" and killed Lacey as a convenient victim? There are no answers, only questions. The case remains unsolved.[xi]

Great Lakes LYNCHING

"String'em up!" "We know he did it." The men surged out of the small jail, several of them pulling a rope with a noose fast around the neck of a protesting man. The victim stumbled and fell as the rope jerked and yanked at the whim of the men holding it.

In a couple of minutes the horde reached a handy lamppost. The free end of the rope was tossed over it. Eager hands grabbed it and pulled hard, hoisting the victim ten feet in the air. After jerking around for a few minutes, he stopped, hanging limp as an old rag. The deed was done and quick justice meddled out to a killer. If sanctioned by a judge's sentence it was an execution. Performed by a group of citizens without benefit of a court, it was a lynching. Regardless, the victim was dead.

The term lynching probably derived from Charles Lynch (1736-96), a Virginia Justice of the Peace who dispensed rough justice in his backwoods court. Lynching was originally a system of punishment used by whites against African American slaves. Its use later became multiracial.

Stretching the neck of a felon with the intention of execution is an old and honored American tradition. Whether done by benefit of a duly appointed judge or by a group of concerned citizens, it is quick, efficient and low cost. All that's needed is a rope, a tall object to "hang" the rope from and of course a victim. As a bonus, the rope is reusable!

Many newspaper editorials approved of lynching, as evidenced by the following from the Cleveland Leader of June 19, 1897. "The people of Ohio have seen murderers tried and convicted of murder in the 1st degree two or three times over and finally set free. They have known many desperate and dangerous criminals to be sent to the penitentiary for long terms and released soon enough to make the whole costly process of the courts seem little better than a farce... That is the real reason why, once in a while, the passion and indignation of the masses break through all restraints and some particularly wicked crime is avenged..." The above was published after a black rape suspect was forcibly dragged out of a county jail and lynched while a crowd of roughly 9,000 people cheered.

Lynching was an expression of violent community feeling.

The true number of lynchings in the U.S. and more specifically Great Lakes region will never be accurately known. However there are some estimates of reasonable validity. Between 1882 and 1968 there were roughly 4,800 lynchings nationwide with 1892 the most active year. About a quarter of the victims are white and 70-percent black. The most popular reasons for lynching were murder followed by rape and theft. The leaders of a lynch mob were very rarely prosecuted. Usually everyone knew who the guilty were but since the community at large agreed with the deed, conviction was near impossible.

Giving a malefactor the chance to dance the Texas Two Step was a legal method of execution in Michigan for many years. In 1763 an Indian woman was strung up in Detroit for the murder of an English trader named Mr. Chapham. The execution was ordered by the local British commander Major Henry Gladwin. It seems in the summer of 1762 Chapham, a Pittsburgh merchant visiting Detroit brought two Pawnee Indian slaves with him, a man and a woman. On the way home, near Sandusky, the three met some other Indians. In a gross error of judgment Chapham gave them all rum. Apparently the slave became drunk, attacked and murdered him. Adding outrage to injury, they also cut off his head and dumped the body into the river. The act so greatly disturbed the other Indians they dragged the killers back to Detroit, turning them over to the British commander. The local Indians despised the Pawnee so perhaps the opportunity to demonstrate their loyalty to the British at the expense of their hated enemy was too good to pass up. After interrogation the Pawnee confessed to the murder but the male was somehow able to escape to the Illinois country. The squaw was duly hanged.

A second neck stretching also occurred in Detroit in December 1775, on the eve of the American Revolution. For unknown reasons a furrier named Joseph Hecker murdered his brother-in-law with a knife. He was quickly apprehended and from magistrate's sentence to dancing the two-step was just a couple of days.

No need for long expensive and time consuming legal appeals! It would be many years before lawyers were numerous enough to require endless government appeals as a way of employing out of work attorneys.

In the early days capital punishment was not uncommon for what we would look at as relatively petty crimes. In 1777, when Detroit was still ruled by the British, an unusual double hanging was scheduled. Jean Coutencinau, a Frenchman, was found guilty of stealing furs from a couple of traders and a female former slave named Nancy Wiley (aka Ann Wiley) of thieving a purse containing six guineas from the same men. The trader's storehouse was also plundered and set fire to but the jury found no evidence the Frenchman or woman was guilty of the crime. Both however were convicted of robbery and sentenced to hang. However, the court couldn't find anyone to act as hangman until the woman volunteered if she received a pardon. The judge agreed. Contencinau took the drop and Wiley walked.

The next hanging, in 1821, was triggered by a relatively minor theft. A Menominee Indian named Kewabishkim filched the hat of a trader named Ulrick and in turn sold it for a few cents. Later when the trader later confronted the Indian and demanded either his hat or a fair price for it, Kewabishkim stabbed him to death. Around the same time an Ojibwa named Katakoh murdered an Army surgeon. The officer was traveling from Green Bay to Chicago when Katakoh reportedly shot him in the back just to see how he would fall off his horse. Certainly this was one of the less common reasons for murder. Both Indians were tried and duly condemned to death. Since the gallows was built just outside their jail window, they had a clear view of the work as well as hearing the hammering. While waiting in jail for the day of their scheduled demise, they gathered tobacco for offerings to the Manitou. They were also able to make a small drum by stretching leather across a water container and on the night before their execution, the pair beat their makeshift drum and sang the mournful "death song." This was well before the invention of TV and quality family entertainment was rare therefore a large crowd gathered for the execution. A single drop was a rare event. A double drop was an incredible bonus not to be missed by young and old alike. A regiment of militia stood by to keep civil order just in case a riot broke out as well as to provide a display of force. When the time came the two men were taken to a nearby Protestant church and given a stern sermon. They then were marched to the scaffolding where they ceremoniously shook hands with the various officials and climbed up the steps. Once on the platform the executioner positioned each over the trap doors, slid the hoods over their heads followed by the nooses. A quick pull on the lever and the pair dropped to oblivion.

Some designated executioners refused to do their duty. In 1829 the recently appointed Sheriff of Brown County, Wisconsin had 20 days to accept his post. Since a prisoner named Hempstead was scheduled to be hung within that period and the sheriff had the duty to act as executioner, the new appointee was in a bind. He didn't want to start his career with a hanging but he couldn't refuse the appointment. The answer came by the temporary appointment of a man willing to do the deed. After the job was done, the temporary was dismissed and new sheriff appointed to his post. When Wisconsin was finally made a state, it's constitution prohibited execution so the problem never arose again.

Wisconsin hangings could be very popular affairs as the Kenosha Advertiser for August 27, 1851 shows. "At Thursday at 1 o'clock precisely Michael McCafferty was hung at Kenosha for the murder of his wife. He made a confession and met his death without manifest want of fortitude. The prisoner was escorted to the gallows by the military, the mayor, the sheriff, etc. The sheriffs of Racine and Milwaukee were present. The crowd attending the execution was not as large as might have been expected. Some females were present."

When William Chaffee was hung in 1840 for murdering a farmer the crowd was much larger. "When the fatal day arrived (for execution) the crowd of sightseers that poured into the village was something wonderful. They began to arrive before daylight and from as far away as 40 miles. They came by wagonloads and horseback and on foot in a continuous stream. Old men and young women and children and babies were there; whole settlements were for a day abandoned. The gathering was larger than any circus nowadays can bring together. The stores and shops of all kinds did a very large and profitable business. The day was long remembered and talked about as "hanging day."

Soldiers weren't immune from committing murder. In 1829 Private James Brown, Company G, Fifth U.S. Infantry at Fort Mackinac became embroiled in a bitter argument with his squad leader, Corporal Hugh Flinn. After "stewing" for a while, Brown became so angry he shot and killed Flinn in the mess hall. Brown was promptly tried and convicted of the murder. When there was some dispute about the original court, he was tried again with the same result – death by hanging. On February 1, 1830 Brown was marched out to a scaffold and stretched appropriately. Where on the island the execution took place is unknown.

Stephen G. Simmons, a 250-pound bully disliked by all who had the displeasure of making his acquaintance, was hung in Detroit on September 24, 1830. When sober, Simmons was said to be a "man of culture and education," but when he drank, transformed into "debauchee." After coming home drunk one night, he beat his poor wife to death when she refused to tip a bottle with him. Even though the murder wasn't premeditated since he was drunk, the court went ahead and sentenced him to a session of stretching the hemp. It was likely a case of good riddance to a bad character. Why get too involved in the details of the law? His execution was good business too, an estimated 2,000 people showing up for the spectacle. The Army band from nearby Fort Wayne entertained with a series of pleasant tunes and merchants peddled liquid refreshments to the thirsty crowd as well as a selection of tasty snacks. When the murderer finally climbed the steps to the top of the scaffold, he was given the opportunity to say a few last words. He took full advantage of the chance, telling the audience he did kill his loving wife and was sorry for doing so, but it was the evil drink that made him do it. He then warbled several verses of a hymn imploring the Almighty's mercy. The hood was dropped on his head, noose adjusted and the trap sprung, sending him to his maker.

Regrettably Simmon's very civilized behavior, his admission of guilt, warning of demon rum and repentance swayed some of the audience toward thinking execution may not be the best punishment. Unfortunately in 1846 the Michigan legislature abolished the death penalty, making it the state the first to do so. No longer would Michigan dispose of it's human garbage. Instead it would just lock'em up at great and continuing public expense in state prisons. In some instances the killers escaped from the pens to murder other innocent citizens but the legislature didn't care. They still don't. In spite of poll after poll showing overwhelming public support for reinstituting the death penalty, the legislature blithely sails along content to coddle cold-blooded killers forever.

Regardless of Michigan's abolition of the death penalty, there was yet one more legal hanging in the state. On September 29, 1937 Anthony Chebatoris, a 39 year old Polish immigrant, tried to hold up the Chemical State Savings Bank in Midland. He was after the payroll of the Dow Chemical Company. He botched the robbery, wounding two employees in the debacle. Fleeing to the street he saw a man in a chauffeur's uniform and thinking he was a cop, viciously shot him to death. The killer was soon nabbed by the police.

Chebatoris' problem was the bank was a Federal Reserve Bank and member of the Federal Deposit Insurance Corporation. The National Bank Robbery Act was also newly passed. This meant he had "messed' with the feds, not a bunch of locals. And the feds did have a death penalty.

A trial in the Federal Court in Bay City found him guilty and issued a death warrant. Until the sentence was carried out he was housed in the federal prison at Milan, Michigan. On July 8, 1938 he was led from his cell to the scaffold built in an empty cell nearby and promptly hung. After assuring he was dead, the body was quickly buried in a potters field in Milan. The trial and execution was over quickly and inexpensively as opposed to the Michigan policy of paying for a murderer's upkeep in prison forever!

So much for executions in Michigan sanctioned by government. While there were many instances where folks just took matters into their own hands and dispensed justice as they saw it, research indicates only eight lynchings in the state, which makes Michigan a very law abiding place. The Great Lakes states in total had 132 lynchings but doubtless as research continues other cases will be discovered. The Lakes states were also "equal opportunity" lynchers too as 77 whites and 55 blacks were summarily hung. Again, these numbers can change as historic research continues.

An 18-year old mulatto named John Taylor is the first identified lynching victim in Michigan so far. The deed was done in Mason, just north of Lansing in 1866. Taylor was working as a laborer for a Lansing area farming family named Buck when he became embroiled in a pay dispute. One thing led to another and one quiet night Taylor attacked three sleeping women members of the family with an axe. He failed to kill them and fled on horseback. The screaming and blood drenched women raised the alarm and neighbors took chase, catching Taylor the next morning and hauling him off to the County jail in Mason.

As news of the terrible attack spread, the good folks of the neighborhood became more "worked up," especially considering the inescapable fact Michigan didn't have a death penalty. "Why, this no good drifter would have to spend his life in prison at our expense." "He damn near killed them poor women-folk!" "Come on men, we know our duty!"

Four days later a mob broke into the jail and dragged Taylor out by his hair. When they reached a big beech tree near the railroad station, someone threw a rope over a strong branch. The noose was quickly dropped around his neck and eager hands grabbed the running end ready to haul him up. Just to be sure he was indeed the guilty party, farmer Buck questioned him and he admitted he was guilty of the attack. The mob graciously allowed Taylor a couple minutes to make peace with his maker, then hauled away smartly on the rope and the miscreant danced in thin air. The body swung in the breeze for a full hour before being cut down and buried in a secret grave close to town. The mob dispersed, their good work finished. None of course were ever prosecuted.

One of the most famous lynchings on the Lakes happened on Sunday September 27, 1881 in Menominee, Michigan on the southern shore of the Upper Peninsula. Two Canadian lumberjacks, brothers (some sources claim cousins) Jack (John) and Frank McDonald, were in town and raising all kinds of hell. Both were well-known local troublemakers and unsavory characters of the first rank. One paper described them as "hard-hearted, villainous men."

The McDonalds just got out of the state prison where they served 18 months for resisting an officer. Supposedly they were boasting about being in town to "pay off some old debts." There is no doubt they were spoiling for a fight.

It seems Jack somehow got into a street brawl outside a Frenchtown bordello with a local named Billy Kittson. When the fight began to go against him, Jack pulled out a big hunting knife and slipped it hilt deep into Billy's back. Unfortunately for Jack, Billy's brother Norman saw the dirty deed and leaped into the brawl. When Frank saw Norman coming to the wounded Billy's help, he jumped in to gang up on him, stabbing Norman twice with his knife. The McDonald's buddy, Tommy Dunn, also joined the battle. Leaving the Kittson brothers bleeding in the dusty street the McDonald boys went back to the saloons and continued to "belt'em down." Billy bled to death in the filthy street, his blood soaking deep into the mud and manure and Norman was badly wounded. Eventually Sheriff Barclay and Deputy Brooks arrested the McDonalds as well as Dunn and tossed them into the calaboose.

Sentiment against the McDonalds ran high. Max Forvilly, the owner of the biggest saloon in Menominee, openly advocated "stringing'em up." They "weren't no damn good anyhow." The more the customers talked and drank, the more they liked the idea. By 6:00 P.M. Monday, an intoxicated mob stormed out of the saloon, marched down the street to the courthouse and jail and demanded that the McDonalds be turned over to them. The mob continued to grow and by 10:00 P.M. the courthouse was surrounded. As one, the mob smashed open the jail and quickly threw a couple of nooses around the killers necks and hauled the men outside. The older brother was defiant but the younger pleaded for his life. A man tied the running ends of the ropes off to the rear of a horse drawn wagon. When the driver cracked the whip, the pair were yanked off their feet and dragged along the ground and past the scene of the murder. As the boys were dragged along, some jacks took the opportunity to stomp on them with their heavy calked boots. Others jumped on them, riding them like a sled.

The brothers McDonald were strung up in Menominee, Michigan in 1881.

When the entourage reached the Chicago and Northwestern Railroad tracks, the boys were unceremoniously hung from a crossing sign. Some of the crowd took the opportunity to throw rocks at the swinging bodies. After a time, the mob cut the long dead pair down and dragged them back to the street in front of the Frenchtown bordello where the fight occurred, stringing them up from a tree. For unexplained reasons the crowd also set fire to the bordello, igniting a conflagration that took the fire departments of both Menominee and Marinette, Wisconsin, just across the river, to extinguish. The bodies swung lonely in the tree until Wednesday morning. When things quieted down, they were buried in a potter's field in Riverside Cemetery, their graves marked only with a rusty piece of logger's chain. Then someone stole the chain. Even dead, the pair were despised. Saloon owner, Forvilly, was indicted for his part in fomenting the lynching but easily acquitted. His fellow citizens saw nothing wrong with eradicating vermin.

The next lynching took place in Cheboygan, Michigan on the Lake Huron shore. In June 1883 a man lured eight-year old Nettie Lyons into the woods and not only brutally raped her, but also beat and stabbed her, leaving her for dead under a pile of leaves. The next morning, a search party found her alive and able to describe the inhuman monster in detail. A posse soon apprehended a black man named Tillot Comstock Warner in Mackinac City. On his return to Cheboygan under police escort, he was duly charged with the crime and jailed.

Public blood was running red-hot over the slaying. Not only was little Nettie so viciously assaulted and left for dead, but the evil doer was safe in jail! If anyone deserved to die, it was Tillot but Michigan had no death sentence.

It didn't take long for a crowd of roughly 600 to gather outside the jail and fired doubtless by liberal application of red eye, decided it was time for action. Under the glare of a torchlight, lynch fever grew. Around midnight on June 15, the angry mob overpowered the jailers, opened the cell and hauled Tillot outside. After a rope was looped around his neck, strong arms shoved him along until reaching a convenient railroad crossing sign. The rope was quickly thrown over the sign and Tillot "danced the hempen jig." After a few seconds of dangling, he was let down to confess his guilt. Claiming he was innocent wasn't what the mob wanted to hear and up he went again. This time the rope was tied off leaving him to flap in the wind until about 5:00 A.M. the following day when he was finally cut down. The body was dropped into a coffin with the rope still tight around his neck and carried to town hall for an inquest. The verdict was "death at the hands of unknown parties." None of the ringleaders of the lynching were ever identified.

Five years later Grayling was the scene of a performance of the "ten toed tap dance." The story goes that Archibald Pelon, a Frenchman known for "engaging in several criminal transactions," raped and beat Mrs. J.S. Crego, an elderly resident living on the outskirts of town. Figuring leaving town was a good idea, Pelon hastily left the scene of the crime but stopped at the home of Arthur Marvin to ask directions to a particular lumber camp. Arthur wasn't home but his young wife was so Pelon raped her too. As soon as Pelon left the Marvin home, all hell broke loose in town, but whether it was Mrs. Marvin or Mrs Crego who sounded the alarm isn't clear. Searchers quickly spread out over the wooded countryside looking for Pelon. Angry citizens finally found him in the Roscommon railroad station waiting for a train to escape the area. It took a couple of stout men to subdue him and drop the cold iron shackles on his wrists but he was soon under guard in the courthouse. An ugly crowd was rapidly gathering in front of the courthouse and doubtless remembering the Cheboygan lynching five years before, the sheriff quietly hid Pilon in a private house where he would be safer. Someone must have followed the transfer because about midnight roughly 30 masked men broke into the house, overpowering the sheriff and dragging Pilon outside to a waiting wagon. Pilon was thrown in the bed and held down by several men while the rest of the masked posse followed the wagon to the edge of town.

Once they found a good stout tree, Pilon was made to stand still while a noose was slipped around his neck and the opposite end of the rope looped over a branch and tied off to the tree. When the driver gave a loud "Giddy Ap," the wagon clattered away leaving Pilon swinging and kicking in the wind. Unfortunately the fall wasn't big enough to snap his neck so he just dangled around a while slowly strangling to death. Death by strangulation rather than breaking the neck was commonplace. Doubtless the crowd preferred to see a slow death rather than a fast, merciful death anyway. Pilon "hung around" until about 3:00 A.M. when the sheriff cut him down. As with most similar lynchings, the men were well known but since the community agreed with the hanging, weren't ever prosecuted or indicted.

A year later Port Huron took it's turn in the lynching limelight. On May 11, 1889 a man entered the home of John Gills just outside of the city. John wasn't at home but his wife and five- year old daughter were. The stranger demanded money. When the wife claimed there wasn't any, he attacked and attempted to rape her. The quick thinking daughter ran for help whose timely arrival drove off the stranger.

One Albert Martin, a mulatto, was soon arrested. Although he admitted being at the Gills home earlier in the day, he claimed he didn't attack anyone. However since both Mrs. Gills and her daughter identified him as the attacker, he was tossed into jail. The authoritie's case was bolstered when it was determined his footprints matched those found outside the house.

Martin was a likely culprit. A Canadian who lived in Ypsilanti, he had frequent run ins with the law and was a graduate of the state prison in Ionia. Some police officers felt he was likely at least partly insane.

With the evidence stacked tall and clear against Martin townspeople began to talk openly of a lynching. Over several days men were openly recruited to make an attack on the city jail where Martin was held. The coming lynching was so well known folks who didn't want to be involved made it a point to be out of town at the appointed time.

In the wee hours of May 27, a group of masked men broke into the jail and grabbed Martin. Seeing the mob coming, the sheriff wisely deserted his post, taking off for his own safety. The prisoner was pulled outside where a yelling mob of 75-100 people hustled him along to the Seventh Street bridge. The prepared noose was dropped around his neck and the rope thrown over the northeast bridge truss. A good pull and Martin was dangling in air and doing a fair rendition of the "gallows dance." Just for good measure an exuberant man ran up and fired his pistol into the body. The following day the body was cut down and taken to the coroner for examination. The official verdict simply stated, "death at the hands of a mob unknown to the jury." The body was later shipped to the University of Michigan Medical School for dissection.

Michigan citizens again took the law into their own hands in Corunna late in 1893. One William Sullivan, a 27-year old Irish immigrant from nearby New Haven, was lounging around the railroad depot supposedly looking for work. A local Duran farmer named Layton Leech noticed the Irishman and gave him a job cutting wood on his farm. For reasons never determined, during the evening of January 1, 1893, Sullivan murdered Leech with an axe while they were outside near the barn. Sullivan then went into the house and shot Layton's wife, Hannah, raping her for good measure as she lay bleeding on the floor. When he finished he left her for dead and escaped into the night. Hannah however was still alive and she later managed to crawl outside where her screams brought neighbors to her rescue. She also identified Sullivan as her attacker.

Sullivan however seemed to have disappeared. To keep the pressure up, townsfolk raised a reward of $1,500 for his capture. Money talks and on May 21 he was arrested in Detroit while drunk and half asleep in front of a Larned Street saloon. Initially he claimed he was innocent but later admitted his guilt. When they heard he was arrested, a crowd of 200 men from Durand arrived in Detroit by train. Surrounding the police station, they demanded Sullivan be turned over to them. While police officers stalled the crowd, Sullivan and several Corunna sheriff's deputies were smuggled away and put on a train to Durand. The secret soon leaked out and word reached Durand, Sullivan was on the train and another mob, this one roughly 300 people strong, waited eagerly at the station to "greet" the killer. The sheriff foiled the mob by having Sullivan and the deputies jump off the slowly moving train a mile or so short of the station. Met by a horse and wagon, they had their prisoner "safe" in jail before the mob realized what happened.

Two days later Sullivan was arraigned for the murder and rape and pled guilty. The judge remanded him back to the Shiawassee County jail for safekeeping. It was a death sentence.

Interest in Sullivan continued to build and reached such a pitch Sheriff Ed Jacobs made Sullivan stand in his cell for ten hours while 2,000 people slowly filed by taking a good look at the cold-blooded killer. If Jacobs thought the look would satisfy people's lust for revenge, he was wrong. It only agitated people to take action. The more they saw of Sullivan, the more they knew they had to do the decent thing. Word soon spread that the people's sentence would be carried out the night of May 23.

Witnesses later said roughly 2,000 people assembled outside the county jail. It was a threatening crowd and loud yells to "hang him" were commonly heard. About 10:00 P.M. a dozen ringleaders showed up with their faces well hidden behind bandannas. The leaders demanded the sheriff give them Sullivan. Sheriff Jacobs and his deputies leveled their guns at the men who were only armed with clubs but the huge mass of people rushed them, sweeping the officers away before a shot could be fired. The mob used a battering ram to smash down the thick jailhouse door and sledgehammers soon beat down Sullivan's cell door. Several men rushed into the small chamber and cinched a noose around his neck. The rest quickly dragged him outside. Sullivan was pulled several hundred feet before ending up at the base of an old oak tree. A quick throw of the rope over a stout branch and the crowd pulled away, hauling the killer up until his head smashed hard into the limb supporting the rope. As the body hung limply from the tree, townspeople "kicked, pulled, punched and otherwise mistreated it." As soon as it was dropped to the dirt, others cut away parts of his clothing as macabre mementos. When the cloth was gone, parts of the branch were sawed away and the tree stripped of bark. Even the rope was cut into fragments to satisfy the demand for keepsakes. Not content to leave Sullivan's body in peace, "hundreds of men dragged it around the grounds" of the jail behind a horse and buggy, finally dumping it front of a saloon. The sheriff rescued it just as the men were preparing a bonfire to roast it.

Sullivan may have been dead before being dragged from his cell. There is a story some Detroit newspapermen were permitted in the cell to interview him and they gave him a bottle of whisky to "loosen" his tongue and give them a better story. When Sullivan heard the mob howling for his blood, he broke the bottle and slashed his throat with a sharp glass shard. The mob may have "killed" a dead man.

The local undertaker soon dropped the body in a cheap coffin and promptly put it on display. He was shocked when an estimated 22,000 people filed past to see it. Visitors came from all parts of the state to see the killer who raised so much community hatred.

No one was ever prosecuted for the lynching. The Governor did his own investigation but came up empty handed. No one would talk. Finally Sullivan's brother convinced the Governor to try again. He appointed Frank Bumps, a circuit court commissioner for Shiawassee County to investigate Sheriff Jacobs for incompetence and neglect of duty. His report was issued on October 8, 1894 in the height of the local election campaign. County voters responded to the allegations of incompetence by returning Jacobs to office by a two to one majority. The locals didn't need any moral lectures from the crooks in Lansing!

Of course local folks were viciously condemned by "holier than thou" newspapers across the state and nation, including such bastions of unbiased and honest reporting as the *New York Times*[i]. The townspeople just shrugged such criticism off, feeling they just did what had to be done. This was also the last known lynching in Michigan.

Lynching wasn't unknown in the cold Northwoods of Minnesota. From 1889-1918 at least 20 people were reported lynched in the state. Nearly all were white.

During the height of World War I, the Minnesota Iron Range was running full out in support of national industry. The ore was vital for steel, and steel was the muscle used to defeat the Huns. Any activity working against the war was seen as something evil and steps taken to squash it.

When workers at a Duluth, Minnesota U.S. Steel plant threatened to strike, the company brought in blacks from the rural south as an alternative labor source. White workers understood the obvious message and backed off their demands.

Minnesota (and the entire nation) also sent thousands of young men off to war and casualty lists mounted daily. Draft age men who didn't do their part were viewed as "slackers" and universally despised. At the end of September 1918 a group of local vigilantes calling themselves the Knights of Liberty took action. According to newspaper accounts, members dragged a Finnish immigrant named Olli Kinkkonen, a logger and dock worker, from his Duluth boarding house and tarred and feathered him as a slacker. Afterward, Kinkkonen disappeared for a couple of days finally surfacing dangling from a tree on the northern outskirts of town, near Lester Park. A police investigation conveniently concluded it was suicide. They thought Kinkkonen was so humiliated by the tar and feathering as a slacker he took his own life. Others thought the "investigation" a whitewash. Kinkkonen was lynched pure and simple. The tar and feathering as a slacker was just camouflage. There was a significant amount of labor agitation going on at the time on the Iron Range and someone mistook him for an organizer. Others said Kinkkonen just didn't want to fight and was trying to return to Finland to get away from the war. Was that any reason to hang him? No one was ever charged with his death.

While there may be some doubt whether Kinkkonen was a suicide or lynch victim, there wasn't any doubt about what happened on June 15, 1920. The day before the John Robinson Circus came to Duluth. Part of the crew included a large contingent of black men working as cooks and laborers. Blacks weren't unknown in Duluth. Of the roughly 100,000 people in the city, 495 (according to the 1920 census) were black. Most worked as porters, waiters, janitors and factory laborers, many for U.S. Steel. After a traditional circus parade through the heart of downtown the show was ready to go!

That evening a 19-year old Duluth woman attended the show with her 18-year old boy friend. Both were known as being "fast and loose," in the parlance of the time. Following the performance they went to the back of the main tent for reasons never explained but certainly not to get an extra cotton candy. The

The Duluth Police station after the mob broke in and removed the prisoners for lynching.

following morning the Duluth Chief of Police was called by the boy's father and told six black circus workers held the couple at gunpoint and raped the girl. A later examination of the girl by a doctor showed no evidence of rape but that was immaterial. The charge was made.

The Duluth Police quickly arrested six black circus workers and tossed them in the city jail on the corner of Second Avenue and Superior Street. The news of the rape charge and arrest spread through the city like wild fire. By evening a mob of between 5,000 and 10,000 people seethed around the station. Many in the crowd were veterans recently returned from the war. Apparently a number were still angry about seeing black soldiers openly cavorting with white French women. Arriving back home only to find more blacks in Duluth, many working at jobs previously held by whites, only fueled their anger. Some of the whites found kindred spirits in the local KKK. Crosses were sometimes even burned to intimidate the black community.

After sparring with the police, including battling with fire hoses, the anger of the mob boiled over and it rushed the police station. Carrying bricks, rocks, axes, sledgehammers, railroad irons and timbers, it smashed its way inside.

The police on duty fought hard, but without the use of weapons, were overwhelmed. The Police Commissioner forbade the use of firearms. It was later charged, since his position was an elected one and the mob was largely composed of voters, he didn't want to "anger" his supporters by shooting at them. The police ammunition on hand was ridiculously inadequate. There were only about 100 bullets between the entire Force. This is reminiscent of the single bullet Officer Barney Fife kept in his upper right shirt pocket on the old Andy Griffith TV show. Regardless, a sharp volley fired over the mob early on certainly would have discouraged them and bought time for other solutions. Ominously the Police Commissioner, who cowered in his upstairs office throughout the entire riot and lynching, refused to call for help from the County Sheriff or ask for the National Guard. A Guard unit was drilling only a couple of blocks away and could have responded nearly immediately.

A hastily run mob "kangaroo court" pronounced three black suspects guilty and passed sentence – death by hanging. All three were hauled outside and promptly strung up on a light pole on the corner of First Street and Second Avenue. The fact that the boy and girl could "positively" identify none of the supposed attackers was not important.

The following morning a contingent of the Minnesota National Guard arrived to restore order. The three remaining prisoners and ten other black suspects were taken to the St. Louis County Jail for protection.

The hangings made headlines around the nation. This type of lawlessness was expected in the Deep South but not in a civilized part of the country like Minnesota! The story even made the front page of the New York Times. A Chicago newspaper railed "...Duluth authorities stand condemned in the eyes of the nation." The Minneapolis Journal moaned the mob put "...stain on the name of Minnesota." Prominent black leaders in Duluth described it as "a horrible disgrace, a blot on its name it can never outlive." But Minnesota Iron Range newspapers were supportive of the lynching, one claiming "while the thing was wrong in principal, it was most effective...." Another asserted, ". . . Mad dogs are shot dead without ceremony. Beasts in human shape are entitled to but scant consideration. The law gives them too much of an advantage." Emotions ran high and deep.

Stunned Duluth leaders, white and black, advocated swift punishment of the lynchers. Compounding the entire issue was the girl's charge of being raped by six blacks. Only three were lynched. The remaining three needed to be investigated and tried on the charge if warranted.

Two days after the lynching a Duluth District Judge convened a grand jury investigation on the whole affair. Determining the identity of the leaders of the mob proved very difficult. Many folks supported the action and didn't want to implicate them. Others thought everyone just got caught in the emotion of the moment and didn't deserve any punishment. Eventually the grand jury issued 37 indictments for those in the mob; 25 for rioting and 12 for first-degree murder. Eight whites ended up being tried with four acquitted and one trial ending in a hung jury. Three were convicted of rioting and went to the state pen in Stillwater for less than fifteen months. No member of the mob was ever convicted of murder.

Seven black laborers from the circus were indicted for rape. Five had the charges dismissed and two went to trial. One was acquitted and one convicted and sentenced to seven to 30 years in prison. He was released after four years with the condition he immediately vacate Minnesota, forever.

The burial location of the three victims was unknown until 1991 when newly found records showed them interred in Park Hill Cemetery. Authorities in 1920 left the graves unmarked to avoid possible desecration. During a special ceremony in 1991, granite headstones were added bearing the victim's names and the phrase, "Deterred but not defeated."

In October 2003 a special monument to the slain circus workers was erected on the site of their execution. A wall ten feet high filled with quotations and featuring life size bronze statues of the men, Elmer Jackson, Elias Clayton and Isaac McGhie projecting from the wall, provides moving testimony to the tragedy.

Mankato, Minnesota has it's own special niche in the "hanging" game. On December 26, 1862, 38 Sioux convicted of murder and rape were hung at one time in the town, the largest mass execution in U.S. History[ii]. Since the hangings were done, "all nice and legal," it wasn't technically a lynching.

During the height of the Civil War, several eastern bands of the Dakota (often called the Santee Sioux) along the Minnesota River in southwest Minnesota rebelled against U.S. authority. Fighting started on August 17, 1862 and in the following weeks claimed hundreds of lives. Estimates of settlers killed range between 300 and 800.

The Indians picked a very bad time to revolt. While deep in the Civil War, the Army had little forces to spare for an Indian war but when the soldiers were finally assembled their instructions were to end the fighting quickly. The troops moved fast and hard and the war was largely over in six weeks.

Initially, 303 Sioux prisoners were convicted of murder and rape by military tribunals and given a sentence of death. Some trials lasted a bare five minutes, and the Indians had no one to explain the proceedings or to represent them. When he reviewed the records of the trial, President Lincoln made a distinction between those who engaged in warfare against the United States and those who raped or murdered civilians. In the end he approved of the execution of 38 of the latter and commuted the death sentences of the others.

The mass execution was performed for all to see from a single scaffold platform. As typical, folks came from near and far to see the spectacle. By no means was a large execution all that unusual. During the Mexican-American War General Winfield Scott hung 48 deserters in groups of 18 and 30. The soldiers were Irish Catholic and fled the American Army to fight for the infamous

38 Indians were executed in Mankato, Minnesota after a failed uprising.

Mexican "general" Santa Ana, the self styled "Napoleon of the West." In reality Santa Ana was a blood-thirsty tyrant, but Mexico was a Catholic country and thus the Irish were easily lead astray by the siren call of religion, reasoning they couldn't fight against a country ruled by the "mother church." The Mexicans formed the Irish deserters into the St. Patricio Battalion, a unit that fought against their fellow Americans in a final display of betrayal. Scott had no compunction about hanging such disloyal men. When many were eventually captured, the sentence was typically the traditional death by hanging. A firing squad, after all, is for honorable men, not traitors. The last group of 30 deserters was "dropped" on September 13, 1847 just as the American flag broke out from the battlements of Chapultepec Castle, the final battle of the war. They were lined up on a hill facing the castle so they could clearly see the American assault and final victory to better comprehend the terrible error of their treachery and make certain the last thing they saw was the flag they so deceitfully abandoned.

There are two macabre sidelights to the Mankato affair. After Army surgeons pronounced the Indians dead, they were buried in a long trench dug in the sand of the riverbank. Before burial, however, a "Dr. Sheardown" supposedly cut away some of the Indians' skin. Afterwards, little boxes containing the skin were sold in Mankato "gift shops." Over the years, many "souvenir" pieces of skin have continued to be sold. Likely most are hoaxes and are just hunks of pigskin.

At the time, obtaining human bodies for medical school dissections were hard to come by, so many doctors attending the execution requested cadavers. In fact, that's why they came in the first place. One of the men was Doctor William Worrall Mayo, who would later help found the famous Mayo Clinic in Rochester,

Minnesota. To fill the need, the mass grave was re-opened and the bodies distributed. Dr. Mayo received Cut Nose, a famous Sioux chief. After dissection the skeleton was cleaned, dried and varnished so other students could benefit from it.

The Minnesota Sioux War of 1862 may have been the first violent clash between the Sioux and the Army but it wouldn't be the last. The Battle of Killdeer Mountain occurred in 1864, Red Cloud's War followed in 1866-1868, the Battle of Little Big Horn in 1876 and Battle of Wounded Knee in 1890 also involved the Sioux.

Today the hanging is commemorated by a huge limestone buffalo in Mankato's "Reconciliation Park."

Indiana was no slouch about stringing up folks either. In 1878 five black men were hanged on the Posey County Courthouse lawn at Mount Vernon by a mob that hauled them out of the jail. Four of them were accused of sexually assaulting a white woman. The fifth man gunned down a deputy sheriff who was trying to arrest one of the four attackers.

The first recorded lynching in Indiana involved a couple of horse thieves who tried to steal from settlers in Clark County who were tired of being robbed. Without a handy jail or judge, the settlers dispensed their frontier justice with a rope and tree.

Five white men were hanged in 1897 by a mob after storming the lockup at Versailles. Three of the men were likely already dead - having been beaten by the mob - when they were strung up. It was just a case of "hang'em for good measure!"

Perhaps the best remembered Indiana lynching involved four members of the notorious Reno gang. This gang of murderers, thieves and cut-throats terrorized the state until good citizens finally ended their evil reign. In December 1868, a group of Jackson County residents took a train south, smashed into the Floyd County jail in New Albany, and hanged Frank, William and Simeon Reno and Charles Anderson from a catwalk. Three other gang members were lynched earlier by the pursuing posse.

Ohio was no slouch at hanging'em high either. One source claims 26 men, evenly split between black and white, were lynched in the Buckeye state.

Canada had it's fair share of hangings too. What was good south of the border worked north of it too. Hanging was a commonly applied punishment for up to 120 different crimes in the "Great White North." It wasn't restricted to murder, rape and treason until 1865. Public hanging was abolished in 1869. While children weren't commonly hung, up to 1834, in Canada, they could be shipped to prison for the crime of being an orphan! Even barring orphans, the prison at Kingston had inmates as young as eight years old.

It took a while for Canadian executioners, as well as the American ones, to figure out the scientific "drop," a technique allowing the condemned to drop through a trap door a distance sufficient to break the neck. If the body dropped too far (or weighed too much), the head "popped' off which was at best very messy. If the body didn't drop far enough, the victim slowly strangled. For folks organizing a lynching, such variations in technique were of little concern. Death was the objective, not proper technique.

This photo in Toronto in 1895 shows the "long drop" in use.

Navies traditionally just hung their malefactors from a yardarm. The hemp rope, usually 1-1/2 to 3 inches in diameter, was just tossed over the yard and the end with the slip knot fastened around the victim's neck. The crew grabbed the running end and on command, hauled away smartly, running the victim skyward. Death was usually by strangulation.

In 1838 Patrick Fitzpatrick was hung in Windsor "all nice and legal like" for the rape of a nine-year-old girl. Although there were a couple of other suspects the girl identified Fitzgerald, so he was duly launched into eternity. Years later another man made a death bed confession that he was the real rapist. Whether this was a true statement or not is unknown.

Not all Canadian hangings went well. In 1831 Cornelius Burley was arrested, tried, convicted and sentenced for shooting Constable T.G. Pomeroy to death during an arrest. The execution took place on Long Point, Lake Erie. Unwilling to perform the role of executioner, the sheriff found a local volunteer willing to do the deed. Unfortunately the volunteer wasn't the brightest light in the land and used a too thin rope. When Burley was pushed off his perch, the rope broke and he plunged to the ground. Stunned by the fall, the victim stood up and staggered around trailing the rope. The hangman promptly guided Burley back to the scaffold with the help of a couple of police and hung him again. According to the strictures of the court, the body was hauled off and given to a local doctor for anatomy practice. It is assumed he was dead before the knife sliced into him.

Women could be strung up too. In 1873 Elizabeth Workman was hung in Sarnia for beating her abusive husband to death with a hunk of wood. In spite of numerous pleas for clemency, no stay came, and she made the drop. Authorities let her body swing in the wind for 20 minutes before cutting it down just to make sure.

On occasion, Canadian citizens also took justice into their own hands. On a bitterly cold night in February 1819, a farm worker named De Benyon, brutally murdered his young stepson. The two lived in a rough log cabin by the side of the road just outside of Toronto. For unknown reasons De Benyon forced the - thirteen-year-old boy out of the house and into the frigid weather. When the boy tried to sneak back into the cabin, his stepfather caught him. His subsequent action was unbelievable. After tying the boy up, he slowly pushed him into the burning fireplace, first burning his legs, and eventually the rest of the lad. Such a despicable action couldn't be hidden from public knowledge and when his neighbors heard of this most despicable murder, they formed into an ugly mob bent on administering justice. De Benyon ran towards Toronto, the mob running just behind, and finally overtaking him near the Don River. A rope was thrown over a handy tree and the damned farmer strung up and left for the carrion to consume, if they would have him.

One of the most famous lynchings involved a couple of expatriates who ran afoul of powerful U.S. cattlemen. It starts with Ella Watson, the oldest of ten children born to Irish immigrants in Ontario. When Ella was twelve, the family moved to Kansas where she grew into a tall and robust woman. One source claimed she stood six foot, two inches tall! At age 18, she married a man who turned out to be an abusive alcoholic. Seeing no value in staying with such a bum, she filed for divorce, a very unusual action at the time, and fled west.

Ella Watson, aka Cattle Kate, was lynched.

She found work as a cook, domestic and some claim, hooker. Regardless, she ended up in the Sweetwater Valley of Wyoming where she met and fell in love with Jim Averill, another wandering Canadian. Averill was a widower and besides having a small ranch, also operated a restaurant. For a time she worked as his cook. Whether the pair ever officially married or not is in dispute, but they certainly were a "pair."

In 1888 Kate later staked a claim near Jim's ranch at Horse Creek. Hers was perhaps the more valuable since it encompassed water rights, something precious indeed, in this miserably dry and inhospitable land. She quickly built a small cabin. Kate was a complete cowgirl, able to ride, rope, hog-tie, shoot and do all of the chores needed to make a ranch prosper. Soon her property was completely fenced in, her land marked out with the hated barbed wire. She also gained the nickname, "Cattle Kate," in recognition of the small but growing herd of cattle she was acquiring, supposedly from passing traders.

The members of the immensely powerful Wyoming Stock Growers Association didn't take kindly to Kate's claim and fencing. They were used to grazing their cattle where they pleased without worrying about whose land it really was.

The association tried to scare Kate and Jim off but neither took the "hint." Finally fed up with interference by the two, the cattlemen acted. On July 20, 1889, a group of six men kidnapped Kate from her ranch, and Jim from his, bundling both into a wagon and going to a nearby rocky canyon by the Sweetwater River. The men claimed both were rustling association cattle and everyone knew the penalty for rustling. They also claimed Kate and Jim were taking association strays and branding them as their own. Such despicable thievery deserved frontier justice.

A couple of lariats were tossed over the limb of a stunted pine tree and the nooses slipped around Kate and Jim's necks. The traditional "hangman's" knot wasn't used but rather the easy running lariat loop. Both victims stood in the wagon and when one of the men slapped the horse on the rump, the wagon lurched forward leaving Kate and Jim dancing together in the air. The drop was only two feet, not far enough to kill them, so both slowly strangled to death.

Perhaps as many as half a dozen folks witnessed the lynching besides the six cattlemen. Some were closer than others but all could identify the killers. In a fit of civic responsibility, the coroner's jury named the six killers but in an equal fit of individual reality, the witnesses all disappeared or suffered amnesia before the grand jury could issue an indictment. No one was ever tried for the murders of Kate and Jim.

The Wyoming Stock Growers Association also made certain their side of the Kate Watson story would be remembered for a long time to come. The local newspaper, deep in the cattlemen's pocket, proclaimed her as a "cutthroat, whore and immoral thief."

Whether Kate and Jim were saints or sinners remains open for debate. That two Ontario natives met their end by frontier justice in Wyoming is fact.

The youngest person legally hung in America was Hannah Ocuish, a Native American. She was a mere 12 years old when the State of Connecticut executed her in 1784 for murdering a six-year old child. The child "ratted" on Hannah when she stole some fruit and Hannah swore she would get even. Remember Connecticut was the same state (then a colony) that hung 13 women for witchcraft in 1692. Death by hanging, whether sanctioned by a judge or judged by the common people, is an old American tradition[iii].

Great Lakes PIRACY & OTHER DESPERATE ACTS

Barratry

The Mariner's Dictionary defines barratry as the willful casting away of a ship. It is a crime as old as sailing and judged extremely serious. In some instances, if the deed could be proved outright, the captain was sent to prison for a long stretch of breaking rocks. If he murdered the crew in the process, he was executed. Other times barratry could be only suggested when the suspicion was present but not the proof. In the case of the small Canadian schooner *Explorer,* the proof was discovered but 15 long years after the terrible and deadly crime.

The story played out like this. In 1866 John Waddell had the 48-foot, two-masted schooner *Explorer* built at Chatham, Ontario. He used her to run freight from Chatham and Windsor to small communities, especially lumber operations in northern Lake Huron. By all accounts she was a well-built vessel, perfectly suited for her trade.

Waddell had an interesting background. Born in England in 1817, he moved with his parents and three siblings to Canada in 1832. He married Nancy Eberts in 1843 and therefore gained entry into Eberts Brothers, one of the areas main trading and merchant houses. Whether it was a love match or a "good business decision" isn't known but it did catapult his "prospects" considerably. The firm was particularly well known for shipbuilding and operation. For a time he worked with the firm but in 1848 became the Sheriff of the united counties of Essex, Kent and Lambton. It was a prominent political position although he still did some work with Eberts. He also owned lumber mills at Collins Inlet, off Georgian Bay, and had a financial interest in various vessels. For a time he prospered but the Panic of 1857 hit him hard as well as the loss of a couple of his ships which were apparently not well insured. When gold was discovered in British Columbia in 1861, he saw it as a way to recoup his fortune so he packed up his family and headed west. He didn't find El Dorado and in 1865 was back in Chatham.

It can be said the schooner *Explorer* was his last chance to pull his failing fortunes out of the sinkhole. Two difficult years passed and in late November 1867 John Waddell arrived at Wiarton, Ontario in a small ship's yawl. He was reported more dead than alive and spent time in a local hospital recovering. He claimed that he and two crew members were bound from Windsor, opposite Detroit, to Little Current on Manitoulin Island in northern Lake Huron in the *Explorer* to deliver a load of sawmill machinery, merchandise and barreled whiskey to his son. The weather turned foul and the cargo of whiskey began to shift. His crew volunteered to go below and try to secure it but as the waves were coming over the deck, opening the hatch was impossible, so they went below to the stern compartment to chop their way through the bulkhead with an axe. This they did and worked at the cargo for sometime before one came topside with a tin cup filled with whiskey for him. He drank some but told the man to lay off the hooch until the job was done. It was dangerous work in the hold and they needed their wits about them. When both eventually came up they were "three sheets to the wind" and said they would be finished in another five minutes. With little choice, Waddell sent them below again. They didn't come back up and without the crew to help manage the schooner, she struck rocks near shore and foundered. He was unable to get the drunken men out of the hold and barely escaped in the yawl himself. He supposed they both were crushed to death when the shock of the collision with the rocks sent the heavy whiskey barrels cascading over them. After ten days of misery, living on a little salt fish he obtained from an old Indian, he reached Wiarton in the yawl. Although he immediately sent a search party out in a Mackinac boat to see if any of the crew survived, they returned empty handed. It was a remarkable story of shipwreck and survival and totally false.

Since the *Explorer* was a new vessel, there was every possibility of salvaging her, if she could be found. Perhaps she slipped off into deep water. If so it could be possible to recover her valuable cargo or whiskey and perhaps even lift the entire ship! Except the *Explorer* couldn't be found. Salvagers searched where Waddell said to look, but nothing was found.

For a couple of years following the loss Waddell would take a small boat and disappear for a while. And the family always had money beyond the relatively small insurance coverage. For a man driven to the brink of financial calamity by the wreck, it was very strange.

He met his personal end in 1870. He and his son were sailing in a small boat from Goderich north on Georgian Bay when it overturned in a sudden squall. The son managed to hold on to the boat and was later rescued. Waddell slipped off and drowned.

A startling discovery was made in 1876 when a commercial fisherman happened to glance over the side and into the depths where he saw the top of a mast projecting upward. He found the long lost *Explorer*. Several attempts to salvage her were made without success. In 1881 a crew from the steamer *Josephine Kidd* grappled the schooner but failed to raise her. Other efforts damaged the wreck. The following year a Mr. Lewis purchased her from the insurance company and dispatched professional salvagers to do the job. The Jex Company from Port Huron worked for ten days to haul her up, including rigging the lifting cables with hard-hat divers. The wreck was only in 94 feet of water, easy working depth for a diver. What the divers found aboard her was startling. Certainly they discussed it with their mates on the salvage steamer. Once the *Explorer* was safe on the surface, the divers no longer had to explain anything. It was plain for all to see.

There wasn't any valuable cargo of machinery, merchandise and whiskey in her hold. The damn ship was filled with rocks! Even worse, Waddell's two crewmen were discovered locked below deck. Closer examination revealed a dozen inch and half holes drilled into the centerboard box near the keel. Plainly, she was meant to sink! It was deliberate murder of the ship and crew.

Since all the principals were dead, no one was around to answer for the crime but speculation ran something like this. Waddell planned to sink the *Explorer* well before he left Windsor and recruited the two crewmen as accomplices. The arrangement was to unload the valuable (and insured) cargo somewhere along the desolate Georgian Bay shore and hide it and fill the schooner with rocks. The rocks would give the appearance of carrying cargo should anyone see them and aid in the planned sinking. Doing this would have been well neigh impossible by just anchoring out and ferrying everything back and forth by the ship's small yawl, so there had to be a dock involved somewhere. Once everything was ready, the crooked trio took the schooner out to deep water and literally drilled holes in her until she sank. Alternatively the holes could have been predrilled and plugged. When the time was right the plugs were pulled and down she went. The rock cargo made certain she stayed down too!

How the two crew ended up sealed in the hold is unknown but the likeliest guess is once the schooner reached the scuttle site, Waddell managed to get them drunk and befuddled to the point he was able to seal them in the hold. No one ever mentioned injury to their bodies, suggesting he knocked them unconscious or murdered them before scuttling the ship. With the only witnesses dead, and the schooner "lost" in an unknown location, all he had to do was make it home in his yawl and spin his tale of disaster.

When Waddell made his quiet and mysterious excursions alone in his small boat, he was really going to his cargo cache where he recovered some and sold it before sailing back into port with his pockets filled with cash. He was simply making withdrawals from his "cargo" bank.

The discovery of the *Explorer* and her gristly remains created a surprising controversy. While everyone was shocked over the situation, a Goderich newspaper claimed it was all wrong. The ship was under insured and Waddell never collected anyway. Plus there were no bodies, rocks or holes in her. It was all nothing but malicious gossip.

This spin was trashed quickly by one of the divers who helped salvage her. He stated emphatically a dozen one and half inch holes were drilled in the hull and the local harbormaster could easily point them out to the editor. In addition, all of the sails, rigging, lamps and compass were gone. Clearly the captain wanted to take as much of the salable ship's goods as he could. Two bodies were found aboard and the hatches were nailed down. He didn't know who scuttled her, but scuttled she was! Since Waddell was "scuttled" himself, there was little anyone could do.

The salvaged *Explorer* was sold to a local man who used her as a coastal schooner for only a short time. She wrecked in September 1883 off Stokes Bay, Ontario, on Georgian Bay.[i]

Piracy

Piracy on the lake never reached the height of Caribbean escapades as produced by Hollywood but it was an illegal activity none-the-less and there was much more of it than is often suspected today. Great Lakes piracy tended to be smaller, less glamorous affairs. Usually it was a band of just a few men. Other times it was a bigger group.

William Johnson was one of the famous brigands from the east end of the lakes, often called the "Pirate of the St. Lawrence." In fact he did some of his finest work in the Thousand Islands near the St. Lawrence River. Born in Trois Rivieres, Quebec in 1793, he was especially resentful against the British.

Johnson was a little bit different than most pirates in that he used his daughter as a major part of his crew. While he ran most of the smuggling going on in the islands, he never missed a chance to waylay a boat with a rich cargo either. It all was fair game to him.

During the War of 1812, much like pirate Jean Lafitte in New Orleans, he helped the Americans as best he could. General Scott, the American Commander, stated he "was worth a thousand men."

When the Canadian Rebellion of 1837 kicked off, Johnson took advantage of the confusion to use his gang to capture a British steamer near Wells Island. Running under the old maxim, "All is fair in love and war," he sometimes used a ruse. When it fitted him, he eagerly wrapped himself in the cloak of Canadian nationality, confusing the issue of who he really was, Canadian or American? Under whose jurisdiction did he fall? He and his men robbed men and women alike on the steamer, acting much like train robbers of the American West. "Just put your valuables in the bag. Keep your hands where I can see them!" Holding two cocked flintlock pistols emphasized his demand. Crew or passenger, it didn't make any difference. He robbed then all. Some of the cargo was also "lifted." After putting the people safely ashore, he and his men burned the steamer.

Later Johnson captained one of the ships bringing American supporters, known as "Hunter's Lodges" to Canada to add support to the rebellion. The entire rebellion later collapsed from a lack of leadership and staunch British action. Johnson was eventually arrested on the New York side of the border and charged with piracy. But the clever old reprobate had a special trick up his sleeve, producing a certificate stating he was "Commander in Chief of the Patriot Naval Forces" and worked for the independence of Canada. Of course Johnson was the signer too! Flimsy though it was, the document was all a New York jury needed to refuse to indict him. A Canadian rebellion wasn't their business.

Johnson soon returned to his old game in the swamps and holes of the Thousand Island area. The police chased him, but never caught the old hare. In 1838 he was appointed keeper of a light a few miles below Clayton, New York and kept it for eight years. He even received a Presidential pardon in 1842 for his multitude of past sins. Strange for a character as colorful as he was, he never smoked, chewed or drank liquor. The old rascal died peacefully in his bed in 1870.[ii]

A Hell of a Fight

In the old days on the Lakes captains didn't take too kindly to some rinky-dink local member of the constabulary trying to "serve papers" on their ship. There were heated fights, sometimes even gun play over such affairs.

Oswego Palladium, May 5, 1847

OUTRAGE AT GREEN BAY. - The *Republican* of the 21st inst. gives the details of a daring resistance of the laws that occurred in that place on the Saturday evening previous. It seems that an injunction had been placed in the hands of the Under Sheriff, with directions to serve it immediately upon the schooner Ottawa, Captain Amos Saunders, then lying near the mouth of the Fox River.

C.H. White, the deputy, proceeded in a boat to discharge the duty, but threats and resistance on the part of Saunders prevented its execution, and White returned to town. Procuring assistance, he again approached the vessel, but was attacked with clubs, poles, oars, boiling water, melted pitch, and indeed with every weapon upon which the exasperated crew could lay their hands.

The Captain then ordered his men to bring the topmast over the bulwarks, that it might be used as a battering ram, threatening death to any one who should refuse to aid in this bold defiance of the laws. After the officer and several of his posse had been bruised and knocked down, a fire was commenced by the party in the boat, with pistols, and the mate of the Ottawa named Foster, a respectable man from this city, was severely, but it is hoped not dangerously, wounded.

The infuriated set scattered for a moment, but soon returned to the conflict. Saunders hurled an axe at White, but the latter at that instant was knocked down by a stick of wood and his life thus saved from the axe. White's party finding themselves unable to board the vessel, retired. A surgeon was sent on board, and soon after four of the crew attempted to land near Devil River, which was certainly an appropriate port for such scoundrels, if there is anything in names. Saunders was on board, and although strict watch was kept, he succeeded in landing. On Sunday morning an armed party took boats and rowed toward the schooner, but as they approached, she hoisted sail and made across the bay. Thus has this pirate captain successfully defied and escaped laws. Such a man should not be suffered to remain at Liberty–*Chicago Jour*."[iii]

The "Stolen" Dredge

People steal many things. The most popular of course is money followed by jewelry and automobiles. But who in their right mind would steal a dredge? The answer depends on how badly you need it and therein is the tale.

From its very beginning Chicago fought the lack of a viable harbor. In the early days a bare two feet of water covered the sandbar at the mouth of the Chicago River preventing commercial navigation. Various schemes were tried to cut a channel through it. Some worked better than others but the answer eventually came down to brute force. Just dredge a channel through the sandbar and keep dredging to keep it open. Every year lake currents filled the channel in and every year a dredge had to open it up again. It was a poor solution, expensive and time consuming but at least it was a solution.

In the spring of 1854 the channel was again blocked with sand and urgently needed dredging. The federal government provided a single big steam dredge to handle all of the harbors on the west shore of Lake Michigan. It operated under the auspices of the U.S. Army Corps of Engineers Officer stationed in Chicago. Then, as now, the Corps of Engineers was charged with maintaining the nation's shipping channels. Unfortunately the local engineer officer was in Washington and no one in Chicago could approve the use of the dredge. The Chicago Board of Trade wired Washington asking to use the dredge and offered to pay expenses but Washington never responded to their plea. Frustrated by the need for immediate action the Board, working with the Chicago Common Council, simply seized the dredge and put it to work. The legalities could be sorted out later. When the engineer officer finally returned to Chicago he discovered a deep channel 600 feet wide cut through the sandbar. Presented with a classic "fait accompli" all he could do was approve the work.

By the summer the sand returned and again the channel needed to be dredged. Now however the dredge was up in Kenosha, Wisconsin where it was also badly needed. Chicago pressured the Corps for its immediate return but Kenosha rejected any attempt to bring it south. The dredge was a huge ponderous machine capable of moving barely six miles an hour and then only on days with calm lake conditions. It couldn't just speed down and do the work, then zip back to Kenosha.

To prevent the dredge from leaving, the folks in Kenosha removed critical items of equipment including the large iron scoop. Just to make certain it stayed put, the Sheriff, with the full backing of the Mayor and city council, took additional gear from the dredge. There was no other way to put it. Kenosha had stolen the dredge! Nine days later, after the Corps officer made the strongest protest, the city council reluctantly returned the dredge to his control and so ended the career of the "stolen" dredge.[iv]

Great Lakes

SMUGGLING, AN OLD & HONORED ACTIVITY

Smuggling Across Lake Ontario

Thomas Jefferson is honored as the primary author of the Declaration of Independence and one of our great American Presidents. He certainly did a fine job with quill and parchment but his accomplishments as President are less brilliant. Jefferson's first inaugural address in 1791 stressed the policy of "peace, commerce and honest friendship with all nations..." It was a good idea but without viable armed forces to back up U.S. policy, hopelessly idealistic. Jefferson had ruthlessly cut the Army and Navy down to essentially nothing, leaving the nation virtually defenseless.

When the Napoleonic Wars boiled up again in 1803 it presented a tremendous trading opportunity and the U.S. eagerly traded with both France and Britain. Since we were neutral, we had every legal right to do so under international law. However France and Britain saw the U.S. as trading with the enemy and seized our ships, cargos and crews. Britain also impressed sailors from U.S. ships, claiming they were British deserters. In some instances they likely were deserters of the Royal Navy for the much better pay and conditions on the U.S. ships, but most of the men seized were honest American sailors. Jefferson protested through diplomatic channels, tried negotiation and finally even threats, but nothing worked. Since he had practically eliminated the Army and Navy his threats were pointless anyway.

In desperation Jefferson imposed the Embargo Act of 1807, which outlawed U.S. ships from sailing to any foreign port, effectively cutting off imports as well as exports. He reasoned by depriving France and Britain of U.S. raw materials they would soon come to their senses and stop seizing our ships and seamen.

Fat chance! The act was a disaster for the U.S. Our exports plummeted from $108 million in 1807 to a pitiful $22 million a year later. The entire nation was thrown into a deep depression. Clearly Jefferson was utterly unskilled in both trade and international relations, much to the loss of honest Americans.

It was only the widespread evasion of the act by shippers, captains and crews that produced the meager $22 million at all. The law did provide an exception for ships on a coasting trip say from New York to Charlestown that were blown off course and forced to land in a foreign port from stress of storm. Not surprisingly it was a very stormy year and many coastal vessels ended up in Europe where they sold their cargo and took aboard another for U.S. markets. The despised act was finally repealed in 1809. Other acts were passed to prohibit trade with France and Britain unless they respected American rights but they too were failures. Reluctantly Jefferson realized an elemental fact of international relations – diplomatic power comes from the barrel of a gun. If you have no military power, you have no diplomatic power and are at the complete mercy of those who do. It must have been a difficult fact for Jefferson to accept. It would take the War of 1812 to finally force Britain to recognize American rights on the high seas as well as the fact that we were here to stay and not be absorbed back into the British Empire. When Napoleon was defeated by Britain in 1815 France ceased to be a world power and faded into the status of a third world country.

Great Lakes ships were also "blown off course" during Jefferson's embargo. For example there was a considerable potash trade with Canada from U.S. Lake Ontario ports. To stop it Jefferson dispatched soldiers to Oswego and old Fort Ontario. When the troops arrived in Oswego to seize the potash it wasn't there. Townsfolk just smiled and said, "potash, what potash?" "We don't have any idea what you are talking about." Local folks cleverly removed the potash to the small port of Vera Cruz just to the west. Vera Cruz was founded in 1796 at the mouth of the Little Salmon Creek River and for a time surpassed Oswego in size and importance. Throughout the embargo period shippers in the area continued to use every possible subterfuge to avoid Jefferson's anti-trade actions and stay in business.[i]

Smuggling Today

Smuggling is not just an historic activity. The Great Lakes are increasingly becoming a magnet for this type of illicit undertaking today.

For example, in August 2005 U.S. immigration officials nabbed 22 Caribbean stowaways from the *NST Challenger*, a rust bucket cargo ship, after it docked on the Detroit River. One official of the U.S. Immigration and Naturalization Service stated, "Because of the sheer numbers, we think that this could be part of a smuggling operation."

Two of the group were held in area jails since one was a 20-year-old Cuban and the other a 42-year-old Dominican wanted on drug charges in New York. The rest were kept aboard ship until their return to the Dominican Republic could be arranged.

The fact they were aboard at all was only apparent after three of them jumped overboard in the St. Lawrence River and swam to Canada. While being interrogated by Canadian officials they related they had not eaten for nine days and they were afraid of crocodiles in the river. They also had no idea were they were.

The men were kept in an 18-20 foot compartment without windows. Once moored in Detroit officials searched the ship for other secret smuggling compartments as well as drugs.[ii]

U.S. and Canadian authorities know Port Huron and Detroit are popular smuggling ports for both material and people. Considering this bias it was surprising when a joint operation between the Royal Canadian Mounted Police, U.S. Coast Guard and U.S. Immigration and Customs Enforcement Office, acting on a tip, nabbed eight people from Red China when they came ashore at Sugar Island in the St. Marys River. Six men and two women were on a small rowboat when it crossed the river from Canada.[iii]

Harsens Island, Michigan, just north of Lake St. Clair is another popular link on the smuggling trail. It is barely a quarter mile across the St. Clair River from Canada to the island and then just a short ferry ride to the U.S. mainland. There is no Customs Service or evident Border Patrol presence. In the summer a rowboat works fine for making the crossing and if the winter is cold enough, it's an easy walk on the frozen river. Professional guides are even available to help illegal aliens across. The alien trade is now the major smuggling product replacing alcohol, drugs and cigarettes. Walpole Island, just over the Canadian line, is a major center of the traffic. Harsens Island residents do a fine job of calling the police when they see illegals but it is a tiring job.

More Smuggling

Any international border invites illegal opportunity. Something on one side is more desirable on the other. The trick is how to get it across and make a buck. The action on the U.S.-Canada border has been constant since well before the U.S. was even born. Smuggling from the French North America to the British colonies to the south and the reverse was always "in play." Nothing has really changed today.

In June 2004 Canadian and U.S. authorities smashed a cross-border crime network responsible for smuggling large shipments of narcotics into the U.S. as well as laundering the resulting cash proceeds. Arrests were made in the greater Toronto area as well as Midwestern and Northeast states including Detroit.

Federal prosecutors laid 157 charges with 49 counts against 24 people at all levels in the criminal organization, including the alleged leaders. Charges included possession of proceeds of crime; laundering the proceeds of crime; conspiracy to possess the proceeds of crime; conspiracy to launder the proceeds of crime; possession for the purposes of trafficking a controlled substance; conspiracy to traffic a controlled substance and conspiracy to export a controlled substance. They really threw the book at them.

The headquarters of the organized crime group was in Canada. The smuggling was accomplished through the Windsor-Detroit corridor and distributed to Windsor, Detroit, Minneapolis, Boston, and Pittsburgh among other cities.

In the early days before the network was "rolled up" authorities seized approximately $5 million U.S. in narcotic proceeds plus 772 kilos of marijuana and 3,000 tablets of the drug ecstasy. Just as in the old days of Prohibition, the U.S.-Canadian Great Lakes border was an open pipeline.

Authorities involved included Royal Canadian Mounted Police, Canada Border Services Agency, Ontario Provincial Police, Michigan State Police, Drug Enforcement Administration, Department of Homeland Security and Federal Bureau of Investigation.[iv]

They're Only Cigarettes

Smugglers have long targeted heavily taxed cigarettes as a way to make a profit. Tobacco is addictive, smokers have to have it. States know it and use a smoker's addiction to slap an inordinately high tax on the product. While in theory this means more tax money for the government in question, it also sets up an opportunity for a smuggler to obtain tobacco products from a low tax state (or country) and bring them to a high tax locale. He profits by the "buy low, sell high" concept and if his high is lower than the normal price, his purchasers are happy since they are getting a bargain. In 2005 Michigan had the fourth highest cigarette tax in the country making it a rich target for smugglers, resulting in cigarette smuggling becoming a big business in Michigan.

Michigan may even be a distribution hub. In May 2005 four Canadians were arrested in Windsor, Ontario just across the border from Detroit with hundreds of boxes of unstamped cigarettes smuggled in from Michigan. Ontario too places an inordinately high tax on tobacco.

A year before the infamous Islamic terror attack on the World Trade Center the FBI raided a house in North Carolina and found cash, weapons (including infamous AK-47 assault rifles, aka Moscow Typewriters), documents written in Arabic and a large shipment of cigarettes. They determined the house was a base for smuggling cigarettes to Michigan and other high tax states. The Michigan distribution network used Arab owned convenience stores in the Detroit area. At the time a weekly smuggling run in a van netted $10,000 and this was based on a 75-cent Michigan tax per pack. In 2004 the tax jumped to $2.00 greatly increasing profits. A smuggler can make about $2 million on a single semi-truck load of cigarettes according to the federal Bureau of Alcohol, Tobacco, Firearms and Explosives. Clearly such profits could be a basis for funding Arab terrorism attacks.

Another FBI sting nabbed a pair of men hauling truckloads of cigarettes from North Carolina to Detroit. The profits allegedly went to support Hezbollah, a terrorist organization in Lebanon with powerful links to al-Qaida. Hezbollah translates to "Army of God." It is the terror group responsible for bombing the Marine barracks in Beirut in 1983, killing 241 U.S. Servicemen. One of the men was also arrested in a different operation and stated he was bankrolling an "orphans of martyrs" program run by the terrorist group. Stated more clearly, Michigan cigarette smuggling was (and is) supporting terrorist organizations working to destroy the free world!

While the tradition of smuggling to avoid high taxes is an old American custom dating from colonial days, today it isn't just the tax issue that is the problem. The terrorist connection of the smugglers means the huge profits made support terror attacks on the U.S. abroad and potentially at home. If it were just wasteful State governments being cheated of tax revenue it would be of small concern to the average citizen. But when the cash generated is supporting terror attacks on our freedom, values and innocent civilians, it is surely a different issue. Is it going too far to suggest that cigarette smuggling cash could have supported the terror attacks on 9-11?[v]

Great Lakes

DETROIT & ENVIRONS

A Gritty City of Crime

Detroit has always been a tough city. Today Detroit and crime are synonymous to most people. It wasn't always that way but for many years Detroit did (and perhaps still does it as a competitive race) lead the nation in per capita murder. If it isn't number one, it is certainly near the top. Regardless, the city never was a quiet and thoroughly respectable community. It always had an "edge" to it, a toughness often translating into vicious crime.

The key feature of the city is the Detroit River. The 28-mile waterway connects Lake St. Clair to the north and Lake Erie to the south. From the very earliest days the river was the highway to fortune. Native Americans gathered on its banks for perhaps a thousand years or more before confused old Chris Columbus stumbled into Hispaniola thinking he had found China. In the 1600s French explorers wandered past the soon to be Detroit and in 1701 Antoine de la Cadillac built a fort on the present site of the city. He dubbed it, "ville d'etroit" which morphed over time into Detroit (aka, Motown, Motor City, Murder City).

It wasn't long before villages were on both sides of the river and both were called Detroit for want of a better name. What little commerce existed was based on fur trading. Following the American Revolution the new United States took over control of the frontier outpost called Detroit.

Everything started to change in 1818 when the steamer *Walk-In-Water* began service between Buffalo on Lake Erie and Detroit. When the Erie Canal (aka Clinton's Ditch) opened in 1825 the floodgates opened. Now commerce flowed between the world via New York and Great Lakes and back again. Travel time for passengers or cargo from the eastern seaboard dropped from two months in a bone-jarring wagon over two track trails to a mere 10 days in a smooth and easy canal boat. Freight rates plummeted too.

Hundreds of immigrants unloaded at Detroit. Most continued west, either deeper into Michigan or further into the vast wilderness of America. Some of the

The old Bucket of Blood Saloon was a famous Detroit watering hole.

newcomers stayed however. City population stood at a mere 1,500 in 1828 exploding to 9,000 by 1840. For a time Detroit never looked back, continuing to add population and industry. It was a city on the go and on the grow! The good days came to a slamming stop with the 1967 riots and ever since the city has plummeted into steep and unstoppable decline. In the mid 1950s nearly two million hardworking people called the city home. Today the population is less than 886,000 and sinking like a rock as anyone who can flees the shell of a once proud community. Nearly a third of those people remaining are at or below the federal poverty line, the largest percent of any U.S. city with more than 200,000 population. By any reasonable forecast, the disintegration will continue but that's another sad story of crime and corruption.

Every step of the city's historic growth was marked by an increase in violent crime. In this aspect Detroit was the same as other American cities but it seemed to find a more fertile environment. Murder, rape, burglary, bank robbing, fraud of various kinds and other miscreant deeds all increased as Detroit grew. But Detroit's greatest claim to fame in the world of crime was during the miserable period of American history called Prohibition.

Michigan, dominated by ultra conservative rural voters without the common sense God gave them, jumped the gun on national Prohibition by passing it's own anti-drinking law. Starting on May 1, 1917 the sale of wine, liquor or even beer was forbidden. Luckily, Ohio still allowed it, and through a fortunate accident of geography, the Buckeye state was only 60 miles south of Detroit. For a while Michiganders made a mad rush south to load up on booze. While law enforcement tried to stop the flood, it was a hopeless effort. Cars and trucks soon had hidden compartments to transport the illicit products to thirsty Michiganders. Boats stopping at Ohio ports made certain to load a few cases for the folks back home to help fight the terrible drought.

Old Henry Ford was one of the great "drys." He realized the advantage to a sober work force and figured he could force his employees to be teetotalers, at work and at home! Reputedly if he found out one of his workers frequented a bar or even took a nip in the privacy of his own house, he fired him! Henry may have been a genius at automobile manufacturing, but he was a miserable excuse for a human relations manager. This is the same Henry Ford who hired Harry Bennett with the specific job of beating the hell out of any employee who tried to join a union. And the same Henry who published the *Dearborn Independent*, a notorious anti-Semitic newspaper. Henry was certainly a "real piece of work." Generations of Ford apologists have remade old Henry into an American icon but the reality is very different.

In many ways Michigan's dry law was a dress rehearsal for Federal Prohibition. As luck would have it, the Michigan law was declared unconstitutional and for a couple of months it was really "Katy, bar the door." Judges were forced to let people previously arrested for violating the law out of jail. It was only a temporary respite. The federal law hit on January 16, 1920 and in theory the national door on booze was slammed shut and padlocked!

Sometimes making an ice crossing was dangerous. How much bootleg booze is still on the bottom of the Detroit River?

Going to Canada to load up with booze was so common the newspapers lampooned it.

Fortunately there was Canada just across the Detroit River. Whatever foolishness the Americans did regarding spirited liquor, Canada could "bail" the thirsty U.S. drinkers out. Individual provinces, including Ontario, had earlier outlawed the retail sale of alcoholic beverages but allowed their manufacture and export. In 1920 there were 45 legal distilleries in Ontario alone. All this meant a boat could legally load a full cargo of booze on the Canadian side of the river and take it anywhere the captain wanted, including the U.S. As long as the Canadian distiller was paid, and all the paperwork and official export forms were in order, it was none of their concern. Many of the boats listed "Cuba" as their destination only to return a day later for another cargo. Apparently they were the fastest boats in the world! Wyandotte and Ecorse were also popular unloading points were the local constabulary could be blinded by a flash of green.

The long Detroit River with its many small coves, bays and islands, was a smugglers dream. Since Lake St. Clair was just to the north and the St. Clair River ran from it to the base of Lake Huron the Michigan-Ontario border was

Happy U.S. customers purchased high quality liquor in Canada.

One of the Detroit Custom Service patrol boats.

porous beyond belief. Soon booze flowed across the river system night and day. It came by car or truck over winter ice and by fast speedboats and slow tugs. Containers filled with booze were even hauled back and forth under the surface from Canada to the U.S. One enterprising smuggler used a hose from shore to shore to pump it to his customers. There was no end to the remarkable ingenuity of the smugglers and rum runners. One estimate claimed 75 percent of all liquor supplied to the U.S. came over the border between Port Huron and Gibraltar at the south end of the river. Canadian booze via the Detroit River went to all points in the Midwest and beyond. Al Capone brought it in to Chicago under his private "Log Cabin" label. His shipments went either by truck convoy, rail or ship. Every mode of efficient transportation was used.

Government corruption was so rampant it is fair to assume an enforcement officer was on the take rather than not. Politicians, prosecutors, Coast Guardsmen, state and local lawmen and judges also took their "fair share" of the offering. There was so much money to be made running booze it was very hard not to take a cut. Customs Officers on the U.S. side of the border were paid to turn an official blind eye to shipments coming across the river. To make sure they weren't cheated, they published a price list of so much money for each bottle by variety and sent an officer to the Canadian side to count off as it was loaded! When it arrived on the U.S. side officers often helped unload as did high school students for the unheard of fee of a dollar an hour.

Detroit boasted having an estimated 4,000 "speaks" (aka speakeasies). Another 400 "ice cream parlors" openly served liquid sundaes and cones.

The Customs fleet was largely ineffective in stopping the flood of booze.

The money made in circumventing Prohibition was staggering. In 1929 illegal booze was a $215 million dollar business in Michigan, second only to the automobile industry. An estimated 50,000 people were employed in it in some capacity.

Prohibition was also nearly universally ignored in Detroit. It was so bad that when the Michigan State Police raided a downtown speakeasy they arrested the Mayor, a Michigan Congressman and the County Sheriff! Had the State Police minded their own business and stayed out of the City, none of this embarrassment would have happened! All the wags could figure out was someone neglected to make a payment on time and the cops made the raid to prove a point.

Hijacking booze shipments was also commonplace as was the killing of gang members running it. Why not just let someone else go to the trouble of bringing it across the border and then stealing it from them rather then do the work yourself. Care needed to be taken however with who was doing the hijacking and from whom it was being hijacked. The absolute rule was never mess with the Purple Gang! The repercussions were always deadly!

Lest you think the good people in Detroit only broke the law by imbibing forbidden alcoholic beverages, prostitution, gambling, racketeering and general murder were prevalent also. One activity tended to fuel the others giving the city the edge it still has.[i]

Someone must have missed a payoff since the authorities managed a successful raid.

Purples

Detroit had the distinction of having the most vicious gang in the U.S. during the Prohibition era. The Purple Gang was well known as the "baddest" of the bad, a bunch of bloodthirsty killers even Al Capone backed away from. Capone killed when business required it. By contrast, it appeared the Purples killed for the pure joy of it.

Their name supposedly sprung from the time when the founding members were kids stealing from local shopkeepers. The killers-to-be snatched ice cream, candy, fruit and all manner of items from stores, beating up other kids and even mugging adults when the opportunity was right. Disgusted with such antics, one observer commented they were "rotten," purple like bad meat. The name stuck.

Unlike Chicago where the gangs were dominated by Italians and Irish, for the most part the members were the children of poor Russian Jews. The Bernstein brothers, Abe, Joe, Ray and Izzy were the core of the gang. Other recruits came from New York, Chicago, St. Louis as well as Detroit. The gang had strong connections beyond the Motor City. For example Abe was a friend of mobsters Meyer Lansky and Jerry Adonis and owned a couple of Miami gambling casinos with the latter. Abe also was connected with Capone and was a critical link in the infamous St. Valentine's Day Massacre, calling Bugs Moran to let him know a big shipment of hijacked Capone booze was heading for Chicago and asking if he wanted it. They negotiated a price and the deal was done. Of course there was no shipment of booze. It was a simple set up to make certain Bugs was in the S.M.C. Cartage Garage when Capone's hit men arrived.

The gang specialized in hijacking booze shipments as they came across from Canada. Let the others do the heavy lifting. If a rum runner objected, mob leader or lowly truck driver, the Purples filled him with lead. Sometimes they killed regardless of what the rum runner did. Their reputation for ruthlessness was unparalleled. To prevent hijacking wise rum runners prepaid the Purples a tax on the booze. Instead of trying to buck the Purples, Capone arranged for his supply through them.

The exception to the Purple's normal technique of hijacking someone else's booze, or taxing a smuggler, was the "Little Jewish Navy." It was a group of ten or twelve hoods financed by the Purples to run booze across from Canada as well as do some "enforcement" work as needed. The LJN kept a fleet of a dozen fast boats to make the river runs.

Like bootleggers everywhere, the gang cut their booze for additional profit, one bottle of the real stuff working out to two and half bottles of hootch. The principal ingredient was water while a dash of food coloring added the right "look" to it. An authentic label was the final touch. During the height of Prohibition 150 "cutting plants" were working in Detroit alone.

The Purples also provided protection for drug dealers for a percentage of the profits. If a pusher missed a payment, a Purple slug didn't miss him!

The bookmaking business also paid a share to the Purples. During the 1920s it was usually called "handbooking." There is a tale about a bookie that refused to pay the gang so they hauled him out to a hole in the ice (it was winter) and dunked him a few times until he agreed. It gave a new meaning to the term "cold cash."

Ever mindful of good profit generating opportunities the Purples also controlled numerous Detroit unions and extorted huge amounts of money from their treasuries. It was a very lucrative racket.

The Purples were never bashful about murder. When three St. Louis gunmen double-crossed the gang the Bernsteins laid a careful plan to get even. The gunmen were invited to a "peace conference" at a quiet Detroit apartment. On entering they were given a fast lead shower by Fred "Killer" Burke, brought in from out of town especially for the job. Burke, who later participated in the St. Valentines Day Massacre, used his .45 Caliber Thompson to do the deed, which incidentally was the first time a machine gun was used in Detroit. Newspaper reporters later counted 110 bullet holes in the now room temperature St. Louis crooks, as well as walls.

In a way the Purples, targets worked in their favor. Since they invariably attacked other gangsters, the police usually left them alone. A gangster rubbing

Coming out of court, gang members hide their faces behind their fedoras.

out a gangster wasn't an inherently bad thing. None of their victims were willing to sign a complaint anyway! In a strange twist the cops suspected the murder of a patrolman was the work of the gang but couldn't prove it. It seems the cop was regularly shaking down the blind pigs on his beat and the Purples took exception to his poaching on their turf. The miscreant officer was given a one-way ride. Should the police be overly concerned if the Purples whacked a bent cop?

The Purples were eventually undone by their own inherently unstable streak of viciousness. The individual members were unable to "get along" with each other regardless of the huge amount of money at stake. The end accelerated when three Chicago mobsters came to Detroit and were taken into the gang. The three had double-crossed Capone and getting out of town was a very good idea. The Purples accepted them even assigning them a territory to run but true to form, the three got greedy and soon were stealing from other members and double-crossing them. In an effort to rake in even more money, they started a bookmaking operation for the ponies, which was OK except they weren't very good at it and kept losing money. When the Eastside mob hit big, winning a parlay worth a couple of hundred thousand dollars, it was a bet the Chicago three couldn't cover. In a desperate effort to pay the debt they bought a large supply of booze from the Purples on credit, *watered it down again* to increase the profit and peddled it at cut-rate prices.[ii] To make matters worse, they accepted a second bet from the Eastsiders, lost, and again couldn't cover it. Making things even worse, the Eastside gang had "fixed" the race! They were just bleeding the Chicago three of money. To bail themselves out, the Chicago Three repeated the watered down booze and under cutting price cycle again. Now the Purple leaders were really "irritated" and a plan was developed to end the problem once and for all.

The booze issue was especially troublesome. The national convention of the American Legion was coming to Detroit and the demand for liquor was sky high. All the bars, speakeasies and cabarets were placing large orders to meet the demand. It was critical to maintain the flow across the river, and since the three had also been double crossing the "Third Avenue Navy," rum runners operating from Windsor to the rail yards between Third and Fourth Avenues, there were delivery problems. The Purples would have to smooth things over.

To solve the problem, Solly Levine, (the man who originally vouched for the Chicago three) as well as the three men were offered positions as liquor agents for the gang. Apparently the Purple leadership was impressed with their ability to water down already water-downed booze and move it on the market. Or so the set-up went. A meeting between the four men (Levine plus the three) and several Purple leaders was set up for the Collingswood Manor Apartments in September 1931. Seeing no reason to bring guns to a meeting where they were going to be "promoted," none came armed. What followed was the Detroit version of the St. Valentine's Day Massacre.

Four members of the Purple gang led by Ray Bernstein met them at the apartment and for a time everything was pleasant; handshakes all around, good cigars and a couple of glasses of real booze made for an easygoing atmosphere. Eventually the senior Purple excused himself and went down to his car. After a minute he blew his horn. Hearing it the other Purples drew guns and opened fire, killing all but Levine. Bernstein wanted him untouched for old time's sake. One of the killers, Harry Fleisher, was a suspect in the St. Valentine Day Massacre and well experienced in multiple killings. Judging from the number of slugs found in the bodies, the killers emptied their guns, reloaded and blasted away again. A job worth doing is worth doing well. On the way out of the apartment the shooters dropped their .38 caliber revolvers into a bucket of green paint to destroy fingerprints. The serial numbers were already filed off.

Police quickly arrested the three shooters. But Fleisher disappeared. All were charged with first-degree murder. Levine, the lone eyewitness, was held in police custody with eight detectives guarding him. After getting the "third degree," he "sang like a little birdie" ratting on the killers. So much for his gratitude for not being bumped off with the others. The case went to trial in November and all three were convicted, given life sentences without parole and trundled off to Michigan's Alcatraz, Marquette Branch Prison. Leaving Levine alive for "old times sake," a rare act of Purple mercy, was not a good business decision.

The following June, Fleisher turned himself into the authorities, claiming he was in a Pennsylvania jail during the killings so obviously had nothing to do with them. Although Levine had sworn he was one of the killers it seems the lone witness had "disappeared." While Levine left detailed written testimony nailing Fleisher as one of the gunmen, since the accused couldn't confront the accuser as guaranteed by the Constitution, Fleisher walked free.

The gang continued to self-destruct literally killing themselves off in internal fighting and by 1935 what was left standing was absorbed into other mobs.

The Purples weren't the only gang in the city. The Eastside mob controlled the area on the upper river east of the city while the Westside mob owned Hamtramck. Both groups regularly shook down gambling joints and brothels and did some bootlegging.

During this period Hamtramck was a seething den of corruption. It was so bad that in the fall of 1923 the Governor of Michigan was forced to react to the tidal wave of complaints by ordering the Michigan State Police to move in and seize control of city government. As a result of the subsequent investigation, 31 men, including the mayor, were convicted of various crimes. The Westsider's activities were badly disrupted but not smashed and when the state pulled out they slid back into place just as if they never left. Chester LaMare, the Westside boss, was given probation on the agreement he stayed out of the rackets. For a while he even sold fruit in Ford's River Rouge factory. It all looked legit but he was really just "laying low" and plotting how to take over the Eastside operation.

When the boss of the Eastside mob died of natural causes, an unusual demise for a mobster, LaMare sent his men in to grab what they could of the bootlegging, numbers, rackets, strong arm enforcement and prostitution trade. Conflict was immediate and clearly some sort of peace needed to be agreed to. Bullets and bloodletting were always bad for business.

LeMare managed to set up a meeting with the Eastside boss, Angelo Meli, at a Detroit fish market for May 31, 1930. Since Meli would bring all his key men, it was a great opportunity for LaMare to rub them all out at once, clearing the decks for his take over. To this end, he hid three gunmen in the market. At the right time the shooters would walk in with Tommy guns blazing and end the meeting. But Meli smelled a rat. Instead of coming himself with his lieutenants, he sent two Mafia counselors. Both sides respected these men and Meli believed that high esteem would keep them safe from harm. Unfortunately as soon as the two sat down in the meeting room the gunmen entered and sprayed them with a fatal coating of lead. Although the shooters recognized the Mafia counselors they were afraid the two hoods would finger them as the planned assassins so they concluded they had little choice but to kill them. It didn't do any good. The three were identified by witnesses anyway as they fled the scene. The cops quickly arrested the three gunmen and the prosecutor charged "murder one." In the end the identification was useless. When they went to trial the witnesses had severe cases of amnesia. The three killers walked.

The murder of the two counselors ignited a major war between the two gangs. Bullets flew across the city with killings taking place on crowded city streets but as in the fish market, witnesses soon forgot what they saw. Amnesia was remarkably catching.

In less than two months following the fish market debacle, 14 mobsters were gunned down. It was a wild and bloody time in old Detroit. The carnage only stopped when WMBC radio commentator Gerald Buckley was gunned down in the lobby of the LaSalle Hotel. In spite of the belief he had close ties to mobsters, the murder of a public figure caused a major police crack down and subsequent grand jury probe. Mob warfare quickly quieted down.

Eastsider Meli was working behind the scenes to end the war but not with a massive bloodbath but instead a single surgical strike. He let two of Westsider LaMare's most trusted men know unless they "hit" the boss, he would arrange to hit them. On February 6, 1931 the pair entered LaMare's house while he was home alone. After kibitzing in the kitchen, LaMare turned around to speak with one of the men and the other pulled a .32 caliber automatic pistol and calmly plunked several bullets into the side of the mobster's head. So ended the war. The Eastside mob later morphed into the city's present Mafia.[iii]

Harsens Island, A Playground for Crime

Twenty miles or so north of Detroit, at the northern end of Lake St. Clair, Harsens Island sits like a plug in the end of the St. Clair River. The island is about five miles by three miles and a short ferry ride connects the island with Algonac on the mainland. Although it isn't much of an island as islands go, mostly flat land and swamp as befits a river island, it is filled with vacation cottages, yacht basins and other destinations for people anxious to flee the crush of the city. In the early 1900s, the area was often called, "America's Venice" in recognition of the many cuts, channels, streams and bays. The State of Michigan owns roughly three-quarters of the island and has numerous waterfowl and wildlife sanctuaries. The area is also home to a wild array of wildlife, including the great blue heron, snapping turtles and red-winged blackbirds. Fish include sunfish, perch, bluegills and silver bass. Today there are roughly 1,000 full time residents and 5,000 summer visitors. The shipping lanes pass close aboard and watching the big freighters is a popular pastime.

The island is rich in history, from the days of the old French voyageurs, English pioneers and American vacationers. The name derived from the first white settler, Jacob Harsen, a Dutchman who migrated to the island from New York in 1779. It was about 1812 the first Harsen related crime occurred. James Harsen went to the Big Bear Creek area to trade with the Indians and was about to enter a cabin owned by John Reilly when Reilly put a rifle ball through Harsen's eye. He died six months later. Why Reilly did it was never determined

The Tashmoo *was the most popular of the Detroit River excursion boats.*

but it was well known he was belligerent and downright ornery when drunk and he was very drunk when he shot Harsen.

Starting in 1900 the 311-foot sidewheel steamer *Tashmoo* carried Detroiters to any one of the island's luxury hotels. Tashmoo Park, opened in 1897, providing vacationers with a dance pavilion and other pleasant activities. The park closed in 1951 and is now part of the Tashmoo Marina. Owned by the White Star Steamship Line, trips ran daily from Detroit to Port Huron, making 13 stops in the Flats area. Round trip cost was .50! Two U.S. Presidents, Teddy Roosevelt and William McKinley, enjoyed a pleasant cruise on the *Tashmoo*.

The St. Clair River and Lake St. Clair were reputedly named in honor of Sainte Clair of Assisi. She founded the Order of Poor Ladies, dying in 1253. August 12, 1679 is her feast day and the day Robert Cavelier, Sieur de LaSalle's ill-fated *Griffon* reached the area sailing upbound for Lake Michigan. The crew evidently thought the tribute would help them survive their journey. It didn't, the *Griffon* becoming the first European vessel to "go missing" on the Great Lakes. Today Saint Clair is listed as the official patron of television since when she was too ill to attend mass, an image of the ceremony was said to have appeared on her wall so she could follow along. This could be considered the first "flat screen" TV. By the way some authorities estimate there are upwards of 10,000 saints up there in the heavens. Competition for jobs must be tough! The river went by other names too. The local Indians called it Otsi-Sippi. When Patrick Sinclair owned the land where the city of St. Clair is today, it was the Sinclair River. Some claim the name St. Clair isn't from the old saint, but rather in honor of General Arthur St. Clair, one time governor of the Northwestern Territory.

Happy passengers enjoying a cruise on the old Tashmoo.

Ownership of the island is still a little "foggy." Following the War of 1812, U.S. and British negotiators agreed the boundary between the U.S. and British North America (aka Canada) ran along the western shore of the St. Clair River, down the North Channel and around Anchor Bay. British North America began on the east shore of the river. The islands in between on "the flats" were left to the Indians. However with the press of shipping in the 1860s, the U.S. Army Corps of Engineers dredged the 6000-foot long St. Clair Flats Canal at the end of the South Channel of the St. Clair River. At this point the two respective governments decided the boundary ran in the middle of the river. The islands that earlier had been "Indian territory" were gobbled up by either country as appropriate, which brings up the argurement whether they were ever legally acquired. Harsens Island is the largest on the U.S. side of the border.

During Prohibition the island was a perfect place to smuggle bootleg booze from Canada. It was so close to the border preventing rum runners from hopping back and forth was virtually impossible. It was also virtually impossible to catch a rum runner once he got into the swamps and canals. There were just too many places to hide. The few Prohibition agents who tried always came back muddy, wet, tired and utterly defeated. It was during Prohibition sixteen resort hotels flourished on the island. When opportunity knocked, good businessmen knew enough to open the door! Today the only one left is the Idle Hour Yacht Club but more on it later. Since all the old hotels were on the water, the smugglers just ran their boats right up to the main dock or, if some discretion was needed, to a pier just behind the hotel. Sometimes guests even helped to unload. It was almost too easy!

The hotels ran the full range of tastes. Joe Bedore's Marshland was a place where "six-bottle" men always had "lusty" escorts. No man ever went away without his thirst quenched and itch scratched at Joe's place. By contrast, families, especially from the South, usually stayed at the sedate and upstanding Island House. The Muir House advertised itself as the "only temperance hotel on the island." It must have been a lonely place. Other hotels included the Old Club, Mount Rushmore, Damer's and Trautz's German Village.

The Idle Hour Yacht Club dates from 1891 when Charles Henry Coulter and a partner had it built to tap into the lucrative resort trade booming on the island. Coulter was one of those "bigger than life" characters who knew everybody, millionaire or shoeshine boy. Originally called the Riverside Hotel it attracted attention due to it's fine expanse of manicured lawn running from the main building down to the dock. One review described it as, "a small but cheerful and home-like hostelry, where popular prices and first-class cooking prevail in a rare combination." Victorian women, fully attired in high lace collars, bustle, long skirts and parasols promenaded on the lawn as lake freighters steamed by. It was an odd contrast.

The Riverside was sold four years later and remade into a hunting and fishing club. For a couple of years during World War II the Coast Guard took over the place for recruit training. There was plenty of room to make it into an ad hoc barracks complete with mess hall and classroom. Following the war it went back

Joe Bedore's place was famous for its "Six Bottle" men and "Lusty Escorts."

The Riverside Hotel was one of the famous Harsens Island "resorts." Today it is the Idle Hour Yacht Club.

to being a restaurant and hotel but business slowly eroded and by the early 1980s it was closed and boarded up. It looked like she would go the sorry way of all the other island hotels.

New life sparked into the old place in 1988 when Ken Baker purchased it, reopening it as the Idle Hour Yacht Club. His work has been well rewarded, creating a wonderful combination of history and style perfectly attuned to the laid back pace of Harsen's Island. The old place is also filled with the steamy side of history. As the old saying goes, "If the walls could only talk," they would certainly "take the Fifth!"

It was claimed during the heyday of the "Roaring Twenties" in Detroit, when the infamous Purple Gang ruled supreme, the Riveside was a frequent rest stop from the tiring business of gratuitous murder and mayhem. Even vicious sub-human killers needed a break once in a while and this hotel on the island fit the bill. When Big Al visited from Chicago for a "sit down" with the gang, it was sometimes done at the Riverside. It was hard for the cops to sneak up on an island!

Rooms in the old Riverside were ideally suited for another form of resort activity, the kind conducted by independent females in contractual relationships with males. The old tales claim the hotel was a popular place for such temporary financial liasons. There isn't any doubt when the joint was hopping with ragtime music in the bar room the beds upstairs were a "squeak'n."

Doubtless the marshy fields surrounding the hotel have all matter of suspect plantings under the tall grass. It was a great place to dump the remains of men who were "taken for a ride." The south wing of the building has an old walk-in cooler that hasn't been used in many years. The cooler is adjacent to the old kitchen dating from the 1920s. Today both are used for storage but when the

Today's Idle Hour Yacht Club still holds the charm of the old Riverside.

Purples stopped by for a little business it was a perfect set up to put someone "on ice," permanently! The killer came up from behind and grabbing the victim firmly around the throat with his left arm to choke off a scream, rammed a knife blade quickly between the ribs with a final twist to assure damaging as much vital tissue as possible. When the struggling stopped, the killer lowered the victim to the kitchen floor allowing the blood to gurgle down the drain. Once the corpse drained out of blood it was an easy job for a couple of hoods to hang it from a meat hook in the cooler until it was time to "dispose" of it properly. Perhaps it was buried in the marsh or wrapped in chains and tossed off the dock into the river. A short boat ride into nearby Lake St. Clair before feeding the fish was a good method too. If the Purples had a special reason, or for that matter the Purples did a lot of terrible things without reasons, the victim could be tied up and hung in the cooler to slowly freeze to death.

Old traditions do die hard. Just four or five years ago the cops noticed a guy stopped on a bridge trying to chuck the dismembered remains of his ex-girlfriend (at this point she must be an ex) off the bridge just down from the Idle Hour and into a canal. They nabbed him just as he was getting set to pitch a leg into the water. For a time her identification was unknown, until a badly decomposed head rolled ashore downriver a month later.

Some of the old hotels later became "hunt clubs," places where rich "sportsmen" could enjoy a weekend or longer of shooting and fishing. The pressures of the business world were great and the opportunity of recharge was important and where better to do it than lonely Harsens Island. The clubs were invariably stag, without wives getting underfoot. Often the men brought their mistresses with them and if a man didn't have one, the club was able to remedy the problem for a price. Over time some of the clubs evolved into more traditional resorts but still catering to the "carriage trade" and their girlfriends. One high school age girl who waitressed in one of the old "resorts" in the 1970s remembered young and voracious wives all through the year accompanied the men until one night one of the men showed up with an older, frumpier woman. Thinking it was his mother (since she had met his wife before) she made a comment to that effect as she was taking their drink orders. When the doughy woman remarked in a huff that she was Mrs. _______, the waitress beat a hasty retreat while the man tried to conjure up a hasty explanation. There was no tip at that table![iv]

Great Lakes

CHICAGO, GOTHAM OF CRIME

"Chicago is unique," lamented Professor Charles Merriam, an early loser in the battle for political reform in Chicago. "It is the only completely corrupt city in America!"

The name "Chicago" is said to translate from the Indian as "swamp filled with rotting wild onions." I suspect a better translation is "crime ridden swamp filled with stinking, rotting wild onions."

The city is steeped in crime. Before the founding of the city to the present, crime is one constant in the windy city. All cities are, to a greater or lesser degree corrupt. Chicago just has a history of being better at it than others!

In the public mind it is linked forever with Scarface Al Capone, Bugs Moran, the St. Valentine's Day Massacre, crooked politics, bootlegging, hookers, gambling and crooked elections. The old joke, "when I retire I want to stay active in politics so I will move to Chicago so I can still vote after my death," isn't a joke in Chicago where the permanently planted manage to vote in every election!

In 1670 old French trader Pierre Moreau had a small cabin at the point where the river ran into Lake Michigan. It was a popular place since he sold his illegal booze to anyone with the money to buy it, including the local Indians.

Perhaps the first vice district was at Wolf Point where two forks of the Chicago River joined before flowing east into Lake Michigan. Over time it developed into a place where local settlers met to drink copious volumes of French brandy, British rum and American bourbon while betting furs, trade goods and other items on any "game" that was available. Horseracing, shooting matches and card games all took center stage at different times. If the weather was conducive, outdoor dances were common with everyone whirling around like a Great Lakes "fandango."

Just to the east, where the river met the big lake, was the site of a "mansion" of five rooms built by pioneer Jean Baptiste Pointe DuSable. An Afro-French fur trader who prospered in the 1790s he was respected by both Indians and whites.

Fort Dearborn protected the growing settlement of Chicago.

For unknown reasons he sold out, "lock, stock and barrel" in 1800 and moved to Louisiana. Perhaps the Chicago winters were too harsh, a lament today's residents still complain about. Sometime afterward Jean Lalime, of mixed Indian and French blood, took over the house. In 1803 trader John Kinzie came to the area after doing business in Ohio and Michigan. A conflict developed when Kinzie moved his family into the DuSable mansion and Lalime objected, feeling the mansion was his. The quarrel turned violent, Lalime ending up on the wrong end of Kinzie's hunting knife!

In 1803 Fort Dearborn, a military outpost, was established at the mouth of the Chicago River. It protected a small but growing community of settlers until the War of 1812. General William Hull, an abysmally incompetent officer, commanded the U.S. Army in the West. As soon as he heard Fort Mackinac fell to the British he panicked and ordered the immediate abandonment of Fort Dearborn. Since Fort Dearborn was well sited and defended, had adequate supplies and no significant hostile threat, the order to desert it was incomprehensible. Regardless, an order is an order, so the commander, Captain Nathan Herld obeyed. In order to leave nothing of value for the enemy, Herld destroyed all excess arms and ammunition as well as the large stock of whiskey. Relations with the local Indians (Potawatomi and Winnebago) were strained but so far controllable so Herld left the excess food, blankets and other goods behind for their use. After negotiations the Indians agreed Herld and his column could pass in safety. Nonetheless, Herld and his men were deeply concerned since once they left the fort's protection they would be badly outnumbered by the Indians and unable to defend themselves in the open. Regardless, Hull's orders were clear.

On August 15 Herld and his small band of 54 soldiers, 12 militia, nine women and 18 children left the protection of the fort heading for Fort Wayne to the south.

With the group was Billy Wells, a white who was captured and raised as an Indian. He led an escort of 30 or so Miami warriors. Wells sensed an ambush was brewing and just when the small column reached a sand dune east of the fort a group of 500 Potawatomi and Winnebago warriors suddenly appeared at the crest preparing to attack. Wells and Herld led a forlorn assault up the dune but the odds were hopeless, especially when the Miami immediately deserted. It was a brutal massacre. All the militia and half the soldiers were killed. One blood-thirsty buck entered a wagon carrying children and beheaded a dozen of them, killing a black slave woman who tried to intervene. Many of the soldiers and civilians taken prisoner were later murdered in cold blood. Others were freed after a year in captivity and the payment of a tribute. Wells was killed in the onslaught, his head chopped off and heart cut out and immediately eaten by the Indians. It was a case of treachery and murder and would help set the stage for Chicago's later history.

By the 1830s Chicago gained the reputation of being a tough and hell-raising town. It was no place for the faint of heart or those unwilling to fight for their "rights." Still an Indian trading post, merchants did a brisk business in furs, fish, guns, whiskey and women. The town had "what ever ya needed bub."

There is a legend about a man named Harper who in 1833 was found to be a vagrant by the local court. Since the law allowed a vagrant to be sold as a slave, he was duly auctioned off for the high bid of .25! In a strange reversal of roles the buyer was a local black man. Supposedly Harper ran off during the night disappearing from history.

Pushed by western migration, by 1837 a community of 4,000 people had established itself around the site. Chicago was on the march.

Justice in Chicago could be fast and deadly. When John Stone arrived in the city in 1838 it was after a stint in a Canadian jail for robbery and murder. While he did some labor as a woodcutter he spent most of his time swilling rotgut whiskey in the saloons. In 1840 he was arrested for the rape and murder of a local farmer's wife and after a quick trial, pronounced guilty. On July 10 authorities laced the killer up in chains and tossed him in the rough bed of a wagon, taking him to the lakeshore. To make certain none of his friends attempted to intervene, 200-armed civilians escorted him as well as 60 Illinois Militia. When everything was ready he was brusquely strung up and left to dance in the wind. Afterward his body was given to a couple of local doctors for dissection.

Chicago really took off in 1848 when the massive Illinois and Michigan Canal, connecting the Illinois River and Chicago River, was completed. While not nearly as successful or important as the world famous Erie Canal, connecting Lake Erie and New York City via the Hudson River, it allowed midwestern farmers to ship their produce to eastern markets and in return, goods from the east to flow to the great western markets. Chicago was all about transportation and within a decade it became the rail crossroad of the nation and population soared to nearly 110,000 people. Great Lakes shipping also boomed; in the 1860s 13,000 vessels a year moored in the city. Population continued to stream into Chicago, reaching roughly 300,000 by 1870. Most were European immigrants seeking a fresh opportunity in America.

As Chicago became the gateway to the west, its businessmen seized advantage of the opportunity to provide the goods and services pioneers needed, especially young bachelors for whom the city was the last example of civilization they would see for a *very long time*. Considering the hardscrabble life many would live on the trackless, soul sapping and mind numbing prairie, perhaps the only civilized place they would ever see again.

Chicago entrepreneurs took full advantage of the opportunity to provide these doomed men with a last taste of the good life. Since the services provided the immigrants were available to all comers, city residents gained too. Saloons, gambling dens and brothels were everywhere. As the city grew more important in shipping, manufacturing and the like, the number of entertainment locations grew dramatically. Popular games included poker and dice with bigger establishments offering Faro, Keno and Roulette.

A rarity, a Chicago "dove" being booked in a police station following a raid.

Not everyone agreed these establishments were a good thing. In a burst of civic reform fever a group of local businessmen advocated hiring the Pinkerton Detective Agency to come in and clean up the city. The idea was quashed after some bickering but the famous detective agency was hired to stop local gangs from digging up bodies from the old City Cemetery and selling them to medical students. It was a Chicago version of Scotland's infamous Burke and Hare enterprise.

As the city grew a number of different geographic vice areas were soon delineated. The area called the Sands was just north of the Chicago River and stretched to Lake Michigan. It was created by lake current carrying sand southward piling up against the pier on the north side of the river. Since the new land was never on any government land survey or map, it officially didn't exist.

Seeing the opportunity, squatters soon moved in and it was filled with gambling joints, saloons and bordellos, many of the lowest variety. Some of the brothels charged a mere 25 cents a "roll." One of the pimps redefined the idea of a family business since he pimped for his four sisters! It was claimed one old hooker, Margaret McGinnis, was neither sober or left her house for five years. She didn't even bother to put clothes on for three years! Ordinarily she "serviced" between ten and 40 men nightly. It was also never suggested she ever bathed. Of course her customers rarely saw soap either. Originally the area catered to sailors and canal men, but as the city crew, the customer base increased. The various dens also became hiding places for all manner of criminals, petty and major.

The city tried to get rid of the Sands via the courts but the owners managed to keep it tied up in various appeals and litigation. In May 1857 exasperated Mayor John Wentworth hatched a truly inspired plan. At the time dog fighting was a major "sporting" and betting interest so he arranged for a fight between two popular mutts at a local racetrack. The event spawned major interest and virtually everyone in the Sands hurried off to the track to see the fight. As soon as the coast was clear, Wentworth led a demolition crew to the Sands and working virtually all day managed to tear down a number of buildings, burning the rest to the ground.

Ultimately Wentworth's "urban renewal" failed. The saloons, gambling dens and brothels just crossed the river moving into other locations, many ending up in the area that would later be the Loop, low class brothels locating on Wells Street and higher class ones to the east on Clark and State Streets.

The Sands later gained more notoriety as "Streeterville," named after Captain George Wellington Streeter, a circus promoter from Michigan. Seeing an opportunity for profit, in 1886 he ran his barely floating boat aground on the sand beach and waited for the current to surround it with sand. Impatient for nature to take it's course, he had construction companies dump their excess dirt and related material there too. For a city growing as fast as Chicago, dumping the material at Streeter's place was far cheaper than hauling it out of town. After a time he claimed his boat was a house and since he had homesteaded the still unsurveyed land, the 168 acres he created was his! He hung out a "for sale" sign and started selling lots. The city tried various legal strategies but he managed to keep them tied up in the courts. Finally after World War I the city managed to nail him for selling liquor on Sundays, in violation of city ordinance. Considering Chicago's reputation as a "hell raising" town, this is truly ironic! It was at best a trumped up charge but did the job. In the end Streeter lost his land but kept the name. The area is still called Streeterville in his honor.

The Willows was another of the infamous early vice areas. Extending for several large buildings near Monroe and Wells Streets, it received its name from a huge willow tree at the end of the block. Roger Plant, an early criminal organizer, ran it as a total business operation. Plant was a bare 5-foot, 1-inch tall but said to be meaner than a junkyard dog. There wasn't a weapon made he couldn't expertly use and always carried a large knife and hidden gun. In his line of work he needed them. Unusual for such a little man, he had a wife that topped the scale (a stockyard model used to weigh cattle to be sure) at an estimated 300 pounds. She ran the hookers, and it was said she often picked him up and carried him around under one arm whenever he became sassy! Plant and his wife also helped Chicago grow, producing roughly 15 offspring. And they made certain each had an employable trade, sending them out on the streets as very skillful pickpockets. After ten years or so in business, the Plants wisely took their money and moved out into the country, content to live off their ill-gotten fortune.

Whatever depravity the customer wanted, Plant could provide. The brothels were of the lowest kind and it was claimed customers were sometimes knocked out, stripped, robbed and dumped into the back alley. His nerve center was a saloon and brothel at Monroe and Wells called the Barracks. City fathers decided to clean it up but instead of using direct action as Wentworth did at the Sands, they would use a form of urban renewal. Like virtually all morality based civic cleanup efforts, it was doomed to ultimate failure and in this instance, self-inflicted. Because the Willows area was very low lying, for practical purposes swamp, it was decided to raise the street level, in some cases as much as ten feet.

The tunnels under Chicago provided a veritable Interstate for illegal activity.

At first consideration in appeared good for the city in eliminating a swampy mess and bad for the notorious Barracks and other dens of sin. What actually happened was in raising the buildings an entire network of underground passages, tunnels and rooms was created, greatly facilitating and expanding criminal activities. Worst of all Plant stayed in control of it all.

Plant had a number of infamous criminals hiding out in his dens. One was Sammy Caldwell, a particularly innovative burglar who is claimed to have been the first to use tape to "bind" his victims.

Chicago really came of age during the Civil War when legions of riverboat gamblers driven off the river by military action migrated north to the lure of easy money. They found a willing host in Chicago, especially as the city was booming with war driven manufacturing and awash in money. There were so many of the riverboat card sharks the area of Clark Street from Randolph to Monroe gained the name "Gamblers Row."

One writer estimated there were 1,300 prostitutes in the city during the Civil War. Randolph Street teemed with saloons, cheap wine rooms, bordellos, and dance halls. The city quickly gained the reputation of being the "wickedest city in the U.S." Besides the expected brothels, some as "reasonable" as two bits a pop, the streets overflowed with bars, peep shows, crooks and pickpockets.

A surprising group of customers came from Camp Douglas, a Union prisoner of war camp located in the northern part of the city. Up to 9,000 Confederate troops were held there at various times, guarded by as few as 500 Union soldiers. Conditions in the camp were bad, with various diseases common but never approached the horror the South inflicted on Union prisoners in hell-holes like infamous Andersonville. Sometimes the boys in gray slipped out of camp and into Chicago to enjoy the various "distractions," especially the very sociable Yankee "ladies." A favorite destination was the Prairie Queen with its brothel and gambling tables. The prisoners usually came back home again once their money was spent. While such sojourns were very embarrassing for the camp commanders, no real harm was done. Having the camp in town did increase the crime rate but the guards, not the prisoners, caused it. The men detached to guard prisoners were never first line troops, north or south but invariably slackers and petty thieves.

One actual prison "break" from Camp Douglas in 1862 was financed by Levi Boone, an ex mayor of Chicago (1855-56). All toll, 60 men escaped and all were quickly captured and returned. Boone wasn't a secret Southern sympathizer, but conditions in the camp were so bad, with disease and short rations killing the inmates, he was moved by pure humanitarian instincts to try to get the men out of such a deadly environment. The camp commander was so livid at such treachery he promptly arrested Boone and tossed him in prison. President Lincoln eventually intervened and ordered his release.

To help newcomers find their way around the city, especially to the various dens of sin and depravation many visitors eagerly sought, a special visitor's guide was published in 1870. It would be the first of many. At the time an estimated 7,000 women were working in 250 brothels and bordellos so the need for an accurate guide was apparent.

Chicago is also famous for inventing the "Mickey Finn," a libation designed to render the consumer senseless in seconds, allowing for a fast and efficient robbery (or in criminal parlance, mugging). Mickey Finn and his wife "Gold Tooth Mary", operated a couple of bars, the Lone Star and the Palm Garden, both located next to a string of cheap brothels. Today the term "slip him a Mickey" is standard dialog in many cheap Hollywood gangster films. And it started in Chicago!

The Great Chicago 1871 Fire killed roughly 300 people and destroyed about a third of the city. Over 17,000 homes went up in smoke and roughly 100,000 people were left without shelter. During the height of the fire many of the 350 prisoners freed from the burning jail quickly broke into a jewelry store. One observer claimed throughout the fire hookers, murderers, thieves and gamblers were in an orgy of "stealing, fighting, and laughing at the beautiful and splendid crash of walls and falling roofs."

The fire certainly demoralized the city. There were those who believed it was punishment from God for the sinful goings on. Other folks saw it as an opportunity to rebuild without allowing the vice districts to again gain a foothold. Committees of clergy and leading citizens organized to fight

Residents desperately fled the Chicago Fire.

The Randolph Street Bridge as crowds surge across.

gambling, prostitution and liquor. Reform Mayor Joseph Medill led the way to build a better Chicago.

The fire certainly destroyed the worst of the vice districts. The flames cauterized disease ridden prostitute cribs, infected gin mills and the like. But just as you can't keep a good man down, they rose again.

It wasn't long after the fire, Chicago bartender Joseph Chesterfield Mackin came up with a new gimmick to bring customers into his saloon – a "free lunch." He tried a variety of devices before taking the fatal step, including adding an extensive library in a back room complete with issues of the latest "sporting papers." Finally he started serving a hot oyster with each drink. It was a hit, and the rest was history. It was also enough of a career boost to propel him to a leadership position in the local democrat political machine. Soon for a saloon to compete in the marketplace a free lunch had to be part of the bargain. Some spreads became very extensive, one saloon went through 200 pounds of meat a day and needing a staff of five men just to serve it. Many joints went broke trying to run a free lunch and still make a profit.

The saloons served a vital service well known to today's travelers – public restrooms. The city provided no public facilities at all. Repeated efforts to have aldermen address the issue met with failure. Saloon restrooms were free, clean, and open on Sundays and at night and everywhere. If you were a temperance reformer arguing against the free restroom was a tough problem. You couldn't close the saloons without offering an alternative for bursting bladders and "anxious" colons. Of course gentlemen who availed themselves of the facilities invariably stopped at the bar for a beer or shot too. It was an unwritten rule as a token of appreciation.

Some saloons featured remarkable attractions. Hester's Fish Camp had a tank filled with live fish swimming hither and yon. Colonel Squire T. Harvey's Ye Wayside Inn had $2,000 in $20 and $5 gold pieces, Queen Victoria Jubilee Coins and silver dollars inlaid in the bar and floor. Heinegabubeler's on State Street was a collection of titillating attractions. Inside was a peep show with such titles as "Night at Vassar" and "Midnight in Paris." It also had gymnasiums, reading rooms and a roof garden for less jaded customers. Another bar in South Chicago had a model coal mine and a working blacksmith shop, both indoors. Grenier's Garden on Madison and Troop Streets ran grueling six-day bicycle races on an indoor track. Whatever brought customers through the front door was fair game.

Chicago police always operated at a disadvantage in trying to enforce the law. Invariably there were too few of them to match up to the vice lords. For example from 1871 to 1894 the city had only one active officer for every 20,000 residents! As the city grew the police became a political arm of the city government, which meant as the owners of City Hall changed so did the police. Keeping your job as a cop meant staying on the right political side of whoever was in power. Since the vice interests often owned the politicians, they also owned the police. Al Capone once bragged 60 percent of the cops were working for him!

Police bribes were a way of life. Since a cop at any time in history is grossly underpaid, when the vice lords (or the mob) offered cash payment for services, it was usually accepted. If it wasn't, either another officer was found to take it, or the one refusing it was eliminated. Sometimes eradication meant a bullet. Sometimes it meant a reassignment to an assignment in the "sticks" or permanent night duty. It all depended on the time and climate.

Entrepreneurs were active everywhere, even among the police. The Superintendent of Police owned one brothel. A combination bagnio and "wine room" a local newspaper editor railed it was "an epitome of hell and an infernal hell-hole."

At various times nearly every official was "on the take." Cops were expected to keep the vice dens out of the fashionable neighborhoods and confine them to recognized tenderloin districts. To help control it local prostitutes sometimes had to register with the police precincts before they were allowed to work and of course a piece of their earnings came back to the police. Periodic efforts to "clean up" the police always met with general failure. The corruption had gone on too long and become too deep for eradication.

To help battle official corruption citizen groups periodically emerged to combat vice, including the threat of anarchy and labor rebellion from the hordes of foreign immigrants. One group in 1880s even bought a Gatling gun and nearly 300 Springfield rifles just in case the anarchists got out of hand!

The police could be just as energetic as the vice lords in looking for way to make a buck or two. In the 1890s the superintendent agreed to hold illegal prizefights to raise money for the "Police Relief Fund." For reasons various and sundry the fights didn't make it so instead the cops published an official history of the force which of course all saloon keepers were expected to purchase. A rash of yearbooks, raffles and tickets to the annual "Policeman's Ball" followed. Selling them was never a problem.

During the 1880s the police established a patrol or call box system. Some 375 wooden boxes were set up on lampposts in the various districts. A dial arrangement inside enabled the cop or citizen, if he had the key, to notify the station of a need for help. The dial had a variety of settings indicating different crimes such as theft, murder, drunk and disorderly, fire, etc. It was an efficient system for summoning assistance.

Getting convictions in a Chicago court on vice matters was sometimes virtually impossible. Officials drew juries from areas near the courts and this often meant local saloons. In 1883 for example there were 14 saloons within 400 feet of the Cook County Criminal Court Building. If a jury was needed, a runner hustled off to a saloon, called for volunteers and led them back to the courthouse. Some men served several times a week and virtually made their living as a juryman!

To fight the "do gooders" the Chicago sin industry organized around one Michael Cassius McDonald, owner of a Clark Street bar and gambling house called "The Store," reputed to be the largest in the city. The saloon was on the first floor with an extensive gambling parlor upstairs. McDonald also enjoyed boxing and was one of the early backers of world famous fisticuff artist John L. Sullivan.

McDonald figured if the forces of civic virtue could organize, so could the legions of vice. He was successful. Come the 1873 election crusading Mayor Medill was bounced out of office by saloon candidate, Harvey Colvin. Under Colvin's protection, McDonald organized the first crime syndicate in Chicago, a tradition continuing to this day. The McDonald organization held together for 30 years with operating funds coming from a tax on vice operators. Reformers won in 1876 but in 1879 the vice gang put Carter Harrison in office and he stayed put until 1887, four full terms! It was a marvelous partnership between crime and city hall and set the pattern for generations.

There is a story told that one time a group of ministers came to Harrison's mansion complaining there were six or seven "gambling hells" as they called them operating full blast, all night, on Clark Street. His honor is said to have replied, "I know. I was down there and it was great."

Harrison had the ability to deal with the base vice lords as well as the pedigreed folks running the symphony. Potter Palmer, one of the wealthiest men in Chicago and a keen judge of city politics, and his wife were major Harrison supporters. Election night they would open up the famous Palmer House for him and allow the "unwashed" to drink at the famous bar.

For many years Chicago had no limit on the number of saloon licenses that could be issued. When they finally clamped down, many operators just refused to pay the fee. One estimate claimed in 1894 over 2,000 unlicensed saloons operated in the city. Nine years later it was up to 4,600. Unlicensed saloons were often called "blind pigs." One of the most famous was one operated by "Black Jack" Yattaw, a black gambler. Instead of being on land, his was floating on water and he called it the Yacht Club House. It was configured with a bar and restaurant on the main deck and dance floor of the roof. To board customers he just slid his craft up to the government pier and customers clambered aboard. Often he had women waving from the deck to entice men aboard. Once filled, he just backed out into the lake and steamed innocently away from the clutches of the city. Since he had friends in city hall, he could usually stay out of deep trouble.

One of several guidebooks used to help visitors "find their way" in Chicago.

Any city with all the "attractions" of Chicago needed a published guide to local services. Several early guidebooks directed men to them while others warned them away. For example, *The Sporting House Directory*, published in 1889, was a guide to the brothels and bordellos. The 1859 *Traps of Chicago* and 1866 *Chicago After Dark* were designed to caution men away. One of the tricks the last two volumes warned of was men stationed at railroad stations to "greet" incoming visitors. Of course the men were all bunko artists working to separate rubes from their money as fast as possible. The 1870 guide was mentioned earlier.

Vice districts didn't have complete free reign of the city. Occasional citizens committees would demand action of the politicians and police and as a result some enforcement effort would be made. Small time crooks, gamblers and madams would be hauled into court and duly charged. Sometimes they received jail time but more often than not, they managed to fall between the cracks, charged but a trial was never held. Part of the reason for lax enforcement was that Chicago's notables including Potter Palmer and Mayor Harrison among others owned much of the vice property.

In the 1870s and 1880s one vice area was directly aimed at the black population. Located near Washington and Halstead, in the midst of a larger tenderloin district, it was known as the "Black Hole." The most popular establishment was called Noah's Ark, an old three-story house owned by a rich and very pious alderman. Perhaps his motto was "God will take care of heaven and I will take care of earth." Like many religious zealots he saw no conflict between owning a black whorehouse and doing God's will on earth. The old parlor was divided into small cubicles with torn curtains, allowing the hookers to work in semi privacy. Their going rate was 25 to 35 cents; the only difference being whether the man took his shoes off or not. If he kept his shoes on the wear and tear on the sheets had to be compensated for. To supplement their meager income, the girls sometimes did a little robbery. While the customer was in the height of "passion" she grabbed his arms, pulling them tight to her while another girl smashed him on the head with a handy bottle or club. Once laid out cold, he was robbed and dumped in the deserted back alley.

One bordello was known as the Library since the furnishings included a bookshelf with half dozen volumes on it. Another brothel was known as Ham's Place, famous for its doxies being outfitted in white tights and green tops. Even here the girls were not above giving a customer a quick smash on the head to get at his wallet. A "house" was clearly not a "home."

The Columbian Exposition drew millions of visitors to Chicago and provided great opportunities to the vice lords.

Prior to and after the Columbian Exposition the area on Clark Street between Van Buren and Twelfth was known as either the Badlands or Little Cheyenne. Theoretically there was a distinction between the two, but even the police weren't certain where the dividing line really was. Brothels, dance halls, saloons and gambling dens lined the streets and all did a roaring business, especially with out of town visitors.

Black Susan Winslow ran one of the worst bordellos, a dive of the lowest variety with constant complaints of customers being rolled. The police had a bucket full of warrants on her, but also 450 reasons why they couldn't serve them. Black Susan was a big woman, in fact a really, really big woman, weighing in at an estimated 450 pounds! She was so fat she couldn't fit through her own doors. Finally disgusted with the whole mess one of the detectives decided it was essentially a problem of leverage. He must have remembered Archimedes, old proverb about "give me a big enough lever and I will move the world." He simply took off her back door, sawed the resulting opening several feet wider and laid heavy wood planks from the doorway to his "paddy wagon." Leaving the wagon in place he unhitched his team and tied a heavy rope to the harness and the other end around her waist. All the while Susan was yelling at the detective and cursing him for the destruction of her door. Her curses turned to screams when he put the team in motion and Susan was slowly dragged literally kicking and screaming from her house, over the porch and up the boards into the wagon. Since the heavy boards were filled with splinters, Susan's ample posterior was filled with painful reminders of her "trip." Once in the wagon it was a simple manner to toss the planks in, hitch the team up and "giddy up" back to the station house with his "big" arrest.

Chicago was reputedly the earliest city in the Midwest to have "concert saloons," the first opening in 1873. These establishments mixed musical performances, booze and sex all under one roof. One wag called them "department stores of vice." The set up was always the same. The main bar was near the front door and the floor was filled with tables and chairs. "Pretty waiter girls" circulated, hustling drinks, and a large stage provided a venue for various musical acts. The more overt sexual performances were in the basement. Hookers also moved through the crowds offering their services and small rooms were set aside on the second floor for them. Suggestive posters around the district advertised the various salons in shocking detail. Famous concert saloons include the Alhambra, Tivoli Gardens, Garden, Park and Foxhall. The famous belly dancer "Little Egypt" once performed in the Tivoli window as a "come on."

The Pacific Garden Saloon was another famous dive in the district. In this case the term "dive" meant more than just the low life of inmates but the saloon/brothel had very low clearance between floor and ceiling so a customer really had to "dive" to enter. The "local talent" hung around the tables waiting for an unwary customer to buy them a drink then it was time for a roll. The Concert Hall and Oyster Parlor were places with high "fa-looting" names but rot gut whisky and really old and ugly whores. A couple of nearby brothels run by Nellie St. Claire and Candy Molly Jones charged 50 cents, a little above the average price but at least they gave the customer a stick of candy as a memento.

Little Egypt was the hit of the 1893 Exposition.

Polk, State, Taylor and Plymouth Streets boarded the infamous Hell's Half Acre. Newspapers claimed the area was so evil even well armed police would only enter in groups of at least two and preferably more. While every available space was filled with a saloon, brothel or gambling den, the center of action was the Apollo Theater and Dance Hall. Wild at anytime, it was particularly so during the infamous masquerade balls sponsored by the brothel musicians. Everyone liked a little music and especially when it could provide some quick rhythm. The parties were really jumping affairs and extremely popular since at midnight the women not only dropped their masks but also stripped "au natural."

During the turn of the century an alley near Polk and Clark Streets had an especially vicious reputation. Hookers would entice unsuspecting men into its dark recesses for a "quickie" but when the customer entered her accomplice slipped out of the shadows and strangled him with a garrote. Even the police stayed clear of "Dead Man's Alley" unless traveling in pairs.

The villainous Custom House district was just south of the area burned by the 1871 fire. Bounded by Harrison Street, Polk and the Dearborn train station, it was a popular stop for out of town visitors, especially those arriving by train. Brothel owners took full advantage of Chicago's train stations, sending pimps to greet the arriving trains hoping both to attract customers as well as recruit new women to the trade. They worked much like Hari Krishnas at today's airports.

While most of the brothels in Chicago were nothing but the lowest sort of dives, there were several that were very high-class places. For example, Carrie Watson's bordello on South Clark Street was internationally famous. How much of Carrie's life story is truth and how much myth isn't known but the popular version goes something like this. Supposedly she hailed from Buffalo, New York from a good middle class family. Not wanting to be stuck in the "wife trap" she fled home, arriving in Chicago in 1866 anxious to learn how to run a brothel. How a young girl from a "good" home decided on such an unusual career is anyone's guess. She worked in a "first-class" house for two years, saving her money. When a madame left town after involvement in a police killing, Carrie took over the business. She immediately ratcheted up the house, putting in new decorations, furniture and of course beds. When she finished, her house had 20 bedrooms, five specially decorated parlors for meeting customers, a fancy billiard room and even a bowling alley in the basement. (All things considered, I can't imagine going to Carrie Watson's to go bowling). Expensive art hung from the walls and on occasion a three-piece musical ensemble entertained clients. Regular girls weren't good enough either. She only recruited young, beautiful and intelligent girls. Her girls always wore expensive silk gowns and "worked" on the finest linen sheets. Catering exclusively to what was called, "the carriage trade" she became very successful. Prices were commensurate with the level of service. At one point she reputedly had 60 women on the payroll, adding even more during the 1893 World's Fair. She also kept two fine white carriages with flashy yellow wheels for her trips "up town" and was known as a generous supporter of city charities. 441 South Clark Street became a very exclusive address well known to her rich and randy clients. Carrie ran her famous house for 25 years before retiring as a very rich woman.

Musicians at bordellos were invariably called "professors." At Carrie's he was a one legged man nicknamed "Lame Johnny." An excellent ivory walloper, he also was a fine singer but was not allowed to sing any love ballads during work hours, since the melancholy songs made the gals cry and their makeup ran. Lame Johnny was very highly regarded throughout the district and for 15 years the Levee staged an annual benefit ball for him at Freiberg's Concert Hall. Upper class doxies and bordello owners as well as aldermen, police and other officials all attended. The custom finally ended when an inebriated cop shot another inebriated cop in a surreal "duel of the drunks." But since the ball was a real moneymaker Hinky Dink and Bathhouse John, two local vice lords, took over the franchise and turned it into the famous First Ward Ball. The intrepid pair first staged it at the Seventh Regiment Armory and later moved it to the larger Coliseum. Crowds of 10,000 to 15,000 were normal and the celebrants were not exclusively as classy as the old Lame Johnny affairs. Pimps, politicians, lawyers, police, gamblers, hold up men, safe crackers, pickpockets, judges, whores and courtesans, all attended the evening of drunken debauchery. Admission was $1 with a mandatory 50-cent hat check to make a little extra cash. Box seats around the perimeter sold for $5 and were used by the upper class attendees. The rich wanted to attend but didn't want to mix too closely with the great unwashed. The 1907 soiree was a masquerade and doxies came as geisha girls, Egyptian queens, Indian princesses and all matter of exotic creatures. The wonderful tradition ended in 1908. The bigger the ball became, the more out of control it became, and finally the mayor would no longer issue a permit regardless of the greenbacks offered.

After McDonald's death in 1907, vice control fragmented to a number of different men and groups. Key among them were "Hinky Dink" Kenna and "Bathhouse" John Coughlin. The pair would reign as vice lords for 40 years! Another important gambling leader was Big Jim O'Leary, the son of Mrs. O'Leary whose cow was blamed for starting the infamous fire when it supposedly kicked over the lantern in the barn. After he apprenticed under a number of gamblers he opened his own place in the early 1890s on Halstead Street just across from the Union Stockyards. He selected his spot well. Once the visiting cattlemen finished selling the herd, they had money to spend and no wives to say no. O'Leary's Horn Palace had an ornate barroom, baths and

The kings of the First Ward, Hinky Dink Kenna and Bathhouse John Coughlin.

barbershop (both needed after a long session with the stinking cows and certainly vital if they intended to have a roll with the classier ladies), concert hall seating for a thousand and of course a gambling room connected by wire to every major sporting event in the country, making it a virtual equivalent of today's "sports book" in a Las Vegas casino. His gambling tables focused on the high stakes gambler, cattlemen with hefty rolls of greenbacks in their wallets. To stymie the rare police raids false doors and passages hid the gambling area. Rapid escape was via secret tunnels, trap doors and hidden exits.

First Ward aldermen Hinky Dink and Bathhouse controlled politics and general vice in the first ward, the downtown and near south Southside also known as the Levee. Hinky Dink's headquarters was his saloon on East Van Buren called the Workingman's Exchange. The upstairs was usually available as a place for vagrants to "flop" but come Election Day they had to be available and sober enough to vote. After feeding them breakfast he marched his army from polling place to polling place assuring they not only voted early and often, but also "right," starting an old and continuing Chicago political tradition. Hinky Dink normally paid 50 cents a vote, a pretty reasonable fee all things considered. Both men were good organizers and also sold "protection" to the various saloons, brothels and gambling dens in the First Ward. Perhaps ahead of their times, they also had two lawyers on retainer to assist any of their clients in the event of arrest.

Before 1890 the Levee occupied the area between Harrison and Polk Streets from Dearborn to Clark. After 1890 pressure from the growing downtown business district forced it to relocate to the area between 19th and 22nd Streets, from State to Clark streets. This was too close to the posh Prairie Avenue homes of the rich and famous so the moneyed folk in turn relocated to the city's north side and suburbs.

The 1890 Levee move pushed into the second ward, which meant Hinky Dink and Bathhouse lost a very lucrative stream of cash. But if somehow the ward boundaries could be "adjusted" everything could be all right. The intrepid pair cobbled together a redistricting ordinance to do just that, which passed with the support of Second Ward Alderman William Hale Thompson. Along with the Levee went the Second Ward's most important business district. This was a very strange ordinance for Thompson to support, gutting his own source of graft unless a deal with Hinky Dink and Bathhouse had been cut and indeed it had. When Thompson was elected mayor it was largely with the support of the two First Ward aldermen. As mayor, Thompson had access to more "boodle" than he ever dreamed possible as a simple ward boss.

The "new and improved" Levee was soon the home of an estimated 200 brothels and bordellos. Key attractions included the House of All Nations, Little Green House, Bed Bug Row, Bucket of Blood, Ed Weiss' Capitol, California, Freiberg's Dance Hall and the world famous Everleigh Club. Freiberg's was often used by Hinky Dink and Bathhouse as their headquarters. Downstairs was a typical bar and dance hall while the hookers operated from upstairs.

Minna Everleigh.

The Everleigh Club at 2131 South Dearborn was a world famous bordello, reputedly more difficult to enter than Buckingham Palace. Clientele included not only the upper crust of Chicago society but also well heeled visitors from Europe. Two young women, sisters Ada and Minna Everleigh, owned and operated the club with rare skill. The pair hailed from Louisville, Kentucky where their father was a very well to do lawyer. Highly educated, they both married young and soon divorced. Since their father gave each $40,000 as a wedding gift, they had private means which they used to buy a bordello in Omaha, Nebraska during the Trans-Mississippi Exposition. They were a mere 21 and 23 years old when they took on the roles of madams. Once the big show closed they saw much greater financial potential in booming Chicago than a dusty western cow town. After shopping around they purchased the house operated by Effie Haskins as well as her stable of girls in 1900 for around $60,000. The three story 50-room building was built in 1890 for $125,000 and was ideally suited to their enterprise. Both bordello and girls were quickly "upgraded." The first floor held 14 separate parlors and even an extensive library of classics intended to "improve the mind." Old Masters hung in the art gallery. The second floor featured themed rooms including Japanese, Moorish, Egyptian and collegiate. The later was decorated with Ivy League pendants and risqué pictures of Gibson girls. To add the proper air of decorum string musicians played gentle strains of Mozart and Hayden quartets. Oriental incense wafted lightly in the air. A $15,000 gold piano stood in a corner, just in case the proper occasion arose for use. Marble inlaid beds and large mirrors on the ceiling were standard.

The girls were the finest in the business. Young, gorgeous and impeccably dressed, they were cultured and able to entertain gentlemen with brains as well as beauty. The sisters took a very liberal attitude toward missionaries. Anyone who wished to come in and try to "save" the girls were welcome to try. Every once in a while they were successful, but invariably they failed. One crusader became a friend of the sisters and once pulled Minna aside telling her "the girls are headed for certain damnation. There is one thing you can do to prevent it." "What," exclaimed Minna? "Make them stop smoking cigarettes!"

During a state visit in 1902, Prince Henry of Prussia, the Kaiser's brother, enjoyed the club's many delights and supposedly started a new tradition too. When one of the ladies lost a shoe dancing on his table, he filled it with champagne and drank a toast to her health! According to local legend, Prince Henry sneaked away from his official escorts after laying a wreath at Lincoln's tomb to rush to the club. One wonders if Kaiser Bill himself enjoyed the favors of the club would it have altered his personality enough to prevent World War I? It remains one of history's unanswered questions.

The Everleigh may also have been the scene of one of Chicago's most famous "murders." On November 27, 1905, 37-year-old Marshall Field II, the son of the Chicago department store millionaire, died in a Chicago hospital from a gunshot wound. That much is fact. How he came to be shot is the story.

The version the family gave to the press was he was cleaning a newly purchased automatic pistol in preparation for a Wisconsin hunting trip when it accidentally fired inflicting the fatal wound. The accident happened on November 22. Reportedly when his father visited him in the hospital he didn't say what exactly happened. Police detectives were refused admission to his room so their questions went unanswered. No autopsy was performed.

And then different versions started to "make the rounds." One claimed he was at the Everleigh when he bungled a suicide attempt. Fearful of the bad publicity of having his body discovered at the club, the sisters hustled him out of the building and home. A variation said he was shot by either a Spanish girl or a gambler. Why he was shot wasn't explained. Perhaps he reneged on promises to the dancer and a woman scorned is a dangerous critter. A variation claimed the owner of the Turf Exchange Saloon was part of a conspiracy of other brothel owners to frame Minna and Ada for Field's death. Competition could be cutthroat! If the Everleigh was out of business then the high end trade would filter down to them. One of the Everleigh girls was supposed to receive $20,000 to testify one of the owners pulled the trigger. Somehow Minna picked up on the scheme and using her police protection contacts, had the gambler hauled off to jail and the plot ended but Fields was still dead.

Nearly 20 years later the sordid affair surfaced again. A former showgirl named Vera Scott claimed she shot Fields accidentally at a party at the Everleigh and he insisted on being taken home alone in a taxi. She further said his father paid her $20,000 to leave Chicago. The Fields family denied her claim.

Fields wasn't the only socially prominent man to perish with a club connection. In 1910 the 26-year-old son of the owner of the Rock Island Railroad died of a heart attack supposedly caused by a prolonged orgy at the club. When his father found out exactly what happened he refused to attend the funeral or even look at him in his coffin!

When Wall Street tycoon W. E. D. Stokes divorced his prominent Park Avenue society hostess wife, he mentioned her previous employment as a "entertainer" at the Everleigh Club. That little tidbit provided a flush of color to a drab social season.

The Everleigh finally closed in 1911. Although the local reformers claimed credit for finally shutting it down, Ada later admitted they gave it up simply because they got tired of paying exorbitant bribes to police and politicians. The two sisters retired to New York with their fortune, living long and prosperous lives. They even brought many of their very expensive furnishings with them, including the $15,000 gold piano.

Madame Emma Duvall's French Elm bordello was almost as famous as the Everleigh. Duvall achieved lasting notoriety by supposedly inventing the "all mirrored" bedroom, certainly advancing civilization to new heights.

The 1893 World's Columbian Exposition, commonly called the World's Fair, was an immense boon to the city and especially the vice districts. From May 1 to October 31, the city hosted an estimated 28 million visitors, fully a quarter of the U.S. population! The exposition was intended to celebrate the 400th anniversary of Columbus's discovery of America by showcasing the country's progress in arts and sciences. Construction delays forced it to open a year late but the public didn't seem to mind, feeling the delay was well worth the result. During this period fairs were extremely popular. The Centennial Exhibition in Philadelphia in 1876 drew over 10 million visitors and the Paris Exposition Universelles over 28 million. These great expositions had everything, from science, art, culture, entertainment and honky tonk. The Chicago Fair went a step farther, introducing visitors to the idea of a "midway" and the unique charms of a belly dancer named "Little Egypt."

The great international fairs also made money, not necessarily for the exposition proper although individual attractions could be very profitable, but for the cities where they were held. People needed places to stay and eat as well as transportation, etc. The horde of visitors brought immense profit to the host city. Chicago competed tooth and nail with St. Louis, New York and Washington D.C. for the right to stage the exposition and only large infusions of cash, $10 million dollars to be exact, convinced Congress to award it to Chicago.

Visitors came to the Fair by either steamboat or train, the latter being most popular. And of course the vice-lords made certain their barkers and shills were at the train stations to steer patrons the right way. Mrs. Visitor may have wanted to see the cultural attractions of the Windy City but Mr. Visitor was more interested in the titillations offered by the Levee. Just think what happened when a local "Hicksville" Elks Lodge (or Odd Fellows, etc.) made a sojourn to see the Fair! There were things you could see and do in Chicago you couldn't even dream about in Council Bluffs, Iowa! When in Rome, do as the Romans do!

Adding to the violence of the city, Mayor Carter Harrison was assassinated at his home on October 28, 1893, immediately after he gave the closing address at the Fair. Killer, Eugene Patrick Prendergast, claimed he shot the Mayor because he didn't give him the job of Corporation Counsel. That Prendergast was utterly untrained and unqualified made no difference, he wanted the job and Harrison didn't give it to him. Left wing lawyer Clarence Darrow defended the murderer and expert witnesses were split whether he was nuts or not, but regardless he was duly executed by hanging.

William T. Stead was a noted English do-gooder.

The Levee came under heavy pressure after an English do-gooder and newspaper publisher William T. Stead visited the city during the 1893 World's Columbian Exposition. Stead was a renowned reformer, one of those people that are always willing to tell someone exactly what they are doing wrong. Back in merry old England Stead enjoyed an especially unsavory reputation. To him the ends always justified the means. For example to prove white slavery existed in London he not only "bought" a 13-year old virgin girl, but was prepared to act as her "debaucher" to prove his case. The revelation caused a great sensation, with crowds outside the paper's office fighting to get copies of the story and others protesting the damage done to the reputation of England's upper class. Authorities prosecuted him resulting in a period of well-deserved jail time. Stead perished when the *RMS Titanic* sank in April 1912. Supposedly he had two premonitions about the disaster. In 1886 he published an article titled "How the Mail Steamer Went Down in Mid-Atlantic by a Survivor." Six years later he published another tale about a White Star liner, the *Majestic*, rescuing survivors of another ship that collided with an iceberg.

Since Stead came from more than 50 miles distant and carried a valise, he was an instant expert. After exploring the Chicago underworld he published *If Christ Came to Chicago* in 1894, a highly charged book focusing on the city's vice. Stead wasn't afraid to name names at least as he saw them through his strait-laced, teetotaler glasses, claiming 66 of 68 aldermen were crooked. He further stated some of Chicago's rich and famous like Marshall Field, George Pullman and Mayor Carter Harrison were nothing but cheap tax cheats. The excitement generated by the muck-raking book spawned another reform movement.

Gypsy Smith, another wandering English reformer showed up in Chicago in 1909. After appropriate speechmaking and the backing of an estimated 60 area churches, he led a mass march of 15,000 people through the Levee. There are two versions to the march depending on your perspective. Of course the revelers sang religious songs and preached the gospel at sinners as they found them. The accepted version of the march claims it made great impact, with sinners eagerly coming back into the fold of goodness and light. Perhaps the second version has a better ring of truth. In seems many of the marchers had never actually been exposed to "adult" entertainment. All they knew about it was the hate spewed from church pulpits. Numerous marchers even ventured into the saloons for a beer or two. Crusading against sin can generate a real thirst! Others enjoyed the delights offered by the various young ladies operating as private contractors. There is nothing wrong with supporting free enterprise. In the end, the marchers suffered a significant loss of members the deeper they went into the temptations of the Levee! One young man told a newspaper reporter he was glad he went since he "wanted to see it all so he could tell the other fellows who weren't so lucky." Hardly a good reformist comment!

Fired up by Smith's haranguing, the next year an estimated 600 church congregations formed the Church Federation of Chicago, which together with the 4,000 strong Women's Christian Temperance Union pressured Mayor Busse to form a commission to investigate vice in the city, resulting in the infamous Vice Commission. Its investigators eagerly took to the streets to find "sin" wherever they could and of course personally "investigate" it! Not a bad job, huh? After a decent period of time the Commission issued a 400-page report claiming among other horrors there were 1,020 "vice resorts" employing at least 4,000 prostitutes, most working in the Levee district. It further reported the district was destroying the "souls" of 5,000 young women a year and must be eliminated. The resorts were reputedly producing annual revenue of $60 million and profits of $15 million.

This brought the concept of a segregated district into conflict with the authorities. Most of the politicians, including Mayor Carter Harrison II, believed it was better to accept the fact that vice would exist and keeping it in one location was the best way to manage it. Chicago was a major tourist town and if the tourists wanted gambling and prostitution, it was the city's responsibility to provide it. Destroying vice would devastate the tourist trade. Plus financial contributions from the First Ward and the Levee were critical to keeping political dominance in the mayor's office. Stopping the vice meant stopping the money and that was not acceptable.

Just to add fuel to the emotional fire stoked by the rabble-rousing reformers, the do-gooders spread lurid tales of white slavery. They claimed thousands of young girls came to the city every year looking for work. When many couldn't find any, they were lured into prostitution. Sometimes the girls went willingly; especially if experienced girls showed them expensive dresses and jewelry they earned "sporting." They said the work was easy and pay was very good, certainly far more then they could earn honestly as a simple store clerk or clerical worker. For the higher-class parlor houses this was certainly true. But the lower dives were much different. Claims were made some girls were drugged, kidnapped and then forced into the trade. A federal investigating committee stated during a two month period in 1907, 278 girls under 15 were rescued from Levee brothels. Girls as young as 14 and 13 were not uncommon in the trade. Whether there was any truth to such sensational charges or not was immaterial. The Chicago churches went ballistic!

Of course brothel madam Mary Hastings didn't help the cause any. By any standard she was not only one of the vilest characters around "Hell's Half Acre," but was one of the worst in the entire city. She boasted no man could possibly imagine an act of perversion or degeneracy, which she and her girls would not perform. Some think the origin of "white slave" is associated with Mary. Supposedly a girl being held against her will in her brothel threw a note out the window on which she scribbled, "I'm being held as a slave." A man passing by the window picked it up and brought it to the cops who subsequently raided the brothel releasing the girl. A newspaper reporter later used the term "white slave" in describing the affair. Hastings reputedly traveled the Midwest looking for young girls between the ages of 13 and 17 to work in her brothel. Once inside her three-story house, they were stripped, locked in a top-floor room, and then turned over to professional rapists to "break them in." Mary was a bit rough even for Chicago and was finally indicted in 1895, but took off to Toledo, Ohio apparently never returning to Chicago.

Once the new girl was in her "house" her clothing was always taken and locked up. Without clothing she had little potential for running away. Instead she was given an inexpensive gown for working in. The house was always careful to charge her for everything, clothing, food and rent, the fees scrupulously recorded in a ledger book. No matter how much she earned it was never enough to cover her debt. Since she was told (and usually believed) it was a legal debt, if she ran away to the police she would be put into jail, so why run? Considering many of the police stopped by the houses to register the girls, and the girls saw them, they easily believed the debt story.

Some girls were brought in from as far away as Duluth, Minnesota. In 1906 one recruiter met his prospect in front of the St. James Hotel in Duluth and told her he was a theatrical agent looking for girls for his new stage show. After meeting her the second night at the roller rink, she agreed to go with him to Chicago. The pair arrived by train and following a tour of the city he took her to the Teco Hotel and told her she would have to become a "sport" and he hadn't worked in five years and lived strictly off his women. She managed to escape and flee to the police.

Some girls were recruited from the various Great Lakes cruise ships by an experienced madam or pimp working the boats looking for likely girls. After striking up a friendship with the girl the recruiter convinced them to visit his home etc, have dinner or drink then spring the trap.

Responding to a *Chicago Inter Ocean* news story claiming a Levee district group was kidnapping young girls from dance halls and selling them to brothel owners, the Illinois Legislature passed a white slave law in 1908. Allegedly the lure was a good looking young man claiming he was the son of a rich meat packer who enticed them back to "his place" where they were trapped. What girl could resist the sex appeal of a sausage sovereign's sizzling son?

The white slaving hysteria was given a boost in October 1909 when Maurice Van Bever, a Chicago brothel and salon owner, was arrested by Federal agents. During the subsequent trial one of his bartenders "sang like a little birdie" testifying how Van Bever and his wife Mollie ran a white slave operation between Chicago and St. Louis. One of the slaves also warbled her tune, telling lurid accounts of her abduction and new "job." Maurice and Mollie received a $1,000 fine and a year in jail.

Responding to public pressure, in 1910, Chicago Congressman James Mann quickly sponsored legislation making the interstate transportation of women for "immoral" purposes a federal offense. Talk about the unwarranted expansion of federal power!

Supposedly dance halls were a major "recruiting" location for white slavery. Reformers charged it was too easy for minors to purchase drinks and police didn't make any effort to prevent it. Masquerade dances were the worst since known criminals could operate behind a mask without being identified. Young girls who became drunk could easily be carried off to nearby vice resorts. Some girls were drugged with cocaine or morphine becoming addicts and later forced into prostitution to feed their habit. Neither drug was illegal at the time and some local druggists were selling as much as four pounds of Morphine a month!

Many of the girls were recruited directly from the streets. Earning a living in the city was tough for a young woman. Opportunities were very limited. Working as a domestic servant for a well to do family had little appeal. Clerking in a department store like Marshall Fields paid very little, perhaps $6 a week and male floorwalkers were often petty tyrants, levying fines for the smallest infractions of store "rules." In some cases the floorwalkers demanded other favors too. If a girl was going to "give it away" for a lousy $6 a week job, she might as well turn pro and earn some real money! Some split the difference, taking on boyfriends on a paying basis.

In a periodic spasm of civic virtue, in 1901 Mayor Harrison pushed the city council to make wine rooms illegal. These were small side rooms in saloons often using a heavy drape as partition from the main floor. Originally they were places for a small group to drink quietly without interruption. Later they became locations for seduction and prostitution. The ordinance of course was generally ignored.

Responding to increased public pressure to clean things up, authorities hauled 24 resort owners into court in 1903. All the cases were dismissed. It seems witnesses had strange "memory lapses." Two years later, in response to powerful reform pressure, the City Council passed an ordinance requiring a 1:00 a.m. closure for dance halls. Efforts were also made to enforce it. Slowly the vice districts were being dragged into reform kicking and screaming.

Sometimes city improvements can work to the advantage of criminal elements. From 1900 to 1909 Chicago built a series of freight tunnels under nearly every downtown street with spurs leading into building basements. The purpose of the tunnels was to expedite delivery of coal and freight as well as remove ash and other debris, thus freeing the streets for more respectable users. Other tunnel connections ran to various railroad stations and wharfs. Of course it didn't take a rocket scientist as the saying goes to figure out there was a real advantage to being able to move "contraband" including booze, drugs, prostitutes, dead bodies, etc. around without being observed. The "underworld" really went underground in Chicago. The tunnels are largely still in place but are now used for utility and communications cables.

Chicago was always on the lookout for new gambling technology, for example slot machines. By 1902 it was estimated the city had 10,000 to 20,000 in use. They usually weren't anywhere in great numbers unlike today's casinos. A saloon might have half dozen or so but they added up and provided a steady and lucrative income to their owners especially since there wasn't any regulation of payout. Some were almost banks for the bars. The patron dropped the coin it, but the machine never paid out.

The gambling interests in Chicago were always innovative. In 1905 a consortium of investors including Big Jim O'Leary, bought the old 214-foot wooden steamer *City Of Traverse* from a bank foreclosure and turned her into a floating gambling palace. It reputedly cost $40,000 to bring her up to operating standards and install the new necessary wagering implements and bars. The main deck was converted to a saloon and restaurant while the salon deck became a gambling room. Most important was a wireless cabin critical to receive the latest racing results. Bookmakers took the bets and paid off on the results, just like the track without the smell of manure.

The City Of Traverse *was a successful Chicago gambling ship.*

The first trip went out on June 29, 1905 and was an immediate success. Hundreds of gamblers crowded on board along with four police to assure no city laws were broken. A small band played the latest tunes to add a festive air. The steamer sailed about 22 miles southeast of the city and dropped her anchor. As long as she was three miles offshore she was safe from Illinois or Chicago authorities. Gambling wasn't against federal law, only City ordinance and state law. By early evening the steamer was back at the dock. Just to be safe, before returning to the dock all betting slips were tossed into the boiler fire to assure destruction.

While gambling on the ship was technically legal as long as she was three miles offshore, the radio transmitter on land, since it was being used for an illegal activity, wasn't. Watchful authorities managed to find one transmitter and shut it down, arresting the operator and destroying the equipment. The ship however had a back-up secret transmitter that was never found!

Chicago authorities, responding to reform pressure, tried to block gamblers from boarding the ship but were usually unsuccessful since it wasn't illegal! If folks wanted to take a boat ride, what was wrong with it?

The *City Of Traverse* ran for three years. The Illinois Central Railroad even ran special trains directly to the dock for the convience of gamblers. The ship wasn't a cheap operation. A local paper estimated the consortium was paying $2,000 a week in protection money. Finally the ship's license was pulled on a technical flaw when reform pressure finally became too great and the consortium sold her to the Graham and Morton Line.

Attracted by the sensation of the *City Of Traverse*, another group purchased the 235-foot steamer *John R. Stirling* as a second gambling ship. However, she never proved successful. Doubtless the *City Of Traverse* group worked hard behind the scenes to keep their monopoly. It was claimed they even arranged to burn down the *John R. Stirling* shore based wireless station.

Entering the vice districts was always dangerous. Temptation was everywhere. Wine, women, song and gambling were beckoning from every open door. Pickpockets were also on the prowl looking for an easy mark. In 1910 there were an estimated 500, many in the districts but also working crowds at ball games, stores and the street. One source described them as the "best looking young fellows in the city."

The Levee had a real scare in 1914. Illinois Governor Edward Dunne signed legislation giving women the vote and for the first time Bathhouse Coughlin not only had a viable opposition candidate for his aldermanic seat but she was a woman! Chicago suffragettes provided massive support for Marion Drake, a court stenographer who passed the bar exam. Bathhouse and his following had to go into high gear to stuff enough votes into the boxes to keep him in office. It was a near thing.

The whole situation was even worse since a County Judge had removed many dead and fictitious voters from the First Ward voting list. Neither Bathhouse nor Hinky Dink saw any reason why being dead or nonexistent should prevent anyone from exercising their right to vote. Chicago political leaders still follow that line of reasoning.

During elections it was common for precinct captains to pull tramps and bums from anywhere and everywhere as voters, registering them using a variety of fictional addresses and names. In one ward the captain used the names of dead British prizefighters! This would be the equivalent today of using "Mickey Mouse" or "Donald Duck." When Election Day came, the captain duly marched his voters to the various polling places and that was that!

"Bummers" became "repeaters" on Election Day by climbing into horse-drawn wagons and driving from polling place to polling place to vote as needed. "Besides repeating, the business of these gangs is to scare voters, and whenever the day is going against them, to attack and destroy the ballot boxes. They also hope in wards where they have large majorities to take possession of the polls in the morning and hold them by brute force all day, so that no decent man can cast his vote against them."

The screws of public morality were slowly turning and increasingly the cops raided the Levee in an effort to drive out the illegal activities. The old vice lords dodged and weaved, trying various gimmicks but each failed. Freiberg's Dance

Hall crew became "Freiberg's Dance Academy." Every night waiters put cards on the tables stating, "Free Instruction in Modern Dance to Our Guests. Hand this card to the head waiter and he will send you one of our competent instructors." Of course the "instructors" were all hookers!

Overwhelming pressure by churches and other reformers finally won out. The last bordello in the Levee was "officially" closed in 1915. Even the election of Mayor Big Bill Thompson, an ardent supporter of the Levee, was unable to muster enough political muscle to make it reopen, at least officially. The old Levee district soon sprouted a new series of "hotels, saloons and cabarets." All served the public demand for the "old" services, but at a much less obvious level.

The low class brothels could be beat down by reformer pressure but the up scale ones just changed their methods. The advent of the telephone, streetcars and automobiles provided the opportunity for the prostitute to travel as ordered. Today we pick up the phone and order a pizza. In 1910 Chicago an upper class customer just picked up a phone and ordered a "trick." Madams were careful not to employ girls who worked in the big brothels or were obvious streetwalkers. They were considered too flashy for the telephone trade where greater discretion was needed.

If you were a conventioneer in town for a few days the doorman, bell boy or desk clerk could take care of your needs. In a lower class saloon the barkeep knew where to send you. It wasn't as noticeable but it was all there and just as profitable.

As the old Levee was papered over, its activities either went underground or just relocated to the suburbs. Some went out to Burnham, 18 miles to the south. Others moved to nearby Stickney and Cicero. With the increasing use of cars and good improved roads, vice didn't need to be concentrated as in the past.

In the meantime the politics of the old First Ward were changing too. Hinky Dink and Bathhouse needed someone to provide a direct link to the underworld while they played city hall politics. After looking around they found an Italian named James Colosimo who they earlier provided a job as a street sweeper. In the language of the time, he "followed the horses" carrying his broom and shovel and while pushing his aromatic cart. After a time he became the leader of the street sweepers union and by controlling their vote gained personal clout. After a time this up and coming hood married a brothel owner named Victoria Moresco. They were a good team and soon expanded quickly eventually running 200 women, virtually all of the cheap $1 and $2 variety becoming the "McDonald's" of the trade. Big Jim and Victoria were soon pulling in $50,000 a month. A chauffeur drove him around town and he showed off his new wealth by building an elaborate mansion. He kept expanding, including opening Colosimo's, a popular restaurant frequented by city notables. Opera great Enrico Caruso always stopped by when in town. Famous left wing attorney Clarence Darrow was another patron who also enjoyed dining and drinking with hoods. Colosimo loved to dress the part of successful mobster, wearing expensive fur coats, sparkling diamond cufflinks and choker rings and of course the obligatory cheap hood gold necklace. Some folks even took to calling him "Diamond Jim." Interestingly while fur coats and cufflinks have since gone out of style, big diamond rings and gold neck chains are still in fashion for the gangland pretty boys.

Diamond Jim Colosimo, one time horse manure picker.

To help him run his expanding business as well as deal with an extortion threat from the Sicilian "Black Hand," Colosimo brought his nephew Johnny Torrio in from New York. Torrio was an unlikely looking mobster. Short, paunchy and colorless, many crime historians consider him the most capable of the Chicago mob bosses. He quickly proved his ability relocating many of Colosimo's operations to the suburbs to better serve customers. Chicago Heights, Calumet City, South Chicago, Burnham and other outlying communities soon were providing all the services of the old Levee.

The Black Hand or Mafia (Unione Siciliana) as it is known today was especially troubling. The evil ones started in Sicily where the low level of culture accepted the premise that it was perfectly alright for men to extort money from others under threat of death. When the mafia slithered into New York it found fertile ground among the thousands of Italians who thought they left this miserable vestige of the old country behind. The mafia system was simple. A letter was sent demanding money or else a bomb would be tossed through your shop window or child kidnapped. The note was signed with a crude imprint of a black hand.

As Italians moved west to Chicago the Black Hand scum came too. Between 1900-1925 there were 300 cases reported to the police and doubtless many more never spoken of. One detective guessed it was a ten to one ratio. In 1910 there were 25 unsolved mafia murders in the Italian section of Chicago. For example in 1911 it was 40; 1912 - 33; the numbers kept climbing as the mafia preyed on the weak and vulnerable. Should a mafia scumbag be caught, there was an unlimited amount of cash to hire a crooked lawyer and as the court date

Colosimo's was popular with the Chicago elite who liked to rub shoulders with "real" gansters.

approached, witnesses "disappeared." If a case actually went to trial, the jury was bribed ensuring acquittal.

The local Chicago Black Hand leader was a defrocked priest named Anthony D'Andrea. He also controlled the red light district in the Nineteenth Ward. The ward had earlier been mostly Irish but they were leaving as the Italians pushed in creating a bloody conflict with gunfire echoing through the once quiet neighborhood. On May 11, 1921 the ex priest was dispatched to hell by a volley of sawed off shotgun fire in an eruption of gangland mayhem. His priest brother had the pleasure of conducting the funeral service for his rotten sibling. The killing was suspected to be Irish retribution for an earlier mafia outrage.

By the time Prohibition rolled around, the Chicago mafia was more or less running the Italian communities. When a freelance group decided to extort Colosimo, it made a very bad decision. When the mafia waltzed into Colosimo's cafe and gave him 24 hours to give them $25,000 or he was a dead man they compounded their gross error. He agreed to deliver the money the next day at 4:30 p.m. under a lonely railroad bridge at Archer Avenue. Instead of Colosimo, Torrio "made the meet" with three of his trusted men. Four powerful shotgun blasts cut the mafia scum into bloody shreds. Colosimo never had another Black Hand threat! Since Torrio was also Sicilian he was soon accepted into the Chicago mafia eventually becoming a "capo."

The more successful he became, the less interested Colosimo was in his business. He eventually divorced his dumpy wife Victoria with a payment of $50,000 and married a vivacious and curvy 19-year old choir singer named Dale Winter and wanted to spend his time with her including providing professional voice lessons. Reportedly Flo Ziegfeld tried to get her to join his famous show but she refused, deciding to stay with her "Big Jim." Victoria, apparently a bit of a cougar herself, quickly married a stud 20 years her junior as a way to one up her ex-husband.

Johnny Torrio was considered by some criminal historians as the most capable of the Chicago mob bosses.

When Prohibition presented golden opportunities to build a highly profitable bootlegging and distribution business, Colosimo laid back, angering the ambitious Torrio. Colosimo was content with what he had. Torrio knew it was necessary to grow or die.

Dale Winter, Colosimo's new wife, was a talented singer.

On May 11, 1920 Colosimo was found dead with two bullet holes drilled neatly through his head. Torrio had set him up. Colosimo was waiting in the vestibule of his restaurant to pay for a shipment of booze that wasn't coming, so he had a large bundle of cash on him. When the cops frisked Colosimo's cold corpse the cash of course was missing. The killers were never apprehended but it was thought it was the handiwork of 22-year old Alphonse Capone, later to be known as Big Al or

Big Al Capone

Scarface Al. The bullet-headed Capone was a graduate of the villainous New York Five Points gang. Torrio brought him to Chicago to help with the growing bordello business.

Colosimo's new wife disappeared following his "offing." Victoria, the old wife threatened to kill her when she stole "her man" so perhaps Dale just took off for her own safety. Or maybe she was too late and Victoria took a quiet revenge. As an old brothel owner she certainly knew the right crowd to give her a hand.

Colosimo's funeral, the first of Chicago's great gangland farewells, drew a crowd of 5,000 people. Hinky Dink and Bathhouse were honorary pallbearers as well as ten other aldermen, three judges, two congressmen and a leader of the Illinois legislature. Big Jim had a lot of friends, at least a lot willing to carry him to his grave.

Capone was born in New York in 1899 to a supposedly respectable and hard working family. The fourth of nine children. His father was a barber and mother a model of love and caring, so goes the story anyway. That Capone turned out to be a vicious killer wasn't their fault. All the politically correct nonsense about his going bad through the influence of his "environment" is so much psychobabble. Capone was just a sadistic murderer. While he developed great "street smarts" and was certainly a natural criminal enterprise manager, academically he never went past the fourth grade.

He received his trademark scars in the summer of 1917 when he was working as a bartender and bouncer at a Brooklyn speakeasy. It seems he made a lewd comment to a girl and it turned out she was the sister of the man on the next bar stool. Her brother took exception to Capone's big mouth, pulling a blade and rewarding the "fat WOP" with a couple of deep slices on his face. According to legend, the exact remark was, "You have a beautiful ass and I mean it as a compliment believe me." Capone was always intensely embarrassed by the scars, feeling justly his courage was tested and like all bullies, found wanting. In later years he claimed he got them with the famous "Lost Battalion" in World War I. Of course it was a bald faced lie since he never served his country in any way. Leeches like Capone take. They do not give.

Capone's first job with Torrio was running a couple of brothels. In effect, Capone was a cheap pimp. After he proved himself adept at beating up girls, Torrio brought him up the mobster food chain.

Without Colosimo's "dead" weight Torrio quickly built an empire much larger and powerful than Colosimo ever had. Torrio saw the key to success was organization and maintaining territorial integrity among the various gangs. There was plenty of money to be made for everyone, as long as they didn't waste resources fighting. For a time everything went as he planned.

Torrio was so "in" with the police he sometimes used them to escort his more expensive liquor shipments. He once boasted, "I own the police." Mayor Thompson was also "in" with Torrio. In fact the Mayor and police chief were frequently seen entering Torrio's speakeasies. Both of course were on the mob payroll.

Governor Small of Illinois was also part of the mob's support organization. Political contributions do pay off. During the first three years of Prohibition, Small's administration paroled 950 prisoners. Roughly 40 percent promptly joined Torrio's gang. At his peak Torrio had 800 men working for him.

Judges too were often in the mob's pocket. On the few occasions when an honest judge set a high bail for an arrested crook, for example $100,000, a gangster "mouth piece" (lawyer) simply took it to a friendly judge who reduced it to a mere $10,000 or less. Friendly judges also granted trail continuances until the cases just "went away." Judges were elected and mob money could make a difference in the campaign, or just go directly into a special and very private "retirement" account.

In 1923 Chicago went through another ill-conceived spasm of public virtue, and reform mayor William Dever ordered the police to strictly enforce Prohibition. 7,000 "soft drink" parlors (which were really speakeasies) were soon shut down. Dever would cause quite a stir but his efforts would ultimately fail. The mob was too well entrenched to be so easily defeated. Dever was essentially only a figurehead anyway. His job was to look good and say the right things while the Democrat machine looted the city and collected mob payoffs.

Regardless of the ultimate failure of the reform mayor, the move caught Torrio vacationing in sunny Italy, leaving Capone in charge. Pressured by the authorities, he quickly relocated the headquarters to the Hawthorne Inn in nearby Cicero. A city of 70,000 people, it was the fourth largest in Illinois and a great place for the mob to homestead.

For a time the tide of reform threatened to overwhelm Cicero too. To forestall such a terrible event, Cicero's local political leaders made a deal with Capone. If he would help them defeat the reform candidate in the 1924 election, they would give him a free hand to peddle booze in the city as well as the brothel franchise. Capone accepted the offer and come Election Day an estimated 200-gang gunmen invaded Cicero, making certain voters voted the right way.

Dion O'Banion ran the North Side of Chicago.

Capone hoods frightened off opposition voters, pulled ballots out of voter's hands and examined them for correctness. Gun battles erupted at polling places when Chicago Police arrived under a court order to drive off the mobsters, Capone's brother Frank being one of those killed in the battle. When the votes were finally counted, the reformers were defeated and Capone and Torrio owned Cicero. It wasn't long before 100 gambling dens; dozens of bordellos and hundreds of speakeasies were doing a "land rush" business. A river of money flowed into the pockets of Torrio and Capone.

Other gangs controlled other portions of Chicago. Dion O'Banion had the near north side. Klondike O'Donnell and his brothers owned the near northwest side. Roger Toughy ran the far northwest side and the six Genna brothers the near west side. Terry Druggan and Frankie Lake had the far west side. All the gangs worked in collusion with the local politicians. The gangs delivered the vote on Election Day and the officials gave the gangs carte blanche to operate for the rest of the year.

Gang members were not always the most psychologically stable personalities. For example Nails Morton was a stalwart of the O'Banion gang. He was unusual, in that during World War I he served as a lieutenant receiving the Croix de Guerre from the French government for valor. Morton also carried himself above the normal mobster and often rode horses in Lincoln Park. While happily cantering along one fine morning a stirrup broke causing a fall and the horse trampled him to death. Incensed at the death of their friend, O'Banion's men put a "hit" on the horse! A couple of days after the accident one of the men rented it and rode it off to a lonely spot on the bridle path where the gang members each put a bullet into the animal's head!

Torrio and Capone were most bothered by O'Banion and the Genna brothers. O'Banion had many friends in City Hall based on his ability to deliver the strong Irish vote making him a powerful ally to be reckoned with. As luck would have it, O'Banion and the Genna brothers came into conflict over booze distribution. They were selling in each other's territory. Worse, O'Banion supported

Republicans and the Gennas, Democrats. Supposedly O'Banion asked Torrio to help him with the Genna problem but wasn't satisfied with Torrio's action. As a way to get even with Torrio, O'Banion offered to sell him the brewery he had in the city for a very low price, explaining he wanted to quit the mob and retire and who better to sell to than his good friend? Taken in by O'Bannion's smooth talk, Torrio handed over $500,000 in cash and the police promptly raided the brewery destroying not only the equipment but beer stockpiles too. Torrio knew O'Banion set him up. Normally Torrio was a very cool character, not apt to make rash decisions, but he was livid and decided to get even. Torrio must have grinned from ear to ear when on November 10, 1924 O'Banion was gunned down in his florist shop. The floral shop was a good cover for O'Banion. The fleet of trucks not only delivered floral arrangements but also booze. Plus O'Banion actually enjoyed arranging flowers! The three killers, who were never identified, greeted O'Banion as an old friend and calmly pumped five slugs into him. The last was fired directly into the head just to make sure he was dead.

His gangland funeral procession included 24 cars filled with flowers plus 122 funeral cars and scores of private ones. The silver and bronze casket reputedly cost $10,000. Thousands of people watched the procession go by and even though the police in the Loop halted traffic, the convoy took 20 minutes to roll through.

O'Banion not only was a former alter boy and member of the church choir, but a newspaper boy too! On the surface he looked to be a clean-cut kid. As a child he was hit by a trolley and as a result, limped for the rest of his life. It was claimed he never drank and went to church every Sunday. He started his criminal career as a singing waiter in a joint on North Clark Street. As a bonus to his act, he deftly picked pockets as he worked through the crowd.. He later graduated to burglary, safe cracking and stick up work before taking over the Market Street Gang. He wasn't a good safe cracker however, once blowing an office wall down but leaving the safe unscathed. An oddity among hoods, he never allowed the gang to run any brothels, finding it a degrading way for a man to earn a buck and never missed a chance to taunt Capone as nothing more than a cheap pimp, which of course Big Al was.

Torrio himself was shot and wounded on January 24, 1925 likely by members of the O'Banion gang. The set up was well planned but poorly executed. Mobsters were usually vicious killers but often utterly inept in the actual deed. The failed killing of Torrio was a case in point.

Torrio and his wife just arrived home in their chauffeur driven car when it happened. After the car pulled up to the curb Mrs. Torrio got out and walked toward the house. Torrio was still in the car. Perhaps he let her go ahead as bait but if so, it wasn't the kind of thing he would tell her anyway. A hit man walked up to the car and fired a couple of rounds from a .45 caliber pistol into the front window wounding the chauffeur. A second hit man came up behind the car and let loose two blasts from a shotgun at the rear window. Neither hit Torrio. Not willing to sit still until he was finally hit, Torrio bolted from the car towards his house. He ran only a few steps before a slug tore into his arm and an explosion of shotgun pellets hit his jaw, guts and lungs, crumpling him to the ground. The 45 shooter walked up and aimed the pistol at Torrio's head and pulled the trigger. The only sound was "click." He was out of bullets. Calmly he started to load a fresh clip when the driver in the getaway blew his car horn signaling it was time to "get out of Dodge." The shooters ran to the car and left, leaving Torrio bleeding in his yard but very much alive. By any standard, it was a botched attempt. Once Torrio recovered he fled Chicago returning to New York to run a small bootlegging operation. Chicago was just too much for him and he happily turned his empire over to Capone.

With Torrio's hurried departure, the old territorial arrangements he had worked hard to maintain crumbled and Capone found himself in a series of gang wars. Irish, Polish and Jewish gangs united with the old O'Banion organization to make a run at him. The Sicilians and Italians stayed with Capone. Shootouts were common as the gangs fought for territory and the resulting income.

One of the tricks hit men used to increase the likelihood of a kill was to boil their bullets in onion water then rub them with garlic. According to legend this improved the chances of the victim getting gangrene if he survived the initial shooting. Apparently they didn't use the technique when they shot up Torrio.

In spite of the gang warfare, mob killings were few compared to the general murder numbers. Chicago and Cook County had 190 murders in 1920. Four years later the count was up to 300 but only 50 were gang killings. A dozen of the dead were also police officers. Murders continued to increase reaching 399 in 1928. All the while the number of gang members going to jail decreased. In the 40 years from 1919 to 1959 there were 929 gang killings but only 17 killers were convicted and several were freed on appeal.

Once Capone was well established in Chicago he invited the rest of his brothers to join him. He found a cash cow and there was plenty of milk for everyone. The only brother that didn't take the invitation was James. He was always different from his siblings. Seventeen years older than Big Al, he decided at age 16 to run away from home with the circus to seek his fortune. He completely cut himself off from the family for many years. Moving west he found he enjoyed firearms and became an excellent marksman. He enlisted in the Army during World War I, rising to the rank of lieutenant. Following the war he drifted to Homer, Nebraska and became a Prohibition agent. He later changed his name to Richard Hart in honor of a popular movie cowboy hero and soon gained the nickname "Two-Gun." He was an extremely effective agent but in 1924 the newspapers "blew" his story. Forced to move from Homer by the publicity, he later surfaced as a special agent for the Bureau of Indian Affairs in South Dakota. When President Calvin Coolidge vacationed in the Black Hills he was one of the guards. Imagine what Coolidge would have said had he known who was guarding him! Hart later moved to Idaho and continued his law enforcement career. After being outed in 1924 he established contact with the family and made annual trips to Chicago around the holidays but never said anything to his own wife and children about his visits. When Prohibition ended in 1933 Hart's law enforcement career largely disappeared. Financially, he was forced to depend on his Chicago connection for support. When he died in Homer in 1950 he was remembered as the "good" Capone.

Capone was the undisputed chief mobster of a city filled with mobsters.

James Capone changed his name to Richard Hart to flee his infamous family of hoods.

Ralph, the second Capone son, was Al's most trusted assistant. Never considered overly intelligent, he was loyal and often a calming influence. Al gave him two clubs to run, the Cotton Club and Montmartre. He spent three years in prison after a conviction of tax evasion in 1930 and later ran a number of businesses, dying in 1974.

Frank was often thought the smartest of the Capone's next to Al. He specialized in managing the gang's relationships in Cicero. He had a violent end, shot to death during the election in 1924. The effort by Capone "muscle" to control the election attracted the attention of law enforcement authorities, which in turn sent carloads of plain clothes Chicago police to chase the hoods off. It was just bad luck Frank was walking out of a downtown Cicero office building when a convoy of cars filled with cops went screaming past. The cops recognized Frank and screeched to a halt, police tumbling out of the cars with guns blazing. Frank never had a chance, riddled with bullets from perhaps 35 cops! One cop joked they needed a magnet to pick up his body. The coroner's jury returned a verdict of death by resisting arrest! It typical gangland fashion he was given a huge sendoff, his funeral cortege stretching for 100 cars long with 15 carrying sumptuous flower arrangements. As a mark of respect, every joint in Cicero closed for an hour during the funeral. Hookers, Johns, pimps, bartenders and gamblers all stood around outside shivering in the cold waiting until they could go back inside.

John Capone was the family "low performer." He couldn't be trusted to do much of anything but did escort beer trucks on deliveries and other low level work. He later changed his name and dropped out of public view.

Albert Capone was the nearest of any of the brothers to an honest man next to Ralph. After Capone bought the *Cicero Tribune* Albert worked in the circulation department. Capone wanted to make certain he always got good press, at least in one newspaper. Like Ralph, Albert also changed his name, dying in 1980.

Matthew Capone was the youngest brother. For a time he helped run a poker game around Downtown Chicago's Loop. When he tried to expand it into a crap game Capone became angry with his initiative and promptly shut him down. He later ran a bar in Cicero and died in 1967.

All things considered, with the exception of Ralph, it was a thoroughly corrupt and rotten family, typical of those families connected with the mobs.

Gangster Bugs Moran ended up taking over the old O'Banion gang and offered $50,000 to anyone able to "put a hit" on "The Big Fellow" as Capone was sometimes known. To demonstrate his resolve to "take on" Capone, on September 20, 1926, Moran led a convoy of eight to 11 cars on a drive by shooting of the Hawthorne Restaurant where Capone was eating. Moran set the hit up carefully and it wasn't his fault it failed. First he had a car drive by and fire some blank shots. Curious at the noise Capone got up from his table and walked towards the door to see, just as Moran planned. Before Capone reached the door, his bodyguard realized what was happening and pushed him to the floor. At this point the cars roared down the street and Thompsons roared their deadly chatter. More than a thousand .45 caliber rounds slammed into the joint, and only one

Bugs Moran tried to put a hit on Capone in Cicero.

hood inside was slightly injured! This is certainly reminiscent of an old comedy movie called, "The Gang That Couldn't Shoot Straight." Outside the restaurant a woman was injured in her eye by flying glass. Reputedly Capone spent $10,000 for surgery to save her eyesight. At least that's the story his publicist put out to the newspapers to promote what a nice guy he was, just misunderstood!

Capone always had trouble with the mafia. Since Torrio was a Sicilian, he could keep good relations with them. Capone wasn't Sicilian thus was always held in suspicion by the mafia, especially when he forced his men into the powerful head job.

When the president of the Unione Siciliana (Mafia), Mike Merlo, died in November 1924, Capone moved to replace him with his man. The Sicilian mobsters wanted to make sure the job was taken only by a racially pure Sicilian. Frankie Yale, an old friend of Capone and the head of the Mafia in New York, wanted Torrio to take it until the various fractions could work out their differences. Instead the Chicago Sicilians put Angelo Genna into the job. He lasted until May 1925 when a hail of gunfire cut him down. The next president, Sam Amatuna, was bumped off in the fall as he sat getting a manicure in a barber chair. Afterwards Capone went to New York to convince Yale to appoint his man Tony Lombardo president. Yale refused to become involved urging the Chicagoans to work out their own leadership solution. Capone returned and claiming he discovered a plot to kill Lombardo and himself installed Lombardo as president. When Frankie Yale later double-crossed Capone on another deal, he arranged a hit on him. A Chicago gunman took the train to New York to take care of the problem with his trusty chopper. Reportedly Yale had 100 .45 caliber slugs in him when the cops finally tossed the body on the morgue table. Torrio replaced him as the Unione Siciliana president in New York.

Lombardo's Chicago reign was short-lived. In September 1928 while walking through the Loop with two bodyguards, he was rubbed out by anti Capone forces. Two gunmen calmly slipped up behind him in the sidewalk crowd and pumped a couple of dum dum bullets into his head and another into his bodyguard, then fled into the crowd. Hundreds of people saw the killing and the second bodyguard recognized the shooters, but "nobody saw nuth'n" when the cops questioned them. The killers were never apprehended.

Capone didn't quit easily, quickly placing Pasqualino Lolordo in the job. His tenure was even shorter. On January 8, 1929 three men visited with him in his apartment, enjoying an afternoon of booze, food and cigars. Lolordo's wife was ironing clothes in her kitchen when a fusillade of shots banged out. The three men ran past her and out of the apartment. Her husband lay dead on the floor, 11 .38 caliber bullets having smashed into his head, chest and neck. Seven more were embedded in the wall and furniture. When the police interviewed his wife she identified the killers but after thinking about it, and considering her own long term health, soon forgot who they were! She was a good mob wife.

The Sicilian faction fought Capone every inch of the way, at one point even trying to have a cook put prussic acid into his soup. They circulated notice of a $50,000 reward for anyone succeeding in bumping him off. Capone's intelligence network was up to the task, keeping him informed of the deadly threats checking their every move.

Capone decided he was tired of dealing with the two bit local Sicilians who were too stupid to see the value of collaboration. He called a meeting of all the senior mafia bosses in Atlantic City and explained to the intellectually challenged Sicilian scum that if everyone cooperated, there was more money for all. Bootlegging was only part of the game. There was also prostitution, gambling, extortion, kidnapping, racketeering and other opportunities. But fighting among themselves was bad for business. Under Capone's prodding they hammered out territories and set up the basis for a crime cartel that evolved into the national organization of today.

Working stiffs knew Capone as a good tipper. Waiters often received a $100 gratuity, the coat check girl $10 and the shoe shine boy $5. He didn't want to be thought a "piker."

A fair number of gangsters also became avid golfers. Because they were supplying the various country clubs with booze, the clubs provided them with complimentary memberships. Some of the hoods were pretty good too. One enterprising killer even started to carry his favorite sawed off shotgun in a golf bag as he went about his business day. It was even better than the venerable violin case.

One of the men "rubbed out" by gangsters was an assistant state's attorney named William H. McSwiggin. Known as an "up and coming" crook buster he was called the "hangman prosecutor." In ten months he obtained death penalty convictions in seven trials. None however involved a gangster. In fact when he prosecuted two gangsters for a murder, he failed and the jury acquitted them. It was a very strange lapse of efficiency for a normally highly successful prosecutor. About a year later, four men just getting out of a car in front of a Cicero saloon were given a powerful dose of hot lead from a Chicago Typewriter. Only one survived. Among the dead was prosecutor McSwiggin. The other three were all well known gangsters. One was one of the men McSwiggin had demanded the death penalty for but lost the case. It was all very strange. Was the prosecutor on the take? Did he fail to deliver? Who paid whom off? The questions were never answered but clearly something was rotten.

The amount of firepower in the hands of the various gangs was impressive. When the police raided one crime lord's house they found an entire wall of filled bookcases. When they started to pull the books off the shelves while "tossing" the joint, they discovered they were all fakes. Behind was a veritable arsenal of weapons and ammunition, including sawed off shotguns and machine guns.

The gangs continued to fight for supremacy. Bombings, assassinations and fire bombings made the city into a battleground. A simple gang hit could be contracted out for a mere $150 cash. A "one way ride" was more costly depending on where the body was to be dumped. The old clay pits and quarries outside the city were favorite places to deposit a stiff. Some of the water-filled sinkholes were 50 feet deep. Just tie up the victim with strong wire, lash on a couple of pieces of scrap iron to make sure he doesn't float back up in a few days and give him the old heave ho! Out of sight and out of mind. The Chicago River and connected waterways were also favorite dumping places and it was easy enough to just stop the car during the dark of night on one of the many city bridges, give the old heave-ho and hear the answering splash. Sometimes the bodies did resurface. In one instance the propeller of a tug running through the Sanitary Canal caught part of the wire wrapped around the body of a gangster. The hood was encased in 40 pounds of wire plus 100 pounds of weight to assure he stayed down. Death was from a terminal case of "bullet disease."

Another technique to eliminate the "opposition" was called the "bump and riddle." The killers chased the victim's car using their car to ride it to the side of the street. Once it stopped the killers loosed a fusillade of machine gun and shotgun fire into the victim's car, leaving it and the victims, riddled with bullets. The deed done, the killers drove quickly away from the scene and later abandoned their car, which was of course stolen, just as soon as possible.

Capone's bullet proof limousine reportedly cost $30,000.

To provide a measure of personal security, Capone took to using a specially built armored car. The big 1928 Cadillac weighed in at a monstrous three and half tons due to the heavy steel plate and inch and half thick bullet proof glass windows. The removable rear window doubled as a "tail gunners" position. A secret gun locker was also hidden behind the back seat. Reportedly the car cost $30,000. Capone didn't use the monster alone. A second car full of his gunmen drove ahead and another behind. If he went to the opera, it was with an armed escort of a dozen and half of his trusted bodyguards. While all wore the expected tuxedoes, their "heaters" were in shoulder holsters ready for instant use.

The vice trade was a growth industry and the profits "earned" by the gangs were immense. In 1923 Torrio and Capone alone split $7 million. Four years later the feds were claiming Capone, now the sole "proprietor" had a profit of $110

The happy wedding party. Big Al, Mafalda and her no name husband.

million, drawn from bootlegging, gambling, dog tracks, vice and labor racketeering. In 1922 there were 12,000 speakeasies in Chicago. Four years later it was claimed they reached 20,000 with 3,000 brothels in the metropolitan area. Such a massive income gave him the ability to play rich uncle. When his 18-year old sister Mafalda married John Maritote, a 22-year old laborer but the nephew of mobster Frank Diamond, 4,000 people attended the December 1930 celebration while a crowd of thousands waited outside the church in a snow squall to catch a glimpse of Capone, not his sister. He presented her with a new car, a home, $50,000 in cash and a vacation in Cuba as a wedding gift as well as a nine-foot tall wedding cake. The marriage wasn't a love match. It was arranged to help heal a rift between two "organizations."

Strife between the different gangs was constant and bloody. On St. Valentine's Day 1930 Capone dramatically raised the stakes. In one move he virtually wiped out the O'Banion gang and sent a powerful message to others who would question his rule.

Certainly it was the most vicious example of gangland killing in Chicago if not the entire country, the inhuman murders set a new mark in mob terror. Undoubtedly the victims were the dregs of the earth, a bunch of thugs whose death only improved decent society. Regardless of being human debris, the callous method of "whacking" them was brutal even for the mob.

The massacre occurred on the morning of February 14, 1929 at the S.M.C. Cartage Company garage at 2144 North Clark Street. The seven men lounging around inside characterized the typical hooligans of Chicago's gangland. There was a safe cracker, two bootlegger brothers and three heavies specializing in enforcing mob policies. Late with a protection payment? These were the bums who would break a leg or two to make certain you remembered next time. None of the men were above rolling a drunk or robbing an honest citizen in a dark alley. The lone exception to the mob members was a gangland groupie, an optometrist who got his kicks from rubbing shoulders with danger. By any measure all of them were human garbage, fiends who preyed on the weaker members of society. It can be argued Capone really did society a favor.

The common element binding the men together was their connection with one of Chicago's most infamous mobsters, George "Bugs" Moran. He often used the nondescript garage as his headquarters. A shipment of booze was supposedly coming from Detroit and the men were waiting to receive it.

The booze shipment was strictly a set up for an ambush. Capone wanted to "rub out" Moran and as many of his men he could at the same time. No sense leaving living witnesses around. Moran was a constant thorn in Capone's side and he just wanted him gone. Moran had tried to "rub out" Capone in Cicero in September 1926 so revenge was a key motive. More important though was Capone's desire to grab the north side vice trade. Moran had it. Capone wanted

Following the killing, a large crowd gathered in front of the SMC Cartage garage.

it. What could be simpler? There was also an issue about Moran hijacking shipments of Capone's best whisky, "Old Log Cabin" brand bourbon. The Detroit Purple Gang was supplying it direct from the Canadian distiller in Montreal but Moran was intercepting it before it reached Capone. In short, there were many reasons Capone wanted Moran stone cold dead!

There are numerous versions of the massacre. This is just one. Apparently a police car pulled up outside the garage and three uniform officers got out and went into the garage. Perhaps Moran's men anticipated a simple arrest for bootlegging, a "pinch" that Moran would easily have a mob lawyer "spring" them from quickly. Perhaps they could have assumed it was a plain shakedown too. Local police were always paid for "protection."

Certainly the faux police expected to find Moran in the garage but he wasn't there. It is thought he drove up just as the police were entering and was scared off. It is also possible Capone's lookout could have mistaken one of the other men for Moran. Regardless his absence saved his life, for a while.

Inside the garage the police lined the men up against a brick wall. Likely the men expected the officers to handcuff them and take'em "downtown." At this point two men in civilian clothing entered. Ominously they also had long topcoats, the type used to cover up BARs (Browning Automatic Rifles) and "Tommy guns." The officers drew their .38 caliber revolvers and the men in long coats pulled out Tommy guns. All five men started firing at Moran's crew. Bullets tore through bone and flesh and ricocheted into the brick wall. When the firing stopped the bullet ridden men lay dead in a pool of blood and the sharp sting of cordite fumes choked the room.

Satisfied with their work, Capone's men calmly left. The murders went undiscovered until a neighbor wandered in and discovered the horror. The

The bodies of the victims lay sprawled on the garage floor.

newspapers howled about the "St. Valentine's Day Massacre." Chicago police investigated and investigated and came up with all kinds of theories but never made an arrest. Although they "knew" Capone ordered the hit, they couldn't prove it and since he was in Florida at the time, he had an iron clad alibi.

The killers were finally identified years later when it was determined Capone's personal killer "Machine Gun" Jack McGurn planned and participated in the massacre. McGurn would later perish in a hail of machine gun fire on St. Valentine's Day 1936. Fred Goetz, a.k.a. "Shotgun George Ziegler" was another of the killers. Goetz was a graduate engineer who served as a flyer in World War I, certainly an unlikely mob enforcer. After raping a seven-year old girl, and jumping bail, he took up a life of crime. He later hooked up with the infamous Barker gang and ran with the nefarious killer Alvin Karpis later known as the "Birdman of Alcatraz." After being sent to Alcatraz Prison, Karpis became famous selling a gullible public a sob story about really being a nice guy just misunderstood! In truth Karpis was one of the most vicious killers ever to walk into "The Rock." Capone eventually had Goetz eliminated to prevent the slim chance he would talk to the wrong people about the massacre. Another shooter was Fred "Killer" Burke who ended his days as a model prisoner in Michigan's Alcatraz, Marquette Branch Prison.

Machine Gun Jack McGurn was one of the massacre's planners.

Incredibly one of the victims survived just long enough to sputter to the police through a blood-choked throat, "Nobody shot me. I ain't no copper." The coroner later counted 22 bullet holes in him.

The hit may not have killed Moran, but he took the hint and backed off from getting in Capone's way. He eventually died in prison in 1957, a penniless small time crook.

One Chicago newspaper estimated Capone was controlling 6,000 speakeasies and 2,000 handbooks (betting parlors) at the time of the massacre. Adding in prostitution and racketeering and it was claimed he was pulling in <u>$6,260,000 a week!</u> Remember, these are 1930 dollars. For example the profit in beer was huge. A keg cost $5 to brew and sold for $55! An army was needed to keep the empire together and authorities claimed his numbered 1,000 men, all vicious killers.

Capone dealt harshly and often personally with members of his inner circle suspected of disloyalty. When he found out three of his men were conspiring to eliminate him, he invited them to a banquet. When it was finished and the plates cleared, he pulled out a baseball bat and smashed their brains out on the dinner table. It was claimed Capone personally murdered between 20 and 60 men. The higher number is likely the more accurate. In addition, he arranged for the rubbing out of at least 400 others. He was never charged for a single one.

Fred Burke, known as "Killer" Burke, ended his days in Marquette Branch Prison.

Corruption was so rampant in the city, the relationship between the mob and local officials so tight, the reformers petitioned the federal government for help. When Big Bill Thompson was reelected mayor in 1927, the relationship was brought into sharper focus, especially when he declared he "was as wet as the Atlantic Ocean." Capone supposedly donated $250,000 to his war chest and many of his men worked on the campaign staff. The mayor's police chief once stated "60% of my police are in the bootleg business." His successor claimed he was offered $1,000 a day to allow bootleg deliveries. The ordinary street cop was getting $5 a day to "not see" passing beer trucks.

While Major Dever was in office trying to frantically beat down crime, Thompson used his enforced exile to build a diesel powered $25,000 yacht named *Big Bill*. Reflecting the height of arrogance, he had his own image carved as the figurehead. The yacht was launched at Riverview Park before a massive crowd. Any time *Big Bill* did something, there were always all the bells and whistles. To kill time while reformer Dever occupied the Mayor's office he claimed to be planning a trip to the South Seas to collect tree-climbing fish for the aquarium. Once the election returns were official (since this was Chicago, the returns were likely official before the votes were cast), Thompson and his supporters boarded a schooner in Belmont Harbor to celebrate. So many fans climbed aboard, the boat sank at the dock from the sheer weight! There was no harm done however. The wet and bedraggled party animals just struggled to shore and continued the celebration.

With Thompson back in power, Capone moved his headquarters back to the First Ward and Levee. Gambling, saloons and bordellos again made the district famous but now under the control of Capone rather than local political leaders. Capone became "one stop shopping" for political deals with the underworld. His men walked through City Hall openly arranging whatever needed to be arranged.

Capone worked the public relations side of life hard. At one point he even hired a press agent just to try to keep a positive spin on his activities. He also donated money to area charities and ran soup kitchens during the Depression. He once even invited reporters to his home for dinner! The big man himself was often seen in the company of movie stars, politicians and businessmen. Everyone wanted to be seen with a "winner" and Capone was hot.

In a dark reflection of the current Hollywood Star tours, he became a minor tourist attraction. Sightseeing buses ran past his Hawthorne Inn headquarters in Cicero, called the "Capone Castle" by the friendly guide. Whenever his immense armored car appeared people crowded around to get a glimpse of the big man.

Capone wasn't satisfied with just Chicago. He also had his tentacles into St. Louis, New York, New Orleans and Atlantic City as well as other locales. His criminal empire was far reaching.

Capone was a frequent first night attendee for new theater performances in an effort to convince people he had "class." He also had a private box at the various racetracks and was a serious bettor. He was a heavy investor in the dog tracks and a major player in the greyhound racing association. Attorney Edward J. O'Hare often represented Capone's dog racing interests. O'Hare was rubbed out when Capone learned the lawyer was apparently playing both sides of the street and providing information to the law. O'Hare's son, Lt. Commander Edward H. O'Hare won the Medal of Honor posthumously in the Pacific during World War II and O'Hare International Airport is named in his honor. Clearly good fruit can come from bad seed.

Finally the federal government acted against Capone. In 1929, President Herbert Hoover ordered a full attack on Chicago crime, dispatching the FBI and Internal Revenue Service as his troops. The famous leader of the FBI in Chicago was Elliot Ness. Together with his gang of agents the newspapers dubbed the "Untouchables" since they reportedly couldn't be bribed, he created merry old hell for Capone. The feds destroyed 25 breweries and distilleries demolishing millions in booze and equipment. Small legal issues like search warrants and due process were ignored. This was war and Capone was the enemy. More ominously, the IRS slowly began to build a case of tax evasion against Capone. "If he made all this money, why wasn't he paying federal taxes?"

To provide extra resources for the fight against Capone, a local citizens committee called the "Secret Six" was formed and raised a million dollar slush fund to fuel the reform effort. Their name came from the very real need not to be identified lest the gangsters take revenge. The money paid to tap telephones (warrant, what warrant?), pay informers, hire private investigators, etc. They also paid $10,000 to send the star witness in the Capone tax evasion case to South America for protection until he was needed for the trial. Eventually Capone was convicted of tax evasion and sentenced to 11 years in the federal pen serving part of the sentence at Alcatraz. Suffering from the terminal stages of syphilis, he was released from prison in 1939 to die at his Palm Island, Florida mansion in 1947. The 25-room palace was garishly decorated including a bathroom sink with solid gold legs. Try as he might, the only class he ever achieved was low. The opulence did Capone no good. He was suffering from deep dementia during the run up to his death and even held meetings with long dead companions.

In defense of Capone and the other mobsters, it has to be remembered that Chicagoans wanted the booze, gambling and women. All Capone did was operate an efficient business to supply a public demand. He couldn't have operated for a day if the demand wasn't there. The hypocrisy of city leaders was staggering. At a public meeting or in the newspapers they would all roundly condemn booze, gambling and prostitution but willingly attended numerous cocktail parties, ordered cases of illegal liquor for their social needs, placed bets with their bookie and occasionally sought the company of a willing female companion to whom they were not married. Big Al just gave them what they wanted.

Capone's sumptuous Florida mansion offered no retreat from the ghosts that chased a syphilis ridden "Big Al".

It is wise to realize too that all the money Capone "earned" was not morally different than the thievery of Chicago industrialists like Samuel Insull and Charles Yerkes. Both men were early advocates of the Ken Lay – Enron School of business ethics. Insull stole many millions from low and middle class investors for various politically inspired transportation and utilities scams. When they invariably failed, he skipped to Europe to avoid prosecution. 300,000 stockholders lost their savings as result of his reprehensible actions. He was finally indicted in 1932 on charges of bankruptcy, embezzlement and using the mails to defraud. Yerkes was a little different using his energy to modernize the city public transit system, including constructing the famous Loop around the central business district. He regularly bribed aldermen and city officials, cheated his stockholders and partners and fought with customers. He too finally fled to Europe but sold his holdings at vastly inflated prices before skipping town.

Big Jim Thompson, always a friend to the underworld, was defeated for mayor in April 1931 by Democrat Anton Cermak. Most city hall observers knew Cermak was no improvement but didn't envision how worse things would get. While Thompson usually had an agreeable relationship with the mob and bankrupted the city with various schemes and maneuvers, Cermak used a systematic approach modeled on the New York Tammany Hall machine. Power, privilege and patronage were exercised on an unprecedented scale.

By this time Capone was in prison but his gang was still operating under the leadership of Frank Nitti. In seems Cermak wanted to take over the Capone gambling operation and rubbing out Nitti was vital. To this end Cermak sent two police detectives, Harry Miller and Harry Lang to kill Nitti. It was nothing more complicated than a straight forward hit and became a fiasco!

According to the story the papers first published the two intrepid flat feet burst into a Capone office on North LaSalle Street and found Nitti who immediately pulled a rod and fired wounding Lang in the hand. The coppers, unfazed by Nitti's gunfire, shot back, hitting the crook in the chest and neck. Lang became an instant hero (just add one crooked cop, equal parts of BS and cash and shake) receiving a $300 award for meritorious service. Miller was also honored. Nitti was promptly dragged off to jail in the full expectation of his imminent death from police bullets. Unfortunately for the two gumshoes, he didn't die. Since he assaulted the detectives with his gun however he was hauled off to trial on a charge of assault with a deadly weapon.

At this point everything went to hell for the police and the Cermak administration. Under tough defense examination Officer Chris Callahan, another member of the raiding force, testified Nitti was unarmed and defenseless when they burst into the room. Nitti in fact promptly surrendered without resistance. Callahan then held him by the wrists while Lang shot him once in the neck and twice in the chest. Clearly he intended to kill him "while attempting to escape." Lang also managed the unlikely and very difficult feat of shooting himself in the hand. When Lang took the stand he claimed the original story was true, he shot Nitti in self-defense. He refused to answer any additional questions, taking the "Fifth Amendment" against self-incrimination to the embarrassment of prosecutors. It didn't take long for the prosecutors to figure out something was radically wrong with the whole case.

Incredibly Lang and Nitti switched roles, between accused and accuser! After a long series of postponements Lang went to trial in September 1933. Doubtless the delays were caused by Lang's insistence that if he went to trial for the shooting he would tell everything he knew about the Cermak administration. Somebody must have had a close and personal discussion with him since he remained lock lipped in court. Lang was found guilty but granted a new trial. Eventually he resigned from the police and everything soon faded away. It's not inconceivable he faded away forever!

In the meantime intrepid Mayor Cermak was in Miami, Florida, ostensibly to attend a rally for President Elect Franklin D. Roosevelt. Cermak was shaking FDR's hand, and basking in the glow of the great man, when Giuseppe Zangara stepped up and fired several shots at close range. The bullets struck Cermak who died three weeks later. At first it was thought FDR was the target and the assassin simply missed. Later many crime historians concluded Cermak was the real target, Capone ordering the hit in retribution for Cermak's attempt to kill Nitti. Cermak was actually in Florida not to meet with FDR but rather to flee Capone's Chicago influence. Regardless, another Chicago crook was dead.

Edward J. Kelly replaced Cermak and held the mayor's office until 1947. While the name on the door changed, business went on as usual. An estimated

7,500 gambling joints continued to operate as did other vice dens. Corruption and racketeering became more organized and efficient and deeper ingrained.

To celebrate its 100th birthday Chicago hosted the Century of Progress Exposition in 1933-34. It ran much like the 1893 Columbian Exposition and like its predecessor, was seen as a great moneymaker for legitimate as well as illegitimate business.

Gangsters operated the Italian Village on the fairgrounds as well as the roller coaster and an illegal roulette wheel. Ralph Capone ran another gambling "concession." The mob also made certain honest businessmen provided appropriate kickbacks and protection payments and "franchised" pickpockets worked the crowds. Of course the full range of vice activities including female "companionship" was available just a couple of blocks away.

Bootleg booze came into Chicago in a variety of ways. Truck convoys from Detroit were common as were boatloads over Lake Michigan. Some even came in by air direct from Canada. Two of the flying bootleggers were Irving Schlig and Harry Berman. Flying from Ashburn Airfield (just southeast of the corner of South Cicero Avenue and West 83rd Street) they made several flights a week. If the weather was too bad they just pulled a few stick-ups to keep the cash coming but flying was their primary income. Once they landed at Ashburn they taxied up to a couple of trucks and quickly transferred their cargo. It was a good system and worked well until they decided to leave Capone's gang. It didn't take long before the intrepid aviators turned up very dead as the result of shotgun blasts to the head. They were almost unrecognizable. One of the men who sometimes hung around Ashburn in the early 20s was Charles A. Lindbergh. He wouldn't become the "Lone Eagle" until 1927. Ashburn Field closed in 1952-53.

With Capone in prison and Prohibition repealed in 1933, the mob changed their business model. Under the direction of Frank "the Enforcer" Nitti running the show, it expanded into "B" girls, narcotics and business and labor racketeering. Since the earliest days various businesses were forced to pay "protection" money. Pushcart peddlers, small shopkeepers, all paid off neighborhood gangs to avoid "problems." Racketeering just took it to a new level of extortion. The list of businesses involved included parking garages, laundries, fish markets, florist shops, and garbage collectors; if it was a business, the mob would figure out a way to extort money. Labor unions were an especially ripe target. Soon many found mob members on their payroll as various officers and filling "no show" jobs. It is a great way to rob a union treasury as well as control the action of the union for extortion. Own a skyscraper in Chicago? Well if you want to make sure the elevator operators don't go on strike it will cost you $1,000 a week. Protection payments to the mob by dry cleaners increased the price of a suit from $1.25 to $1.75, which meant each customer was paying more money to support the crooks. As early as 1928 Chicagoans "lost" an estimated $136 million to the racketeers.

Should a victim decide not to pay off the mob there was an immediate cost. The racketeer could have the shop bombed with a simple black powder device for an economical $100. A more difficult job with a dynamite bomb could run as high as $1,000. Bombing in Chicago was commonplace. From October 11, 1927-January 15, 1929, a short 15 months, the city echoed with 157 bomb explosions. Not a single bomber was ever convicted!

Don't be naive enough to think it isn't still happening today. Just read the papers. But it all began during Prohibition. In 1928 the Cook County State's Attorney reported 91 Chicago unions were dominated by the mob. The Coal Drivers Union, Motion Picture Operators Union and Elevator Operators Union are a few of the early ones taken over by the mob. The mob activity in unions today dates from this early period and is more sophisticated and effective than ever.

Prostitution branched out into call houses; flats and other covert locations set up through taxi drivers, saloonkeepers and hotel bellhops. In effect vice was freed from geographic boundaries and went citywide. In the 1940s and 50s Clark Street and Chicago Avenue were a hot spot and B-girls solicited openly in bars

From 1839 to 1926 the method of execution in Illinois was hanging. Its great advantage was simplicity. A length of rope, a tall tree or light post and you were ready to go. All in all it isn't a bad method for most circumstances. Things got complicated when electrocution was introduced in 1927. Special equipment was needed which added to the expense and of course there was the cost of electricity. From 1983 until the present lethal injection is the legal method of execution, which is infinitely more complicated than using "Old Sparky." Somehow as a society we lost track of the old KISS (keep it simple stupid) principal. Where we used to just "string up" murderers, we now go through a complicated mechanical and chemical process to assure a quick and painless death.

Although the death penalty is still in effect in Illinois, there is a moratorium on executions, which was introduced by Governor George Ryan in 2000 and continued by Governor Rod Blagojevich in 2004. It is reportedly the first such moratorium to be instituted by a state in the United States. Other states have since imposed moratoriums on the imposition of capital punishment. The Illinois moratorium was followed by the publication of a comprehensive Commission Report on the history and status of capital punishment in Illinois. In January of 2003, Governor George Ryan unfortunately granted clemency to all inmates then under a sentence of death in Illinois, more than 160 persons, an unprecedented act of clemency in the history of criminal law in the United States. While cheered by such miscreant groups as the American Civil Liberties Union, the family members of the innocent victims murdered in cold blood by the vicious killers that Blagojevich and Ryan allowed to go unpunished, roundly condemned it. The action of the two governors speaks volumes of their moral corruption but also follows the historic tradition of miscreant Illinois politicians.[i]

Sally Rand

The 1933 Chicago Century of Progress Exposition was famous too for a notorious "fan dance" performed by a beautiful nymph named Sally Rand. She scandalized the local strait-laced set while attracting thousands of males to her daily shows.

Sally, born as Harriet Helen Gould in the hillbilly burg of Elkton, Missouri in 1904, ran away from home as a teenager to join a carnival. She wanted bright lights and action, not the mind numbing nothing of rural Missouri. Eventually she worked her way up through jobs as a nightclub cigarette girl, artist's model and cafe dancer. Slowly she climbed the ladder of success, dancing with a Chicago ballet company and Ringling Brothers Circus. Ending up in California when a touring company failed, she made her way into the movies working in some Mack Sennett and Hal Roach comedies. When Cecil B. deMille formed a stock company he made sure she was part of it and suggested she change her name to "Sally Rand." When Cecil suggested, you agreed! She appeared in a few of the new "talkies" but her vocal lisp kept her from movie stardom.

Leaving Hollywood she combined her flare for dance with the strong male desire for sexual titillation and started performing at Chicago's Paramount Club in 1932. Using a pair of seven-foot ostrich feathers purchased at a second hand shop she "showed" everything and revealed nothing, cleverly using the feathers to hide behind. Her act was a smash hit! Sally was considered the sexiest thing to ever hit the city. With her 36-24-36 inch measurements stacked on a small 5 foot, 1 inch body, she had all the "right stuff" in all the "right places." She was of course, a natural blonde (aren't they all?).

Sally Rand scandalized the strait-laced matrons of Chicago in 1933.

When the Fair opened in 1933 she reprised the historic Lady Godiva role by riding a white horse from the

Loop to the fairgrounds by the lake in the buff. Unlike the classic tale of Lady Godiva where only one man became a "peeping Tom" in Chicago there were peeping, staring, ogling, gaping, gazing and gawking Toms, Dicks and Harrys too! It was a great publicity gimmick and she soon was the featured act in the "Streets of Paris" concession. She wasn't a modern "bump and grind" dancer but rather performed to the strains of Claude Debussy's *Clair de Lune* or Fredric Chopin's *Waltz in C Sharp Minor*. Whether she ever actually danced nude is open to question. What is unquestioned is everyone at least thought she was nude. Was it a body stocking or a full coat of theatrical cream? She never revealed her secret. While men hooted, howled and packed every show, the local "protectors of the public virtue" had her arrested and hauled into court for behavior "lewd, lascivious and degrading to public morals." Judge Joseph P. David listened courteously to the rants and raves of the do gooders and handed down his verdict. "There is no harm and certainly no injury to public morals when the human body is exposed, some people probably want to put pants on a horse." The gavel thumped down and the case was dismissed.

An estimated 39 million people visited the Fair, a large number because Sally was doing her exquisite dance with her wondrous fans. She was grossing $6,000 week, a remarkable amount considering it was still the height of the Depression.

She returned in 1934 for the Fair's second year but feeling the need to keep her act fresh, used five 60-inch diameter transparent bubbles. A supporting revue of 24 dancers and 16 showgirls backed her up. Again testosterone filled males flocked to see her while old bitties and stiff-necked preachers ranted against her performance. Asked later about her life, she made the dry observation, "I haven't been out of work since the day I took my pants off."

Sally continued her career with stints at the California Pacific Exposition at San Diego in 1935-36, Frontier Exposition at Fort Worth in 1936, Golden Gate Exposition in San Francisco in 1939 and many others. She once took her act to sea, dancing on William Randoph Hearst's sumptuous yacht. She finally retired in 1967 at age 63 and was still turning heads with her mini skirts in 1974. She died two years later but remember, it all started on the shores of Lake Michigan![ii]

Great Lakes PROHIBITION

Driven by the strong anti-German atmosphere of World War I, organizations such as the Anti-Saloon League and Women's Christian Temperance Union working with both major parties, rammed a Constitutional amendment through Congress and the states initiating national Prohibition, taking effect in 1920. Previously many states, especially in the Bible thumping South, enacted local prohibition on the county or community level. Thanks to the national Prohibition from 1920 to 1933, the manufacture, sale, and transportation of alcohol was prohibited in the United States. As a loophole the private possession and consumption of alcohol was not prohibited. The Eighteenth Amendment to the Constitution, ratified January 16, 1919 and the Volstead Act, passed October 28, 1919, provided the legal framework for national Prohibition which officially began on January 16, 1920. The 18th Amendment was repealed by the 21st Amendment on December 5, 1933, making it the only Amendment to be repealed by another Amendment of the Constitution.

By any standard Prohibition was a unmitigated disaster of epic proportions and the direct result of what happens when a group of radical "do gooders" drive public policy without regard for "common sense."

The impact on communities could be devastating. For example, in 1918 Milwaukee had nine breweries employing 6,540 employees generating $35 million a year in product. When Prohibition came in it not only knocked out the entire industry but also a host of supporting concerns manufacturing goods like boxes, barrels, glassware, etc. The resulting loss of nearly 2,000 taverns not only threw the employees out of work, but cost the city roughly $500,000 in annual license fees. All just to satisfy a radical fringe group!

While Milwaukee is an extreme example, this was an era when brewing was more localized than it is today so every town or city of any size had a brewer. When they closed the domino effect was powerful.

Liquor in its many forms has long been a part of the country. From the earliest colonial days rum was the product of choice, both as a trade commodity and libation. The "holier than thou" Puritans were the first major distillers of rum in America and although they railed against drunkenness, they imbibed freely themselves. Western farmers soon learned to convert bulky grain into highly portable (and palatable) whisky. Crying babies were often given a simple and effective mixture of rum and opium to "quiet" them. A teaspoon of whisky also helped take the edge off teething children. A mint julep was as common as a breakfast drink in the south as orange juice today.

Congressman John Volstead of Minnesota authored the infamous Volstead Act.

The idea of the modern coffee break has its roots in liquor. It was common for businesses to keep a keg of rum or whiskey on the counter and when a little pick me up was needed, a glass was poured and everyone had a snort. When having a little "touch" became politically incorrect, the idea of a "coffee" break was born.

The drive to national prohibition took years. It wasn't accomplished overnight. There were areas of the country were prohibition was the norm for decades under local option. Invariably these were rural areas where rabid evangelical Christian groups stifled dissenting opinion and rammed their beliefs down the throats of others.

The various Christian groups were not above using any skullduggery to force Prohibition on the masses. For example, Yalie Charles Foster Kent, a professor of Bible History was given the job of "cleaning up" biblical references to drink. Under his imagination biblical verses such as "And the vine said unto them, should I leave my wine, which cheereth God and man?" (Judges 9:13) to "Shall I leave my juice that gladdens gods and men." The learned expert who knew absolutely HE alone knew God's word, swept out all references to alcohol, producing a sanitized Bible the radical Christian sects could be proud of. That it was grossly inaccurate was of small consequence.

America's entry into World War I impacted Prohibition too. The same groups fighting for Prohibition also fought hard to remove any possible adult

Before the passage of Prohibition female advocates of dry laws regularly busted up innocent saloons.

entertainment from military bases or the civilian community surrounding them. With the passage of the Selective Service Act in 1917 (aka the Draft Act) President Wilson (a straitlaced, dour faced, fun is never allowed character) and his Secretary of War received new authority from Congress. It didn't take long before both slammed the American military hard. All brothels near military bases and all saloons within a half-mile of urban bases and five miles of rural ones were closed by official decree. Soon even a military man couldn't even legally have a drink in a private home! Talk about the intrusion of big brother!

Certainly the local civilian community took a major hit too. Now even an innocent civilian worker couldn't even get a beer in his favorite tavern if it fell within Wilson's infamous "circle of sobriety."

Under the guise of needing the grain to feed the "starving masses of Europe" Wilson tried to forbid the manufacture of all fermented or distilled alcohol except that used for religious, medical or scientific purposes. Only the timely threat of a congressional filibuster prevented complete implementation of Wilson's idiot plan but the compromise was nearly as bad. Wilson banned the importation or manufacture of all hard liquor and reduced the alcoholic content of beer. It was a

A group of men enjoying a libation.

brutal slap in the face of Americans who enjoyed a nip or two as well as those brave American soldiers and sailors denied the simple pleasure of a drink.

Looking back from today's vantage point, it is amazing how a law as sweeping as national Prohibition slipped by the American people as quickly and easily as it did. When the 18th Amendment came before the Senate, reputed to be the "great deliberative body," it passed with a one sided vote after a mere 30 hours of debate! When the House took it up, it passed in a single day! Talk about reckless legislating!

But we are a democracy and the necessary 36 states ratified the amendment in January 1919, despite opposition from the metropolitan areas. Eventually every state ratified it but two, Connecticut and Rhode Island. Considering Rhode Island's historic role in the colonial rum trade, her opposition is understandable. Prohibition went into effect on January 20, 1919. Andrew John Volstead, a sour faced dust dry Minnesota Congressmen sponsored the infamous Volstead Act, the enforcement arm of the 18th Amendment, The ill-famed Anti-Saloon League largely wrote the actual legislation. Incidentally Volstead was voted out of office in the next election. Even Sven and Ole couldn't stand him.

How national prohibition became the law of the land is a study in strong arm lobbying. Apply enough pressure, find the congressman's weakness, mix in a little blackmail and it all works well to force a supporting vote.

The dry forces were very organized and had been lobbying publicly and behind the scenes for decades. The forces of the Women's Christian Temperance Union and Anti-Saloon League were very powerful and when combined with various evangelical Christian groups and social do-gooders, irresistible. In the same manner a rum runner's money would later buy police, prosecutors, judges, juries and elected officials, so were crooked legislators "bought" by the "drys." In effect, "If you want to continue to be our senator with all the cushy benefits, you better vote dry." The result was the same, the "currency" was just different. Frankly, I think the rum runners were more honest about the whole thing. They didn't have a "high minded" moralistic agenda. Their only goal was making money.

When national Prohibition started 24 states already had prohibition laws by local option. The first was Georgia in 1907. North Carolina, Tennessee, Mississippi, West Virginia and Oklahoma soon followed. All were states with large rural populations easily swayed by the fire breathing rants of evangelical groups. Local legislators, ever swayed by righteous pressure, caved in like a punctured balloon and prohibition became state law.

Once Prohibition passed, its biggest supporter was the rumrunning fraternity. The drys as well as crooks worked to keep incumbent dry politicians in office. The mob often provided a little backroom donation. Mobsters made a great deal more money with Prohibition than without it. And everyone was getting a drink if they wanted it. It was even easier for a politician's rich supporters who just made a phone call and a case was quietly dropped off at the back door. Liquor by the case was also regularly delivered to the Senate cloakroom for those "in need" of a stiff one (or two) during or after their most difficult deliberations.

Even when the public clearly wanted Prohibition repealed, politicians were unwilling to admit the mistake (or forgo the crook's periodic donations) and vote it out. The political power of the drys was too strong to openly challenge anyway. Prohibition was often ignored and virtually anyone who really wanted to could get a drink. This all allowed the legislator to huff and puff about the necessity to enforce the law and perhaps vote a small increase to the Prohibition Bureau making his dry supporters happy and still wink at the real situation.

The "wets" were also not well organized. Generally they were the companies making the liquor and beer and seen as money-grubbing concerns willing to ruin honest Americans through evil drink.

The World War directed the attention of the public away from domestic issues including Prohibition. Although America had no real reason for involvement in the bloodbath, under Wilson's persistent campaigning it was seen as inevitable and necessary. He cleverly managed to convince the people the very existence of the country was at stake. If it is a choice between a drink and the nation, there is no real choice.

Many of the big brewers were also of German origin. Pabst and Busch for example. Since Germany was our new "enemy" all things German must be bad, including "Hun" beer.

If winning the war was vital, then improving efficiency was a needed virtue. America required sober soldiers, sailors and factory workers. Eliminating alcohol would achieve this critical goal.

The American people never miss a chance for a good party and the last night of legal drinking provided a great opportunity. Many places fancy and low, displayed black drapes and somber funeral decorations. Some even had a coffin available since it was the official wake of old John Barleycorn.

Somehow the country thought citizens would just meekly obey the new law. After all, we weren't a nation of outlaws, or were we? Congress knew some enforcement would be needed to prevent backsliders from breaking the law, so they appropriated $2 million to fund a Prohibition Bureau under the Treasury Department. The new agency promptly hired roughly 1,500 "agents" to enforce the new law.

Prohibition agents were also notoriously corrupt. Since the Bureau paid very little; in 1920 $1,200-$2,000 a year and even in 1930 only $2,300-$2,800, many looked to supplement their official salary with "unofficial" bribes. The agents also didn't come under the provisions of Civil Service, they could be hired and fired at will. When an effort was made to bring them under the protection of Civil Service, three-quarters couldn't pass the simple entrance test! The Bureau hired indiscriminately. There were no background investigations and in some instances, criminals just released from prison were handed a revolver, box of bullets and sworn in! The professionalism and competence of the agency was certainly open to question. All that said, there were some good men in the Bureau but it is fair to say most were a laughable bunch of crooked clowns.

Some of the agents were laughably blatant about their crookedness, even riding around town in big limousines with a flashy blonde showgirl on each arm! In an effort to weed the crooks out, one Prohibition Bureau captain brought all his agents into his office and had them place both hands on a table. He then announced, "Everyone of you sons of bitches with a diamond ring is fired." Half the men walked out the door. He figured only men on the take could afford a diamond.

When Prohibition started it was assumed everyone would blindly fall into line. The first Prohibition Commissioner, John K. Kramer, stated the law, "...will be obeyed in cities large and small, and in villages, and where it is not obeyed it will be enforced. The law says liquor to be used as a beverage must not be manufactured. We shall see that it is not manufactured. Nor sold, nor given away, nor hauled in anything on the surface of the earth or under the earth or in the air." Clearly Mr. Kramer was the type to buy a "really good bridge" if offered.

Congress's original appropriation of a mere $2 million for enforcement was ludicrous. Eight years later the Prohibition Commissioner was asking for $300 million for a single year! Still, he admitted, there would be leaks.

As an early demonstration of coming problems, a bare 59 minutes after Prohibition went into effect six armed men broke into two railroad cars in Chicago and stole a load of alcohol valued at $100,000. During the crime they bound and gagged two trainmen and locked another six in boxcars.

The problem of enforcement was enormous. The coastline of the U.S. stretched for 18,700 miles. The Prohibition Bureau started with a bare 1,500 agents. Even as late as 1930 it only had 2,836, working out to one agent every seven miles or so. This didn't take into account the use of the agents doing anything else but standing guard 24 hours. Assuming an eight-hour shift, it worked out to one man for every 24 miles. Plus of course there was desperate need for the agents to chase down rum runners and bootleggers inside the country, bust up stills, smash speakeasies, kill innocent civilians and cause all manner of general disruption and harm. The entire federal enforcement scheme was absurd.

In theory the U.S. Customs agents worked to cover the border points of entry and the Coast Guard patrolled the water. Since both groups were grossly underpaid there was great temptation to just "look the other way" for an hour. Many men did.

Stills didn't need to be large or complicated to be efficient.

State, county and local police were also supposed to enforce the law. The results were at best, spotty, the prevailing thought being, "it's a federal law, let them enforce it." If the drys were locally strong, enforcement was better. If the local wets held sway, then it was weak. Such is human nature.

It didn't take long for a fleet of liquor ships to anchor just off the U.S. coast and sell their illegal product to hordes of fast cabin cruisers dashing out from shore. The fast boats moored up to the mother ship and their operator passed greenbacks up with a shopping list. In a short time down came burlap bags filled with their order. And unlike what the public bought from their local bootlegger ashore, this was the "real McCoy." In fact one of the popular captains was named McCoy and he guaranteed his product. And why shouldn't the liquor be the good stuff. The ships that made up "rum row" picked it up at Bimini, Belize or St. Pierre. Legitimate distillers were happy to sell their goods to the rum runners, after all the price was right and it wasn't their job to enforce crazy American law.

Profits from bootleg booze were immense. With the right contacts a barrel of beer cost $7 and sold to the speakeasy for $55. A case of Canadian whiskey cost a Chicago rum runner $45 and sold of $90, however it was cut three times by the operator. Usually the new mixture included one third water, one-third 80-proof industrial alcohol and one-third the original Canadian whiskey. Sometimes mineral oil was used to "smooth" the taste out. The proper color came from burnt sugar or caramel. In effect the one case of real Canadian whiskey became three, complete with fancy labels and the rum runner's assurance it was "the real thing, right from the distillery." If plain alcohol was being converted into gin a little juniper juice provided the right taste.

The liquor all didn't come in by boat. Entire boxcars packed full of the best brands crossed the Canadian border. It didn't take much effort to have a customs agent miss a car or two or "pencil whip" an inspection. Even airplanes flew hooch in by the caseload. And all the Canadian customs paperwork was complete and proper. Their laws didn't prohibit export anywhere so it was perfectly legal to send it to the U.S. There were also gaps in the Volstead Act that could be exploited. It allowed the manufacture of "cereal beverages" with alcohol content of less than one half percent. The basic ingredients were legally available and soon everyone was home brewing. One estimate put a hundred stills in every block of West Madison Street in Chicago. Of course the alcohol content of the beverage "tended" to exceed the legal limit.

Many saloons switched to selling ice cream. The present day Antlers Restaurant in Sault Ste Marie, Michigan is a fine example of this. Reputedly before Prohibition it was called the "Bucket of Blood" and served a local cliental as rough as it's name. Once the dark days of dryness arrived the name changed to the "Bucket of Blood Saloon *and Ice Cream Parlor*." The clientele never changed and it somehow made it though Prohibition on a single order of ice cream! It was rumored the Revenue Agents shut it down when they discovered it operated an entire month and only sold a single quart of ice cream! Considering the saloon was in the Soo, if she was shut down, it was only for a very, very brief period.

Policing efforts were grossly inefficient. In 1925 the Assistant Secretary of the Treasury in charge of enforcement estimated less than five percent of the illegal

State authorities pose with a pile of stills discovered in Munising, Michigan. Who missed the payoff?

booze was intercepted. The value of the liquor coming into the U.S. in 1924 was set at $40 million. Before Prohibition was repealed in 1933 the value increased every year.

The profits made by the bootleggers were staggering. A 1931 federal study estimated bootleggers were getting $10 million <u>a day</u> from the public. The price of a drink increased dramatically too. Before Prohibition a shot of whisky sold for 15 cents, after 75 cents was the norm.

Prohibition also had a major impact on the crime rate. A study of 30 cities showed a jump of 24 percent from 1920-1921. Arrests for drunkenness increased 41 percent and drunken driving arrests 81 percent. Thefts rose nine percent and assault and battery leaped 13 percent. Federal prisons were hit hard by Prohibition. Prior to it taking effect the prisons held 4,000 convicts. By 1932 the number of prisoners increased 561 percent. In 1930 over 66 percent were there on alcohol and drug charges.

In 1925 Chicago with a population of 3 million had 16,000 arrests for drunkenness, more than the entire country of England with 40 million people! Drunken driving arrests in the city increased 476 percent by 1927.

In 1932, the year before repeal, 2,000 civilians and 500 Prohibition agents had been killed in the booze wars. In Chicago alone, 23 absolutely innocent citizens had been gunned down by over zealous federal law enforcement agents. Although indictments were given in every case, not a single federal agent was ever punished. It was an astounding abuse of power by the prohibition agents, district attorneys, state and federal courts.

While gangsters and bootleggers usually walked off with acquittals if tried for violations as the result of their large bribes, ordinary citizens were often given absurdly severe sentences, especially if dragged in front of a dust dry judge. For example, a Lansing, Michigan man was given life imprisonment for processing a pint of gin; a deputy sheriff in Aurora, Illinois killed a housewife and clubbed her husband when he sniffed liquor in their home; a Michigan mother of ten received a life sentence for having a pint of gin. Clearly such action by the forces of the law only turned more and more of the public against them.

The amount of liquor consumed during a single year of Prohibition was staggering; 200,000,000 gallons of booze, 684,000,000 gallons of malt liquor, 118,000,000 gallons of wine. Prohibition became a major U.S. industry, some folks argued it was the largest!

One of the methods used to circumvent prohibition was the ability of a pharmacist to provide whisky by doctor's prescription to patients. It was good stuff too, in many cases bottles of Old Crow whiskey were labeled "for medicinal use only." It wasn't unheard of for a doctor to provide a pad of pre-signed prescriptions to a trusted pharmacist for a fee. In turn the pharmacist would "sell" the prescription to a customer for an appropriate fee. One pharmacist reputedly filled over 1,000 prescriptions in a single day to just 50 customers!

A set of confirmed drinkers enjoying a beer in Houghton, Michigan, far from the forces of law and order.

Industrial alcohol was a major component of homemade booze. There was a valid need for alcohol for industry, science and medical purposes and certain factories were licensed to manufacture it. Policing how much was actually made and where it went was virtually impossible and much was diverted to bootleggers where it was used to "cut" good Canadian whiskey or to quickly mix up a batch of rotgut booze. In an effort to stop the flood of industrial alcohol to illegal use, the federal government required toxic wood alcohol be added. It didn't stop the bootleggers but did poison to death many customers.

The term "cocktail" dates from Prohibition. Drinks like whiskey sours, old-fashions, various gin fizzes and the like were necessary to kill the taste of the bad booze. Some of the alcohol was even cut with mineral oil to "smooth" it out.

Breweries were allowed to make "near beer" or as it was often called, "soapsuds." Beer was brewed in the conventional method, then run over a heating element to de-alcoholize it. There were a couple ways of defeating the low alcohol content. Most easily of course was to not turn on the heating unit so the brew was bottled at original strength. A few bucks assured the inspector took a break during the critical period. A second method was to boost the near beer with alcohol. The speaks were sold the near beer and given a supply of wood alcohol. The beer was either charged with alcohol while in the keg with a compression style pump or boosted in the glass with a needle filled with alcohol, gaining the name "needle beer."

Not just content to kill citizens with poisonous alcohol, the government pushed enforcement agencies harder to stem the flow of booze, even issuing shoot to kill orders. Usually the firefights resulted in death or injury only between the "good" guys and the "bad" guys. Sometimes innocent people were killed. In March 1920 the vessel *I'm Alone* was chased by the Coast Guard and finally apprehended and sunk 215 miles off the Atlantic coast. Since the international boundary was 12 miles offshore, this was a wanton violation of international law. Even worst, she was a Canadian vessel! Such unpopular actions resulted in many instances of negative press, leading one editor to write, "Who's Watching the Coast Guard While the Coast Guard's Watching the Coast?"

The judicial weight of prosecuting citizens apprehended for Prohibition violations was staggering. By June 1920 there were 500-600 Prohibition-related charges waiting trial in Chicago. Waiting for a trial took years.

In notoriously wet areas prosecutors often failed to prosecute and when they did, juries returned innocent verdicts. Sometimes states's witnesses also "failed to clearly remember" during testimony. Judges also set extremely low bail, especially for well connected mobsters. Everyone was on the take.

Prohibition introduced a new attitude towards booze. Since it was now illegal, more people wanted it, especially young boys. Drink was seen as a rite of passage

What a waste! Prohibition authorities dump barrels of wine in Iron Mountain, Michigan.

and bragging about getting "blotto" was important to their ego. In the big cities speaks sprang up around high schools to service the demand.

Pressure to repeal Prohibition gradually increased. When the stock market crashed in 1929 and the Depression swept over the country additional pressure was generated since the brewing and distilling industries would add workers and jobs were desperately needed. Plus there was the additional tax revenue for the government to consider. Finally in December 1933 the 21st Amendment repealed the 18th and if all wasn't right again with the world at least a man (or woman) could mull over problems with a legal drink.

The financial loss to the federal government during the 14 years of Prohibition was staggering. An estimated $363 million was spent in a hopeless effort to enforce the law and throughout the period the normal alcohol tax revenue was nonexistent. State and local government also committed an estimated $3 billion trying to enforce Prohibition.

Prohibition changed the face of American crime. Prior to it the criminal scene was dominated by hold up men, safe crackers and just plain robbers. Most would be eventually caught and sent to the "big house." Once the criminal element became involved with rum running and related alcohol crimes, the money became so plentiful it was common to buy off the legal system. The crooks became largely untouchable.

Police, prosecutors, judges and juries all came under the influence of the mob. Bootleggers who needed the police to look the other way when a convoy of booze passed, needed an indictment quashed or jury to find an acquittal were usually able to do so. Money talked and the crooks had an endless river of cash to spread around.[i]

Rum Running Forever

The booze came into the Great Lakes in a variety of ways. If the mind of man (or woman) could conceive it, it could be done. Planes, trains, boats and autos all had their place in the smuggling scheme.

One of the unique methods involved a small buoy in the St. Clair River just off St. Clair, Michigan. All the locals knew it was there and knew its purpose, including the local police and Coast Guard. With the exception of the users, it was left strictly alone. Every so often a boat from Canada pulled up to it and grappled a hose aboard and connected it up to a small pump. A few pulls on the starter rope and thousands of gallons of booze flowed through the hose to a tank ashore. The underwater hose was quick and efficient.[ii]

U.S. Customs agents were often on the take. Sometimes it was obvious, like when the agents helped a smuggler unload the booze from his boat to a truck. Other times it was far more casual. For example, it seems a fellow who had been working in Canada shipped a trunk back to his home in Grand Rapids, Michigan via the Railway Express Agency. Since he had five bottles of booze and didn't want to waste them, he carefully packed them deep in the trunk. When the trunk arrived at Grand Rapids he eagerly looked for his hidden treasure but instead found a note from a customs agent. "We took three and left you two. You tell on us and we'll tell on you."[iii]

Bootleg Bars

It is fair to say virtually the entire Great Lakes region was involved in bootlegging and rum running. The U.S. shares thousands of miles of border with Canada, still the home of good whisky. Regardless of the law, state or federal, the "real McCoy" still flowed in to thirsty folks across the Lakes.

Although I know of no accurate count, there were certainly thousands of bars and saloons that kept serving alcoholic beverages during Prohibition. Some did it openly and others were somewhat more circumspect. Most of their stories have been lost to history. It was so common, no one bothered to record them for future generations. But there are joints we do know about.

Shipwrecked Brew Pub (Egg Harbor, Door County, Wisconsin)

Door County today is Wisconsin's trendy vacation retreat, sometimes described as the Cape Cod of the Great Lakes. Bed and breakfasts, boutique hotels, wineries and intimate restaurants mark the area as a paradise for the legions of yuppies that make it a favorite destination. Generations ago the Door was very different. It was a working class region, with small fruit farms, commercial fishermen, lumberjacks and sailors. Having a good saloon or two around was essential for morale.

The Shipwrecked Brew Pub started out in the late 1800's as a workingman's bar. It wasn't any different than the many others dotting Peninsula. Good beer and a good meal became its staple attraction. Sometimes things did get a bit rough as might be expected. It is thought a lumberjack was killed in the place sometime during the early years but the details are scarce.

During Prohibition the alcohol never stopped flowing. Egg Harbor was a very long way from the law, at least the law that couldn't be persuaded to look the other way. It was said the saloon became a favorite for Al Capone and his minions to hole up in when things got too hot in the Windy City. Supposedly there were tunnels running under town to allow him to flee unseen if needed. There is a tale that Capone once showed up with his girlfriend and her young son. Whether the son was related to Capone wasn't known. The tale goes the child kept crying and the girlfriend kept nagging Big Al and after a day or so both were "gone." Whether they went back to Chicago or were wrapped in some heavy chain and dumped into the depths of Green Bay is unknown.[iv]

Nelsen's Hall Bitters Pub and Restaurant (Washington Island, Door County, Wisconsin).

Washington Island is at the tip of the Door Peninsula. A small ferry makes periodic trips to the island from the small village of Gill's Rock. It is to say the least, remote.

The original bar was built in 1899 by Danish immigrant Tom Nelsen as a community center for the small island settlement. Over time it saw use as an ice cream parlor, medical office, drug store and movie theater and of course, tavern. The structure has been modified several times and gone through a number of ownership changes.

Nelsen's Hall is the world's largest dispenser of Angostura Bitters, certainly a strange honor for a Door County bar. German Dr. J. Siegert developed the bitters, intended as a tonic to treat fatigue and stomach ailments, in 1824. A hopeless romantic, the doctor journeyed to Venezuela to join Revolutionary Simon Bolivar in his fight against Spanish oppression. Realizing the doctor was more valuable as a doctor than soldier, Bolivar appointed him Surgeon-General of the Military Hospital in the town of Angostura. It is there Siegert developed his remarkable tonic which is now the single most widely distributed bar item in the world. Angostura Bitter is named for the port town of Angostura, Venezuela, and not for the bark of the eponymous tree. The bitters are made from a secret blend of tropical herbs; plant extracts and spices - reportedly over forty ingredients carefully selected by Doctor Siegert for their healthful properties.

When Prohibition started Tom figured there had to be a way of still serving his loyal public without attracting too much attention. Washington Island was far; far from the enforcement flagpole but why take chances? So he became a distributor for Angostura Bitters. He claimed he drank a pint of the concoction every day and it was the secret to his good health. The bitters were also 90 proof which didn't hurt the bar business one bit! Tom also received his pharmacist's license allowing

The Blossom Heath was a famous roadhouse in St. Clair, Michigan.

him to dispense "medicinal" alcohol by a physician's written prescription. If the patron desired to take his required medical treatment while seated at the bar that was his prerogative.

The bar's special relationship with Angostura Bitters continues today. Every year more than 10,000 people take a dose and become a card-carrying member of the club! Nelsen's Hall is also the oldest "legally" continuously operating bar in Wisconsin.[v]

Yachtsman Matthew Kramer built the **Blossom Heath Inn** in St. Clair, Michigan in 1911, naming his new roadhouse the Kramerhof. William McIntosh purchased it 1920 changing the name to the more appealing Blossom Heath Inn. McIntosh also added two new wings including a very ornate ballroom. It quickly gained the reputation of being one of the most opulent roadhouses in the state. Nationally known big bands often played there and the clientele was a who's who of the Midwest, including members of Detroit's notorious Purple Gang. Hollywood stars like George Raft, Claudette Colbert and Sophie Tucker also stopped by to enjoy the "atmosphere." Good booze and mixing with vicious killers was a powerful attraction and the inn buzzed with guests and excitement.

During Prohibition the laws of the nation and state didn't apply to the Blossom Heath. The bar ran full blast and any kind of booze was readily available. Rum runners from Canada brought boatloads of booze up the canal behind the Blossom Inn for ease of unloading. The inn was also famous for it's gambling with high stakes roulette, poker and other games enticing sporting men and women from near and far. Rumor claims the upstairs rooms were also used for illicit liaisons with "professional ladies of the evening." The local police of course managed to always look the other way where the Blossom Heath Inn was concerned. When Prohibition finally died a well-deserved death in 1933 business at the Blossom Heath died too and it was sold in 1943. A roadhouse not used is a roadhouse in decay and in 1946 the village of St. Clair Shores purchased it eventually reopening it as a civic and recreation center. What a horrid use for such a great old building! Apparently the city was embarrassed by it's colorful past! In 1986 the building was renovated into a banquet and meeting hall, bringing back much of the old glory to a new generation. Reputedly the Blossom Inn is still honeycombed with storage areas and secret passages including one hidden by a full- length mirror in an upstairs wall. A secret button concealed in a banister was wired to an alarm system to warn if the cops were making a raid. Almost always such raids were for show only, a way of proving to the "dry" members of the community the police were doing their job. Today the Blossom Heath is in wonderful condition and very popular as a banquet and wedding and reception facility.[vi]

Roadhouses – Windsor

The term "roadhouse" was a spin off of Prohibition meaning "an inn, restaurant, or nightclub located on a road outside a town or city." Usually there was an illegal activity involved of some sort including gambling, bootleg booze or "women of the night."

Many roadhouses lined both sides of the Detroit and St. Clair Rivers. Just north of the city on the St. Clair places like the Blossom Heath Inn attracted the best (or worst) of society. On the Canadian side of the waterway the roadhouses pulled customers from both Canada and the U.S. Many folks from the Detroit side came over by boat, pulling up to private roadhouse docks and wharfs. There wasn't any foolishness about customs and immigration inspectors either.

Just to the west of Windsor, Ontario was the Chappell House. A sign over the door "At All Hours" clearly stated it was ready whenever the customer was! The Albars Island View, Edgewater Thomas Inn, Rendezvous and other roadhouses ran off to the east. While food was good at all of them, it was the gambling and drinking folks came for.

The Edgewater Thomas Inn specialized in all you can eat chicken for a mere 50 cents. Liquor and gambling were just up stairs. Of course booze was illegal in Ontario too during the Prohibition era so the operators had to be wary of over enthusiastic local police just like on the American side. Cooperation among the joints was vital and each was carefully wired with a buzzer system connected to four other roadhouses. If the cops headed for one, all would be instantly alerted to the danger. Spotters also kept guard in the second floor windows to monitor police movements.

The Edgewater Thomas Inn, owned by Bertha Thomas, was also equipped with secret passages and concealed wine rooms. When the cops were heading over for a raid, moving a lever collapsed the liquor shelves and bottles disappeared down a chute to be magically replaced with soft drink bottles. Musicians had the job of quickly grabbing customer's glasses and dumping the contents into the very thick floor carpet where it vanished. Bertha wasn't above using bribery with the police if needed. On one occasion she placed a trail of $10 bills from the front entrance through the club and out the rear exit. The cops dutifully followed the bills, picking each one up as they went. Doubtless they were seizing them as "evidence." When the rear door slammed behind they went directly to their patrol cars and never returned, at least that day.

The Rendezvous Bar was owned by the very flamboyant Mrs. Herbert who always stationed herself in front to welcome patrons often including the Fishers, Dodges, Fords, Al Capone, Detroit Tigers or New York Yankees. These folks didn't want to be seen in Detroit speaks, so dashing across the river was a great alternative. Herbert was typically dressed to the "nines," sparkling with jewels and wrapped in costly furs.

The Chappell House near Windsor was another great roadhouse. Built in 1897 by brothers Henry and Harley Chappell, it had a well-deserved reputation for good food. In 1919 they sold it to Beverly (Babe) Trumble and it became a rousing center of the Roaring Twenties trade. It is claimed even Scarface Al Capone once visited the place. The roadhouse was also the scene of a most despicable murder. In November 1920 a Provincial Liquor License Inspector, one Reverend J. O. L. Spracklin, of the Methodist persuasion, viciously shot and killed Babe Trumble on the front steps during a raid. The two had known each other since childhood but there was no love lost. The newspapers had a field day with the murder, calling Spracklin the "pistol pack'n preacher." Doubtless Babe's many friends called the murdering Methodist minister much worse. The killing was certainly not justified as evidenced by the fact that the reverend was hauled into court on manslaughter charges. Incredibly he was acquitted of the charges and set free to lead the charge against the evils of demon rum. Spracklin claimed Trumble flashed a gun, but considering his shoot first and ask questions later attitude the death was inevitable. His heavy-handed enforcement effort evidently continued but perhaps the courts were less inclined to be lenient as in January 1921 a lawyer was awarded heavy damages when the reverend attacked his yacht. He frequently led vigilante raids on smugglers and speakeasies, often apparently without due regard for the law. He railed and ranted from the pulpit about the evils of drink and made it his personal mission from God to eradicate it, the public be damned.

Legend always claimed there was a tunnel running under the Detroit River to the U.S. but it was never found. Like many old Prohibition stories, it's a good story but the facts are short. The building went through a number of changes in ownership but finally burned down in May 2006. It was known as the President's Strip Club when flames finally ended its storied life.[vii]

Great Lakes

THE ROARING TWENTIES

Choppers Forever

The greatest symbol of the gangster era has to be the Thompson Sub Machine gun, aka "Tommy Gun, Ukulele Music, Chicago Organ Grinder, Chicago Street Sweeper" and just "Chopper." Having a Thompson of his very own seems to have been the ultimate status symbol for the up and coming "torpedo" of the era.

The .45-caliber Thompson is one of the world's classic firearms. Originally designed by Brigadier General John L. Thompson to "sweep" German infantry from the trenches of World War I, it was initially only slowly adopted by the tradition bound U.S. military. Production by the Colt Firearms Company began in 1920, too late for the war and it languished in military limbo until 1938 when the gathering storm of World War II forced it's purchase as "nonessential limited procurement." The Army was still enamored by the single shot, bolt action 1903 Springfield rifle and buying a machine gun as a personal weapon for an individual soldier was a difficult concept for them to grasp.

During the late 1920s the Thompson was also available to the general public for $200 each. While this was a considerable amount of money, it was peanuts to the gangsters of the "Roaring Twenties" and soon the principal markets were the cops and the robbers. Each wanted Tommy Guns. The first time a mobster used

The .45 Thompson was also called a "Chicago Typewriter."

one appears to have been in Chicago on September 25, 1925 when gangster Frank "Spike" McErlane opened up on Edward O'Donnell, a bank robber and bootlegger. O'Donnell and his gang had been highjacking Torrio-Capone beer trucks which was a gross error in judgment. Torrio ordered McErlane to "take care of the problem." McErlane duly "rubbed out" eight of the O'Donnell gang. Eventually McErlane who had a brand new "Tommy gun" cornered O'Donnell. To O'Donnell's immense luck, McErlane's had apparently never used the Thompson before and he emptied an entire drum of bullets at O'Donnell who was standing in front of a wall and MISSED! When the cops arrived they assumed at least several shooters were involved judging by the huge number of holes in the wall. O'Donnell promptly ran off to Torrio and begged forgiveness for his sins. Torrio amazingly forgave his impertinence and sent him on his way.

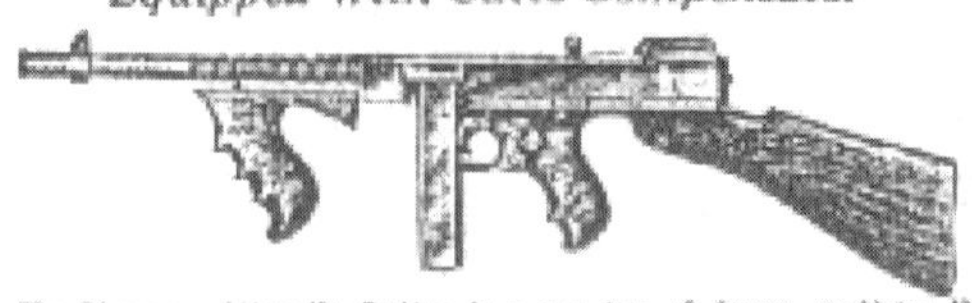

The Thompson was sold on the civilian market too.

McErlane was considered one of the busiest contract killers in Chicago. Fat and red-faced, he was utterly without compassion. Once he and a companion were drinking at a Crown Point, Indiana bar and his chum questioned his shooting skills. An inebriated McErlane drew his revolver, picked a man at the end of the bar and using him as a human target, coolly drilled him with a slug. Presumably McErlane eventually learned to use the Chicago Typewriter.

It is thought the Thompson was largely responsible for the National Firearms Act of 1934, which was intended to keep machine guns, concealable weapons and silencers out of the hands of mobsters.

The Thompson was an excellent weapon and became a mainstay of the U.S. military during World War II. It was extremely reliable. From the miserable jungles of Southeast Asia to the frozen forest of the Ardennes, it always worked. Between 1939-1945, 1,750,000 were manufactured. Many were used by Allied nations since they were far better than anything else available. Their only real drawback was expense. Later in the War a British 9mm STEN gun could be stamped out of cheap steel for $10.59. It wasn't especially reliable but it was low-cost. A .45-caliber M5A1 "grease gun" of U.S. manufacture was just as inexpensive and unreliable but again, factories with low skill workers could turn them out quickly and cheaply.

The Thompson was capable of either single shot or full automatic at a cyclic rate of 700 rounds per minute. Three magazines were available, drums of 100 or 50 rounds or a stick of 20. Considering the gangster's tradition of carrying their "choppers" in violin cases, the flat magazines (or sticks) were very popular.

Legend claims the Thompson is hard to fire, the recoil throwing bullets all over the place. In truth it is very easy and accurate. Most of the recoil is taken up by the weight of the gun, which at 10-3/4 pounds is fairly hefty. At 40 yards distance a nice 5-inch shot group is easy and at 80 yards a 12-inch group is standard. This assumes of course the shooter has adequate training and understands machine guns are fired in bursts of 5 rounds or so. More than that the barrel will climb, and bullets go wide of the target. Certainly many of the reports of mobsters firing hundreds of rounds at an enemy only to miss him reflect an abysmal lack of training and practice.[i]

The Handguns

Two handguns were in common use during the gangster era. Both law enforcement and the crooks had .38 caliber revolvers and .45 caliber automatics. Uniformed police officers invariably carried the .38. Special federal agents sometimes used the .45. Crooks could have both.

The .38 was usually a Smith and Wesson revolver with six bullets and a five-inch barrel. A short-barreled "snub nose" or "special" was available but its only advantage was easy concealment. The short barrel gave it abysmal accuracy.

The .38 caliber revolver was reliable but didn't pack a big punch.

The .45 was the renowned Colt M1911A1 of U.S. Army fame. The magazine held seven rounds and could be rapidly changed. The .45-caliber slug was far more powerful than the 38, which meant the higher likelihood of a kill. The 45 virtually never jammed but was larger and heavier than the .38 so concealment was more difficult.

While the design and manufacture of the M1911A1 is critical to its great success, it's use of the .45 ACP (Auto Colt Pistol) round is equally so. The round was designed by John Browning specifically for the M1911 although General John Thompson, designer of the Thompson sub machine gun, pushed him towards the size.

Following the disastrous performance of the Army's standard .38 pistol in the Philippines during the insurrection (1898-1913) it was recognized that the military needed a pistol firing a more capable "man stopper" cartridge. Time and again charging Philippine natives took multiple hits from the issue .38 caliber pistols without immediate effect. Clearly a bigger and more powerful round was needed and the Army Ordnance Corps set forth to solve the problem. The first issue was to define what a "man stopper" was and here Chicago becomes the scene of the action. In 1904 Thompson, then a Captain in the Ordnance Corps and Major Louis Anatole LaGard of the Medical Corps, conducted an extensive series of experiments at the Nelson Morris Company Union Stockyards. Using live cattle and deer as well as human cadavers, they fired away with a variety of cartridge sizes and loads. As a result of their experiments they recommended a .45 caliber with 230-grain bullet at a velocity of 840 feet per second. The Army

The M1911 .45 caliber automatic pistol provided both the police and mobsters with a powerful weapon.

adopted the recommendation and the rest, as they say, is history as the .45 soon gained the reputation of being the finest combat pistol ever made.

In 1985 the Army switched to the Italian Beretta Model 92F chambered for a 9mm round. The move broke many old soldiers hearts (including this old vet). The good old .45 was still performing at a very high level but the political pressure was overwhelming. Politicians wanted the U.S. military to accept some kind of NATO standard weapon and the Beretta fit the bill. The old .45 also had the reputation of being a "man's gun" and as the military was being feminized, the same politicians wanted a gun with minimal recoil that the women could easily handle. The Beretta proved a dismal failure with a significantly short life span. At this writing the Army is moving toward a new sidearm under the "Joint Combat Pistol" program. It will be chambered for the .45 ACP![ii]

The B.A.R.

While the legendary Tommy Gun may have been the favorite of the average gangster, the discriminating hood, especially one who appreciated both firepower and accuracy, favored the B.A.R. or Browning Automatic Rifle. The B.A.R. fired a powerful .30-06 slug with an effective range of better than 800 yards. Like the Thompson, it operated in either a single shot or full automatic mode. A box type magazine held 20 rounds. Although relatively long at over 47 inches, crooks often cut down the barrel to make it easier to handle. A factory modified short-barreled version was also sold to police agencies. The B.A.R. was a favorite target of mobsters when they stole weapons from police stations and National Guard armories. John Dillinger frequently used a B.A.R as did Clyde Barrow. The heavy .30-06 bullet was powerful enough to slice through a car's body, a valuable characteristic if the police (or mobsters) were using it for cover.

In 1917 John Browning originally designed the B.A.R as a light automatic infantry squad support weapon. A bipod was fitted to the barrel in 1937 to provide a steadier firing support when lying prone. Although available for use during World War I, it was not issued to U.S. forces for fear one would be captured and fall into German hands. It was considered such a revolutionary design it was better to have American soldiers die using a vastly inferior French

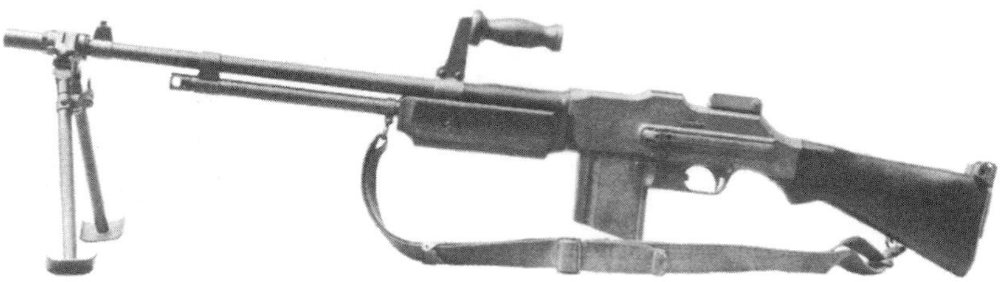

The Browning Automatic Rifle was a devastating weapon for the cops and crooks.

machine gun rather than the B.A.R. This very capable weapon remained in service with U.S. forces into the 1970s.[iii]

Moral Decay

The same do-gooders who rammed Prohibition down a thirsty nation's throat eagerly attacked the changing values of the younger and not so younger generations during the Roaring Twenties. If enforcing Prohibition itself was a hopeless endeavor, trying to drag people back to the social values of the Victorian era was doomed to failure.

Do-gooders complained American women were lifting their skirts far too high and the hem was inches above the ground. Young women called "flappers" were wearing thin dresses with short or even no sleeves. Stockings were rolled below the knee and providing fleeting glances of bare knees and even shin bones! Some women even used cosmetics too! Applying rouge and lipstick was common as was "touching up" their face in public. The number of "beauty shops" increased dramatically. Soon everyone was getting a facial, plucking and trimming eyebrows, applying disappearing creams for wrinkles and blemishes. Some experts estimated American women were spending $2 billion on cosmetics by 1930. In a spark of things to come, pioneer plastic surgeons began performing "facelifts."

The old "cover up" bathing suits of the 1890s gave way to a new style.

Horror of horrors, young women also threw away their corsets, claiming men wouldn't dance with them if they wore them. The do-gooders were also offended by the new style of dancing. Instead of the old romantic sound of the violin, the "barbaric" saxophone dominated the orchestra. The new-fangled foxtrot was scandalous, dancers moving in tight embrace without an inch of space between them. The *Catholic Telegraph* of Cincinnati wailed, "the music is sensuous… the female only half dressed… absolutely indecent." Other religious newspapers trumpeted it was "impure, polluting, corrupting, debasing, destroying spirituality, increasing carnality." The Charleston gave the do-gooders apoplexy!

The University of Florida President railed and ranted, "low cut gowns, the rolled hose and short skirts are born of the Devil… and are carrying the present and future generations to chaos and destruction." (Author's note… considering the current state of the female student body at UF, it is a remarkable complaint.) Some places took action to correct the problem. In Philadelphia, always a bastion of liberal and progressive thought, a "Dress Reform Committee" of leading citizens polled over a thousand religious leaders as to what proper dress for young women should be. The result was the "moral gown," a long, loose fitting garment with sleeves reaching below the elbow and hem nearly to the floor. The wearer looked like a refugee from a Jesuit nunnery! Pandering legislators were just as activist. In 1921 a bill was introduced in Utah calling for imprisonment for women wearing a dress in public with a hem higher than three inches above the ground. (Remember this is Utah… a place where the pervasive religion approved of a man having as many wives as he wanted but lightning bolts from above would rain down if a hemline reached to high.) Not to be outdone, Virginia legislators introduced a measure forbidding women from wearing shirtwaists or

"Lord Almighty" the new style showed SKIN!

evening gowns showing more than three inches of their throat. Ohio legislators upped the ante of silliness to no more than two inches and preventing the wearing of a dress by any girl over 14 years of age that didn't reach the instep. Today we look at this legislation as being totally in line with the draconian dictates of radical Muslims like Osama Bin Laden and his fellow rag heads.

Women changed their hairstyles too forsaking the old long tresses for "bobbed" heads. The new haircut was simply a blunt cut, with the bottom of the ears usually level all around the head. It was worn either with bangs or with the hair brushed off of the forehead. The short hair was shocking many of the old generation as well as Do Gooders. But it wasn't just girls getting the new style but women in their 20s, 30s, 40s, 50s and even a few in their 60s. It was also convenient and easy to maintain, but so "unlady-like." It also created a conflict between traditional hairdressers and barbers. Many gals just went to the barber for the new bobbed style. The barbers liked the business and after all, it was just a haircut. The traditional stylists hated it and for a time refused to "bob" women's hair. Part of the problem with women going the barbershop was the atmosphere was seen as too relaxed. It was no place for a woman. Why they might even have a copy of the *Police Gazette* on a table! Going to a barber shop was simply not suitable for the "high standard" of American womanhood.

The controversy still raged as late as 1925. A teacher in Jersey City, New Jersey was actually ordered by her Board of Education to let her hair grow, claiming women waste too much time fussing with bobbed locks. Evangelical preachers warned parishioners, "a bobbed woman is a disgraced woman." Some men divorced their wives over bobbed hair and one large department store reputedly fired all employees wearing bobbed hair.

The changes in the way the younger generation behaved were largely caused by World War I, or as his many detractors named it, "Mr. Wilson's War." An entire generation of Americans was deeply affected by the war and it's aftermath. There was a real feeling of "eat, drink and be merry for tomorrow we die." It wasn't only among the soldiers actually experiencing combat, but also among those people who watched them march off and return. The two million men who reached France had lived through events folks at home could only imagine. The filth of the trenches, rampant disease, death by shell and bullet, horrible disfigurements, choking gas attacks, all worked to change the men forever. The "Mademoiselles from Armentieres" also transformed them. The easy access to French prostitutes gave them a different view of sex than the traditional Puritanical American culture. American women who went to France as nurses, telephone operators and other war workers experienced their own sexual awakening. The continental attitude towards sex as well as male-female relations in general were entirely different than what they were used to at home. *And they liked it!*

When the Army returned to America its members were far different than when they departed the U.S. Everything had changed and it would never be the same again. To return to the hum drum lives they left behind was unthinkable. They were restless and discontented and questioned everything they earlier thought good and true. They also knew just how fragile life really was and wanted to take every opportunity to experience it.

Even though few American women participated directly in the war, they too were affected by increasing independence. Winning the vote in 1920 was important since it made them the political equal of men, but gaining their freedom to grow as human beings was far more important. In the 1920s, the women's rights movement died down. This was due, in part, to the achievement of the goal of suffrage, but also because of a general retreat from activism in post-WWI America. Feminists of the time made three alarming discoveries.

Perhaps surprising to era feminists, women did not vote as a bloc; there was no such thing as the "women's vote." Younger women were more interested in rebelling against traditional social restraints than national reform. Their focus was on smoking, drinking, going without corsets, bobbing their hair, reading daring literature, and dancing the Charleston. They wanted their part of enjoying new economic and sexual freedoms following America's prosperity in the years immediately following the War

Women were growing away from the traditional chain to housework. New labor saving devices were available and food preparation vastly easier. Local stores provided all kinds of canned goods, dresses and other products. Commercial laundries were in every town and the telephone spawned the ability to call in store orders. No longer did women have to labor all day at simple household chores as their mothers did.

Finally women could also live their own lives instead of blindly supporting their husbands. Middle class women could seek employment in business. Previously they were limited to social work, nursing, clerical jobs and teaching. Now the sky was the limit and they wanted to "fly high." Some went into business for themselves, opening small shops, selling real estate and other items. Others trooped in from small towns all over America to work in large department stores. It wasn't always the best work but it was theirs. It wasn't only single women who "went to work." Many married ones did too and it wasn't always a decision the men agreed with.

Those who thought they could turn back the clock were appalled by what was happening to American women. The new woman was radically different than America's old Victorian ideas of what a woman should be, especially between the upper and middle classes. The old thought held women to four virtues:

<u>Piety</u> - Women were supposed to be far more religious and spiritual in nature than men.

The new generation was far more promiscuous than the old.

Purity - Women were supposed to be pure of heart, mind, and body, never engaging in sexual intercourse until marriage, and even then not enjoying it. After all sex was wifely duty, not something to be pleasurable.

Submission - Women were supposed to be passive, responding only to the actions and decisions of men. They didn't think on their own.

Domesticity - Men worked away from the home and women kept house.

Psychobabalist Sigmund Freud provided a boost to the women's revolution too. By 1909 his work began to infiltrate to America and following the war it exploded. Sex was the major force of mankind. Sex was natural. Sex was subliminal and was part of everything. Good mental health meant having an uninhibited sex life. "Urges" shouldn't be controlled, but rather followed. Self-control was the wrong thing to do.

Prohibition fueled the revolution too. Drinking became the thing to do. A generation before the saloon was the exclusive home of the man. Now renamed the speakeasy, it was used by both sexes. The cocktail party became very fashionable and middle and upper class families all used a local bootlegger in the same fashion as the trusty milkman. The new cocktails also served to make strong liquor (and in many cases really bad bootleg booze) more appealing to women by disguising its taste with other ingredients.

The car opened up entirely new horizons not only for transportation but also for exploration. It let people take quick rides to the beach or lake for a picnic or dash to a party 20 miles away. The new closed cars also offered what moralistic critics claimed was a portable bedroom. Couples could park on lonely roads and lanes and "pet" or even worse; "do it"! One judge claimed it was a "house of prostitution on wheels." Previously such behavior was controlled by a lack of available privacy. The closed car changed it radically.

Mass Entertainment thundered onto the American scene with powerful impact. America had never seen anything like it.

Young women even had the nerve to make long cross country camping trips too.

Radio sales boomed during the post war years, from $60 million in 1922 to $426 million in 1929. From a humble start in 1919, the nation's airwaves filled with musical variety shows and comedies. The new radio pulled the nation together by bringing news, entertainment, and advertisements to more than ten million households by 1929. Regional differences softened and the concept of similar tastes and lifestyles took hold. Stereotypes became common.

The phonograph also changed American culture. The popularity of Jazz rode right along with it. Powerful new recording artists brought the blues, with their emotional and defiant reaction to life's sorrows, to a vast audience.

The movies were easily the single most significant new instrument of mass entertainment. Attendance soared, from 50 million people a week in 1920 to 90 million weekly in 1929. According to one estimate 75 percent of the population went to a movie theater every week.

Movies increasingly featured glamour, sophistication, and sex appeal. Stars like the mysterious sex goddess in the form of Greta Garbo; the passionate hot blooded lover, exemplified by Rudolph Valentino; and the flapper, with her bobbed hair and skimpy skirts pushed the limits of moral values. Swashbuckling adventures films, sophisticated sex comedies, and tales of flaming youth and the new sexual freedom pulled in hordes of fans to the castles of fantasy. Some girls claimed the torrid love scenes were so "hot" they had to leave the theater with their boyfriends to find "release!"

Although American values were changing all around them groups like the Society for Suppression of Vice continued to be vigilant. In 1927 the zealots had actress Mae West arrested and thrown into jail for ten days for "material and suggestive ad libs" in her Broadway show "Sex."

Rudolph Valentino in the Sheik with Agnes Ayers set a new standard of depravity according to some critics.

Racks of sex and confession magazines fired the imagination of impressionable young women. Story titles like, "Indolent Kisses" and "Confessions of a Chorus Girl" stoked the dreams of girls set on experiencing the adventure of "illicit love" for themselves. *True Story* magazine exploded from 300,000 readers in 1923 to over a million by 1926.

Clara Bow, shown here in the movie Dancing Daughter, epitomized the changing values. Known as the "it" girl, no one was sure what "it" was but knew she had "it."

The great symbols of sin, cigarettes and booze were commonplace. Even "nice" girls started smoking cigarettes and in public too. The advertising industry picked up on the trend and soon slick billboards showed stylish women enjoying a smoke with husbands and boyfriends (but never at the same time – reminds me of the famous toast, "to our wives and girlfriends, may they never meet"!). Ashtrays soon appeared between the chairs in women's shoe departments and rest rooms. Smoking was expected and accepted.

Young folks were also drinking and getting "blotto." Hip flasks became part of every young man's attire. At dances, football games and in the movies, boy and girl enjoyed a snort. "Going out" usually meant heading for the local speakeasy or roadhouse.

Sex was the biggest change. Boys and girls were becoming sophisticated about sex much earlier than older generations. Girls started carrying contraceptives in their pocketbooks. "Everyone" was "doing it." Prostitutes were facing amateur competition of unheard proportion. Although there was no way of accurately measuring it at the time, it was thought infidelity among married couples was higher than ever before. The divorce rate was climbing too, going from 8.8 percent in 1910 to 16.5 in 1928. Divorce also no longer had a social stigma, especially for women. In fact there was a romantic notion to being a gay "divorcee."

The famous Ziegfield Follies helped lead America to a new era of openness of thought and behavior.

Men and women of the country club set sometimes had illicit liaisons with other club partners. With traditional inhibitions dulled by bootleg booze, and passions fired by the "wild" saxophone, mature men and women paired up and enjoyed the moment. Unmarried men and women often enjoyed sex before marriage and one-night stands were common. Both men and women were expected to be "experienced" before committing to marriage. Sexual freedom was in the air and it shocked the older generation to their core.

Some lawmakers tried to reverse the new sexual freedom though legal means. In Norphelt, Arkansas in 1925 an ordnance was passed that:

1. "Hereafter it shall be unlawful for any man and woman, male or female, to be guilty of committing the act of sexual intercourse between themselves at any place within the corporate limits of said town."

2. "Section One of this ordnance shall not apply to married persons as between themselves and their husband and wife unless of a grossly improper and lascivious nature."

I guess no one was supposed to "do it' in Norphelt, or at least not enjoy it.

Regardless of the pressures from various lawmakers, church and religious leaders, the new generation concluded chastity and fidelity were vastly overrated. They would be free to take pleasure in the sex experience. Remember though, this was a period when birth control was not legal but still generally practiced by all but the lowest and most ignorant classes of society.

The newspapers were filled with titillating tales of sexual scandal. The adventures of 51-year old Edward West ("Daddy") Browning, a New York real estate tycoon and flamboyant millionaire playboy of alleged lewdly amorous leanings and his 15-year old child wife "Peaches" captured the nation.

While there are many versions to the story it seems Daddy wanted a playmate for his daughter Dorothy after a messy divorce so he advertised for a "pretty, refined girl, about fourteen years old..." Supposedly he interviewed 12,000 applicants using the special Daddy technique of bouncing them on his knee and giving a pinch or two. When his first choice turned out to be a 14 year old who was really 21, he started over. I suspect he didn't mind another round of "testing." A while later he met Frances Heenan, a 15-year old Irish colleen, at a sorority dance in a New York hotel.

Daddy fell for the teenybopper like a ton of bricks, saying, "You look like peaches and cream to me! I'm going to call you Peaches." Next day, and for many following, she was vigorously inundated with glaringly expensive gifts, flowers, jewelry and clothing.

The impulsive romance caught the scandal-focused eyes of the press, radio and general public. In fact it was better than any soap opera! People on the street were captivated by the antics of the May-December romance. Ominously the ever-watchful child welfare agencies were also watching and waiting to pounce. With threats of dapper Daddy having to appear in Children's Court, the debonair swinger and his little girl ran off to Cold Spring, in upstate New York via his blue Rolls Royce. They quickly obtained a marriage license from a local merchant who also owned a plumbing shop.

The lovebirds were married on April 10, 1926 in a farmhouse at Nelsonville, a village just east of Cold Spring. It was exactly 16 days from the couple's first meeting. A local Justice of the Peace, who doubled as a part-time cab driver, performed the ceremony. Since Peaches was now his wife, the child welfare agencies could go to hell!

Supposedly the pair retreated to a house in Cold Springs to enjoy their honeymoon. The howling pack of press dogs yapping around outside all fighting to get the "story" must have made it an unpleasant interlude. There also were claims "Peaches'" mother watched over her daughter night and day, whether in or out of the house, and she'd sleep in the same room with her dear Frances.

Within six months Peaches tried to obtain a divorce. The national newspapers had a ball with it all, from the hunt for the child bride to the very sloppy divorce. It was all grist for the daily mill of ink and paper. Among many titillating accusations Peaches claimed her "daddy" kept a honking African goose in their bedroom. Frances also claimed Daddy mentally and emotionally abused her and he continued to chase young girls! During the divorce trial beginning in January 1927, fiery accusations of degrading passion, depravity and lewdness spewed from both Peaches and Daddy. Hundreds of frenzied newspaper reporters, radio correspondents and a morbid public tried to fight their way into the courtroom to get their daily dose of dirt.

Peaches wasn't as innocent as portrayed by her lawyers or in many cases, newspapers. She took a cool $1,000 from the *New York Graphic* newspaper to tell why she left her Daddy. The paper printed it under the headline, "Peach's Shame Story in Full." Peaches had her predilections too. Ex New York City Congressman Adam Clayton Powell in his book *Adam by Adam, The Autobiography of Adam Clayton Powell, Jr.*, remembered working as a bellhop at the San Remo Hotel when she and Daddy checked in. They had so many trunks and suitcases it took all afternoon for Adam and a coworker to move them to their suite. Daddy gave Peaches a $100 bill to tip them, but she switched it for a ten spot. When she went to present it to the bellhop she let her dressing gown fall open revealing her "charms" in all their glory in an effort to distract them. Adam remembered he had seen better so he ignored the free show and instead pried the C note from her clenched fist.

When the trial ended in March, Daddy found himself exonerated on grounds he had been "taken" by a crafty mother and daughter who had envisioned and sought after a gold mine at the end of their ruse. The judge's decision must have been difficult since public opinion was strongly in favor of Peaches, believing "Daddy" was nothing more than a spoiled, wealthy playboy into whose clutches was drawn a poor, defenseless and innocent lass. "Peaches" eventually was awarded a portion of her hubby's fortune through several ensuing legal manipulations after Edward's passing. Peaches eventually became an "actress" of a sort and died in 1956 at age 46.

Taken together all of these social and cultural changes provided the fertile ground to accept new ideas including the notion of breaking the law, especially an unpopular one like Prohibition. Living in a whirlwind of change made all things possible.

It was a different age![iv]

Prohibition Vocabulary

Bathtub Gin - A form of homemade liquor mixed in a bathtub.

Blind Pig (Jimmy, Blind Tiger) - A place were booze was sold illegally. The term supposedly came from someone putting a blind pig in a box inside a tent and urging people to view a blind pig for ten cents. For every dime the customer got a drink of liquor.

Bingo - (blue pig, demon rum, hooch, juniper juice, booze, monkey swill, moonshine, panther piss, panther sweat, mule, red eye, rye sap, shoe polish, squirrel, squirrel dew, white coffee, white lightning, all names for intoxicating liquor.

Bootleg liquor - Illegally alcoholic beverages.

Bootlegger - A person who illegally made or imported alcohol beverages.

Bump Off - To murder.

Cement Overshoes - Prior to being dumped in the water (river, lake or ocean as appropriate), the victim had his feet encased in two buckets filled with cement. When the cement set, he was ready to "feed the fish."

Chicago Typewriter - Tommy Gun, Ukulele Music, Chicago Organ Grinder, Chicago Street Sweeper, Chopper) Gang term for a Thompson sub machine gun.

Dry - A person opposed to the sale of intoxicating liquor.

Fall Guy - victim of a frame-up.

Frame - To give false evidence, to set up someone.

G-men (government men) - FBI special agents.

Giggle Water - An intoxicating beverage; alcohol.

Gin Mill - An establishment where hard liquor is sold; bar.

Hard Boiled - a tough, strong guy.

Hooch - Bootleg liquor.

Hoofer - Dancer.

Moll - A gangster's girl.

Moonshine - Illegal alcohol, usually in context with homemade alcohol.

On the Take - Having accepted a bribe.

Pop Highball - Soda water with alcohol added.

Pocket Pistol - A hip flask.

Policy - Small time gambling game. Although the bets were nickel and dime, the profits for the mob were large.

Prescriptions - A doctor would be paid a set amount of money to prescribe a certain amount of liquor a day. His signature became extremely valuable and sometimes gang wars were fought over who owned what doctor. Forgery was common and gangsters often stole stacks of blank prescriptions for later resale.

Ritzy - Elegant (from the hotel).

Rub Out (Take for a Ride, Whack) - To kill.

Rumhole - A saloon.

Rumrunner - Someone who smuggles alcohol: bootlegger.

Speakeasy - A place selling liquor illegally or after hours. The term was taken from the requirement to speak softly when ordering drinks. Codes, passwords, and secret handshakes were usually needed to gain entrance. They were not just a bar but usually contained at least one brothel, gambling den, or drug dealer. These combinations made for popular venues around the cities and many were disguised as nightclubs, where the patrons could dance, drink, and spend a night of pleasure with a "woman" (women) of his choice. All in all, the speakeasy was the central piece in the jigsaw puzzle of the Prohibition underworld.

Take for a Ride -To drive off with someone in order to bump them off.

Torpedo - A hired gun.

Temperance - Self-restraint or abstinence in the use of alcoholic beverages.

Tenderloin - Another name for a vice district. Supposedly the term came from a New York City Police captain who transferred from a nice quiet residential precinct to one with much greater graft potential, causing him to exclaim, "I've been eating chuck steak but now I'm going to get a slice of the tenderloin."

Three Fingers in a Bathtub - A large drink of whisky.

Volstead Act - The act implementing the 18th amendment. It made the 18th amendment enforceable.

WCTU - Woman's Christian Temperance Union: a group against saloons and alcohol.

Wet - A person favoring the sale of intoxicating liquor.

Great Lakes BITS & PIECES OF THIS & THAT

The Drinks' the Thing

As W.C. Fields said, "Reminds me of my safari in Africa. Somebody forgot the corkscrew and for several days we had to live on nothing but food and water." It seems there were some fellows in Presque Isle Township Cemetery near Alpena, Michigan that really understood what old W.C. meant. The story goes something like this.

In the early days of Presque Isle Harbor, say the 1920s - 40s, there were three men that hung out together, Fred Piepkorn, Charlie Priest and Bill Green. All were supposed to be great friends but it is also possible they just chummed around with each other because there weren't a lot of other folks around to hang out with. Beggars couldn't be choosers.

Fred ran a local fish tug out of the harbor. Charlie owned an unlicensed bar (also known as a blind pig). What Bill did is unknown but perhaps he just staggered between the blind pig and an occasional job on the fish tug.

As three friends are prone to do, Fred, Charlie and Bill often sat down and imbibed a little hooch once in a while, or even more often as the situation required. If the sun came up today, it is time to celebrate! If it successfully set, its time to celebrate too! With this crew it didn't take much to get a party going.

In any case the three made a pact. When the first one "assumed ambient air temperature" and was firmly planted six feet down, the others promised they would pour a drink down to him on holidays. When the second one followed the first, the survivor would do the honors. To keep it simple they arranged to be buried side by side. And indeed that's what happened. Three graves, each covered by a cement slab, are side by side at the back of the Presque Isle Township Cemetery. Each also has a neat hole in the center of the slab, to facilitate pouring a drink down![i]

A "Brewing" Battle

Governments will take any opportunity to grab money from hard working citizens, all of course in the name of the "public good." The City of Chicago is no different in its grasping ways.

In 1855 Mayor Levi Boone, elected on an anti-immigrant, anti-Catholic ticket with heavy support of temperance forces, saw an opportunity to steal (er, acquire) more funding for he and his cronies at City Hall to misappropriate and at the same time please the local dry population. First off he increased the liquor license fee from $50 to $300 and made it a quarterly tax not an annual one. In effect he increased it by a factor of 24! To top it off he began enforcing long ignored laws requiring saloons to close on Sundays!

Most neighborhood services were private or accomplished at the local level, so city politics were not part of an election. Previous Chicago elections were nonpartisan affairs with little interest to anyone except real estate operators. And quite by chance Boone made his fortune in Chicago real estate. Boone's supporters were able to vote him in without wide support since turnout was invariably low. They didn't even need the local graveyard vote.

The new law wasn't applied evenhandedly either. Hundreds of ethic Germans were arrested for violating Sunday closing laws while the transgressions of native Chicagoans were ignored. It was a double standard. Considering the Germans and Irish too had a long cultural tradition of enjoying Sunday leisure time in a neighborhood tavern, it was a very directed attack on immigrants. It was also an attack on freedom of speech since it was in the German beer gardens and Irish pubs the men met and spoke politics, discussing the issues of the day and their plans for the future. The Germans and Irish had also formed their own neighborhoods, churches, trade unions and even theaters. As an anti-immigrant mayor, this was clearly something that could not be allowed to continue. These alien groups needed to be broken up.

The police promptly hauled the law breaking Germans off to jail. Since Boone also "reformed" the Police, including putting them in uniform for the first time, he had a loyal force to execute his orders.

To make an example of the Germans, on April 21, 1855 they were scheduled to be tried in the courtroom of Judge Henry Rucker, one of the mayor's loyal lackeys. In protest a horde of hundreds of angry Germans marched to courthouse to support their countrymen but were rebuffed by the police and scattered but only after nine were arrested. An armed group of Germans from the north side also attempted to rescue their countrymen but the Mayor outsmarted them by keeping the Clark Street Bridge raised until police reinforcements arrived. When the bridge lowered a throng of 200 angry Germans charged across and a general melee ensued including shooting firearms. It is known for certain one officer was wounded and a German protester killed. There were likely many more injuries on both sides unreported.

Alarmed by the violent German reaction, Mayor Boone called for the State Militia. While there were no further protests the Germans made their point. The law applied to everyone or no one, crooked politicians and good for nothing reformers like Levi Boone notwithstanding!

Perhaps most important, the Germans and Irish learned how the game of politics would be played in Chicago. They organized well for the next election and threw Boone and his men out on their butts. The $50 license fee was restored as was Sunday openings.

Mayor Boone was an interesting character. Born in Kentucky and the great nephew of Daniel Boone, he arrived in Chicago in 1835. A physician, he helped organize the first medical society. Boone was in the city during the great cholera epidemic, which he blamed on immigrants. He also claimed slavery was sanctioned by the Bible and fully supported it.[ii]

An "Unofficial" Buoy

Sometimes what the government does is in itself a crime, especially when it insists rules must be followed regardless of how much sense they make as the following piece from the July 9, 1891, *Detroit Free Press* illustrates.

"Among the other points touched at by the steamer *Greyhound* on her up and down trip between here and Port Huron is Algonac. In the river, between Algonac and the Canada shore, is Harsen's Island. Half a mile above the island is a buoy set by the lighthouse department to mark the navigable depth of water. It was found that as the *Greyhound* is not a deep draft boat, she could run pretty close to the head of the island. So soundings were taken and a barrel placed by the Star Line, owners of the boat to mark the water she could safely use at that point. In rounding the head of the island to come into Algonac she could run close to the barrel and it is claimed she saved at least two miles per day in doing so. The Lighthouse tender *Marigold* on her last trip removed this barrel and the owners of the *Greyhound* are asking questions in consequence. They will once more place a barrel there and if it is removed they will drive a spile in the mud at the point named. They say the *Marigold* would have no right to remove the spile as it will be on land and out of her jurisdiction."

Dueling to the Death

Dueling, either with pistols or swords, is usually thought of as a gentlemen's sport. The Hollywood version is fairly simple. The two antagonists meet at dawn with their seconds. All the men are formally dressed and a physician with his small black medical bag stands in the background ready to treat the wounded or pronounce death as needed. Sometimes the reality was far different, especially on the raw frontier of the Great Lakes.

In the fall of 1791 a trading party was slowly moving west along the south shore of Lake Superior bound for the Ontonagon River. They left Mackinac Island in October, very late in the season to travel and were intending to spend the winter trading with the Indians. The leader of the group, Albert Graveratte, was ill and had to be carried by his men much of the time slowing the party down considerably. The faster the men wanted to travel to make the Ontonagon and winter camp, the slower Graveratte seemed able to go. By November the band reached the small river just west of the Keweenaw Peninsula known today as "Graveraet River." It was on the banks of this lonely stream pressures came to a head.

Graveratte had a particularly combative time with Louis Drouin. They constantly argued, especially about an Indian woman Drouin brought with him. It was going to be a long cold winter in Ontonagon and perhaps Graveratte was jealous. Regardless of the woman, it looked to Graveratte like Drouin was challenging him for the leadership of the group. On the way to the Ontonagon River the group did some trading with the Indians, Graveratte dispensing rum at full strength instead of diluting it with water as was typical. Drouin objected to the practice, arguing there wouldn't be enough to last through the winter if it wasn't "cut." Graveratte viewed Drouin's argument as insubordination and it could not be tolerated.

While camped at the small river Lake Superior kicked her heels up in typical November weather. When it calmed a bit, Graveratte sent the Indians accompanying them on ahead but held his canoes back unwilling to risk losing or damaging any of the trade goods in the still roiled waters. Drouin immediately objected, saying the weather was fine and ordering some of the men to launch the canoes. Fed up with Drouin's rebelliousness, Graveratte had one of the men tell Drouin to come see him. When he arrived Graveratte told him, "my friend it is necessary that one or the other of us mark the encampment here." (Graveratte was saying one of them would need to die in effect, "marking" the camp with his corpse.) Drouin took the comment as a joke and sat down near his hut. Graveratte wasn't joking, picking up his gun and without further warning fired at Drouin, the ball just slicing through his cap. Drouin hastily fired back but missed. Since honor was apparently satisified, Drouin suggested they stop fighting. Graveratte would have none of it and reloaded his gun. Two of his men tried to subdue him but he fought them off, threatening to smash in their heads with his musket butt. When he leveled his gun to fire again Drouin fired his, the ball hitting Graveratte in the stomach. Graveratte also fired but his shot went wild. Being gut shot is always a miserable wound and Graveratte was soon a dead man.

Graveratte was hastily buried along the small stream and the traders continued west to Ontonagon for a winter of trading. When they stopped on the way back to Mackinac Island they discovered animals had dug up the grave and consumed much of the body. After reburying the bones they continued on for Mackinac.[iii]

Mackinac Island was also the scene of a duel. In 1808 John Campbell was killed there in a duel with trader Redford Crawford. Both men were former business associates. What prompted the fight isn't known but Campbell left behind his seven Metis children to fend for themselves since his Dakota wife died seven years before. Campbell was well known on the frontier having been appointed Indian Agent at Prairie du Chien in 1792 and a justice of the peace by Indiana Territorial Governor Harrison. Whether it was pistols on Market Street at dawn, knifes on the waterfront or a down and out axe fight is unknown.[iv]

Counterfeiting Iron

Counterfeiting is an old crime. When the first coins were minted out of gold or silver, somebody was certainly trying to figure out how to make fakes from base metal. After currency moved to paper, counterfeiting became a bit more involved but yet more rewarding too. Up on Lake Superior it was all a little different.

The move to paper money instead of coinage presented both problems and solutions to the country. Congress established a national mint in 1792 but it was for coins not paper money. During the Revolutionary War many states printed and issued paper money and most ultimately proved worthless since it wasn't backed by specie. No one wanted to go back to that kind of problem.

As the U.S. grew, the need for currency grew too but the coinage tended to end up in cities, not in the developing areas where it was badly needed. In an effort to help solve the problem, when the Michigan Territory was organized in 1805, a bank was chartered in Detroit. It promptly printed huge amounts of paper money with very little gold and silver to back it up. Like most things in Detroit, it failed leaving worthless paper in the hands of investors. Politicians are incapable of learning from history so when Michigan became a state in 1837 legislators allowed any group of a dozen men to start a bank, adequate reserves not required. Within two years 49 banks graced the new state with another 21 in the process of forming. While an effort was made to provide for state bank examiners to keep everything on the up and up, the legislature provided far too few to do the job. The result was chaos and a well deserved reputation for unscrupulous banking. The paper money was in wide circulation and some was valued at par, some at a steep discount and some utterly worthless. Many people and businesses refused to accept the paper money issued by the new banks since they had no way of determining it's actual value. Although the state Supreme Court declared the banking law unconstitutional in 1842, the damage was done. It was 15 years before banks would again have the ability to print money.

Money was especially sparse on the Upper Peninsula Iron Range. Even though there was some gold, silver and copper coins as well as bank notes from other states and even Canada in circulation, money was in short supply and of questionable worth. As the mines expanded, hiring more and more workers, the problem became acute. The men wanted to be paid and the currency available to do so was difficult to find.

The answer was "iron" money, the mining companies printing their own paper draft notes in various denominations including $1, $2, $3 and $5. Since the companies had good reputations and the public had full faith in their worth, the system worked well. It was claimed between 1852 and 1858, fully three-quarters of all the money in circulation on the Marquette Range was "iron" paper.

The U.S. Treasury Department didn't start printing paper money until the Civil War. The tremendous need for funds to pay for the war soon pulled the available coinage out of easy circulation so the only real option was for the feds to start the presses. The distinctive green ink used gave the new bills the moniker, "greenbacks."

When the war ended the Treasury wanted to keep public confidence in the new federal paper money and not have it compete with a host of local bank issues. To achieve this, the government did what the government does best, namely throw a ruinous tax on any "non-federal" money. In reaction, state banks stopped printing bank notes but the iron mining companies continued since they issued draft, not notes. This point later became a major issue between the Treasury Department and Internal Revenue Commission and the mining companies and was only settled by a special Congressional relief bill. The oppressive power of the Federal government is nothing new.

Just because it was "iron" money doesn't mean it wasn't a lucrative target for counterfeiters. It seems a local Negaunee miscreant, Dr. James Crucial, decided it was easier to make a living by passing bogus bucks than treating ill people. Negaunee was in the heart of the iron range, an ideal location for his scheme. A little art work, a little printing, a few accomplices to help pass the "iron" drafts and he was in business. It wasn't long before the local constabulary caught on to him and in May 1874 showed up at his front door just to "ask a few questions." They nabbed the good doctor just as he tossed a valise filled with $16,000 in bogus bills out his back window. Investigating further the police found the ring had passed bills in Marquette, Ishpeming, Negaunee, Michigamme and L'Anse. The bills were counterfeits of Jackson Mining Company drafts and looked good until they were compared with the genuine article and then certain errors in size, serial numbers and quality were apparent.

The county prosecutor duly charged the doctor and his men with having counterfeit notes, falsely and feloniously forging promissory notes and uttering and publishing forged counterfeit notes. Although all pled not guilty, it seemed like an open and shut case. During the trial the defense counsel cited a federal law as part of his argument that the Jackson Mining Company had no authority to issue "notes in similitude of bank notes." The lawyers tangled for two days over the issue and in the end the judge held for the defense and the case was dismissed! The doctor and his minions went free. A clever lawyer once again managed to have criminals freed to prey on society. The local paper ranted and raved on the injustice of it all, but the ruling held, a judge again triumphed over good sense.[v]

Swindles, Large and Small

Sisters of Mercy

Various scams were common in big cities as well as small in the early 1900s. Many are still in vogue today proving P.T. Barnum's famous quip "there's a sucker born every minute."

One used in Chicago involved an imaginary home for epileptics. Since there was a real home for these unfortunates and it engendered great local support, the scam was easy to pull off. Professional women solicitors dressed as prim and pious nurses went house to house seeking "donations" for this most worthy cause. The "nurses" were all very sad and austere looking which increased the sympathetic reaction among donors. A great deal of money was collected by this simple method. While the women received a healthy "commission" the promoter got the majority.

The scam was so well done in Chicago the great blowhard lawyer William Jennings Bryan was touched for $100 as well as the Governor of Illinois and others. Today the same gimmick is largely worked by telephone and email.

Fake nuns were always excellent fund raisers.

Matrimonial Agents

Today the rage is finding a "soul mate" by computer analysis via an Internet-based dating service. A century ago it was done by letter through "matrimonial agents." Most were scams. The schemes were not just in the Midwest but operated throughout the country, big cities and small villages. The flame of hope

Matrimonial agencies provided "love at first letter."

burns eternal and the marriage bureaus were there to keep it going, for a fee.

The operators were smooth, sharp and utterly without scruples. They went after rich and poor alike but certainly the more money the greater the attraction. If the marriage bureaus were crooked, those folks that gave them money to find the mate of their dreams were gullible beyond belief. Widows and widowers looking for a last fling at true love, young women from the country hoping to meet an exciting young beau from the city, old maids hoping to find the "right" man to manage their financial affairs, all were willing victims of the scam.

The method of operation was simple. The marriage bureau placed advertisements in papers claiming to be able to find ideal mates. Often they stressed, "golden-haired young ladies worth half million dollars," or "blue-eyed widows of languishing temperaments" and "wealthy farmers" were all available through their agencies.

The lonely were encouraged to write in with their "particulars". In reply they received a form to fill in and return. After due course, a mate was found and correspondence started through the bureau. The lonely soul never knew the "mate" they were writing was someone in the bureau, male or female it made no difference. A variation had a fee collected for a subscription to a matrimonial paper filled with descriptions of men and women looking for "love." Sometimes an additional fee was charged for a photograph, which of course, was of a mythical person. The money could build up quickly. If it actually got to the point of marriage, the applicant was charged a hefty fee up front before the ceremony. Of course the contracted bride or groom never appeared and the broker disappeared. It was common for a matrimonial agency to operate under different names from the same address using the same staff "correspondents," the operators shifting addresses to keep a step ahead of the cops.

Incredible as it may seem, thousands of otherwise intelligent people in Chicago, Milwaukee, Detroit and other Midwest cities large and small, were taken in by the scheme. Across the nation the take was massive.

Spooks and Spirits

Mediums or spiritualists were as common as the marriage brokers and just as "bent." "Want to talk to your dead Aunt Ida? Wait a minute and I will call her up for you." There truly is a sucker born every minute.

These fakes bilked gullible people out of thousands of dollars. Occasionally police raided the seances and swept up the charlatans and their stage props needed to produce spirits on demand. But they or others always came back. The public was demanding to be bilked and the crooks were ready, willing and able to do the bilking. The book "Revelations of a Spirit Medium" by A. Medium published in the 1870s describes the methods used by the crooks in detail, techniques still used today.

Harry Houdini was a famous enemy of the mediums, constantly exposing their trickery.

Pickpockets and Shoplifters

All pickpockets and shoplifters were not males. Women were amazingly successful. One of the cleverest in Chicago was Bertha Lebecke, known by the police as "Fainting Bertha." She was considered one of the most remarkable pickpockets, diamond snatchers and shoplifters of her day.

If caught shoplifting by a police officer or store floorwalker, she promptly fainted causing a large crowd to gather around her. Many shoppers begged the police to let her go, surely this woman did nothing wrong. Regardless of the evidence, she evoked enough sympathy to frequently cause a release, perhaps with a stern warning.

The fainting trick was also used to distract attention from a "lift." She would faint into the arms of a man or woman and in the confusion remove the jewelry by secreting it on her person or if a man, steal his wallet or watch. Her deft little hands were so nimble and quick the victim was clueless to her manipulations. Sometimes she even bit the diamond off a stickpin and swallowed it. If the item was noticed missing, she even helped look for it after she recovered from her "spell."

Bertha Lebecke was famous for her fainting routine.

Only when actually arrested and taken to a police station did a police matron discover her secrets. A strong waist pocket resembling a petticoat was cleverly concealed under the folds of her voluminous dress. Made of two pieces of material gathered at the top it had a strong cord or string run through and sewed together around the edges. The front had a two foot long slit opening from the top to within a few inches of the bottom. Each side of her skirt had a long slit concealed in the many folds of the garment allowing her to slip the stolen material through the skirt and into the petticoat bag.

Police described her as a young woman with baby dimples and peaches and cream skin, innocent blue eyes and a vivacious sense of humor. Men flocked to her aid whenever she beckoned. They usually left lighter their valuables.

She made such a nuisance of herself in prison the warden managed to transfer her to the state insane asylum at Elgin. Doubtless his reasoning ran the only explanation for her bizarre behavior was insanity. She slept all day and spent the nights screaming curses at one and all. It didn't take long for the warden to conclude she was indeed insane. The resourceful Bertha escaped from Elgin on Christmas Eve, 1904 by fainting in the arms of an attendant and causing enough of a distraction allowing her to "lift" the keys. Later that night when all was quiet she calmly unlocked the doors and strolled out, taking an electric car to Aurora and boarding a train to Peoria. On the train she picked up spending money by slipping $30 out of the conductor's pocket. Within two days in Peoria she stole $1,000 in goods from local stores. Police finally apprehended her on a train for Omaha as it was waiting to pull out of the station.

Authorities now shipped her to the Asylum for the Criminally Insane at South Bartonville, Illinois. Although the records are a bit murky, she apparently escaped from there too! To this point she had already made seven escapes from various prisons and asylums so why not continue?

Bertha was certainly just one of many female "boosters" working American cities. Some altered dresses to include a "hoisting kick," a short shirt over a regular dress sewn such that the lining and skirt formed a bag around the body from waist to hemline. A clever slit allowed the booster to slip merchandise into

Bertha escaped from the State Mental Hospital at Elgin by "lifting" the keys from an unsuspecting attendant.

the bag with ease. A variation of the kick included a long pocket sewn the full length of a skirt or into a loose blouse. Bloomers with elastic at the knees were also handy places to drop hot goods. When bustles were in fashion they were a remarkably good place to conceal purloined items.

An unopened umbrella was a favorite tool of many shoplifters. Small items like gloves, lace handkerchiefs and jewelry were dropped in and the owner sauntered out of the store without a care in the world.

Some shoplifters, male and female, used special belts with hooks worn under their coats, a handy place to park goods. Women with especially talented legs were called "crotch workers," able to hold stolen goods between their thighs and walk out of the store without a worry or a change in gait.

Jewelry counters were special targets for the thieves. In one con the crook "palmed" a valuable diamond ring and stuck it in a hunk of chewing gum he earlier jammed under the counter. If he was searched after leaving the store, of course he had no ring and was quick to sue them for false arrest. Later he returned to the counter and retrieved his booty.

A surprising amount of turn of the Century shoplifting was by young women from "good" or prominent families. They were strictly amateur and invariably caught by the department store dicks. The first time they were caught the store required them to write out a full confession which was held as a warning for good behavior. Prosecutions were rare. The publicity reflected worse on the "big bad store" than the "poor innocent girl who obviously just forgot to pay for the item."

Sneaks and Forgers

Joseph Cook, aka George Havill, aka Harry Thorn, although Canadian born made his "bones" in Chicago working with some of the best sneak thieves of the day. When things got too hot in the Windy City he went east and plied his trade in Gotham (aka New York City). After being nabbed in 1880 in an attempt to pass bad checks drawn on a local bank, he received a four-year vacation in the state pen. Within a year of release, he was back behind bars again.

John Tracy

John Tracy, aka Big Tracy, aka Reilly, was a plumber by training but had the reputation of being an excellent "second story man" in Chicago and Buffalo as well as various eastern cities. He was caught in a couple of robberies receiving paid vacations from time to time in the big house. In 1885 he was sentenced to a railroad work gang but managed to escape, supposedly heading to the West to find "work."

David Goldstein, aka Sheeny Dave, was an accomplished shoplifter and sneak thief. Among his accomplishments were lifting jewelry in Buffalo, silks in New York and picking pockets whenever the opportunity presented itself. In the 1880s he spent some quality time in New York's Sing Sing.

John Cannon, aka Jack Cannon, aka Davis, aka, Stewart, aka Bartlett, born a Pennsylvania Dutchman, was one of the most widely known and dangerous thieves in the U.S. His resume included robbing hotel rooms, stores, safe blowing and jewelry heists. He was arrested in New Orleans in 1886 and charged with robbing one Effie Hankins of Chicago of $8,000 in diamonds while in the city.

David Goldstein

Margaret Brown, aka Young, aka Old Mother Hubbard, Irish born, this grandmotherly looking woman worked as a pickpocket for fifty years. Her expertise was in opening handbags and removing purses before the owner had an inkling of the danger. Once caught in Chicago, she was sentenced to Joliet prison for three years but while trying to climb over the wall, fell and was seriously injured. When she was

John Cannon

Mary Hollbrook

freed in 1879 she went East and worked in New York, Philadelphia and Boston. Who ever would suspect such a nice grandmotherly lady?

Mary Hollbrook, aka Molly Hoey, was considered the most successful female thief in America. In spite of her achievements she saw prisons in Chicago, Boston and New York from the inside out. Molly was once married to Buck Hollbrook, the owner of a Chicago brothel. It was apparently a good marriage until Buck was ventilated with a blast of buckshot fired by a state prison guard when he was caught trying to escape. Since old Buck was gone, Mary had to fend for herself, which she duly did in Chicago's finest stores including Marshall Fields. Sharp-eyed store dicks sometimes nabbed her resulting in her incarceration. Her greatest career accomplishment, at least as far as is known, was when she lifted $25,000 from a western visitor to Chicago.

A Gambler's Ways

There is no such thing as an "honest" gambler or a "fair" game. Never has been and never will be, yet people are anxious to throw their money away in one crooked game after another. Whatever game you play, roulette, poker, slots or faro, the list is endless, the odds are always stacked in the favor of the house. So why play a game you know you have to loose? It makes no sense but people did and still do judging by the success of state lotteries, Indian casinos and of course Las Vegas. Perhaps it is as one famous gambler, Canada Bill, answered when someone asked him why he was playing in an obviously crooked poker game, "I know it's crooked, but it's the only game in town."

Virtually all of the card games were crooked.

Professional gamblers during the heyday of the big city vice districts all worked with an edge, whether they operated a single game or ran an entire casino. Everything was rigged so the house won the lion's share. There was considerable overhead in the big dens; free lunches, drinks and cigars for players, entertainment, payoffs to the cops and miscellaneous politicians, all ate into expenses. Playing the game fair didn't cover the costs, let alone turn a profit.

Working the various table games required partners, mirrors, words, signs and hold-outs (mechanical devices to "hold a card out into a players hand, gave credence to the old phrase, "a card up his sleeve.") and other illicit techniques. A player dealing from a "stacked" deck (one in which the cards are prearranged to deal in a certain pattern) will tell his confederates how many cards to draw based on a coded word in conversation. Likewise a "lookout" will signal the house player what cards the "fish" has by silent signals. Cards can also be marked in ways invisible to the innocent "marks." Professionals call the marked cards "paper." Life isn't "fair" and neither is gambling.

When the country rubes ventured into the gambling dens in Chicago, Detroit or Milwaukee, the gamblers rubbed their hands in expectation. The hicks were just so many sheep to be clipped! Sometimes it was a city man caught in the net who should have known better. Stories of bank tellers dipping into the till to feed a bad run of the cards were common.

Weighted dice assured the house of a winning night.

Marked cards, stacked decks, mechanical card deliverers, weighted dice, fixed roulette wheels, non paying slot machines, fixed numbers games and horse races, all formed part of the gambler's arsenal of weapons liberally used against the rules.

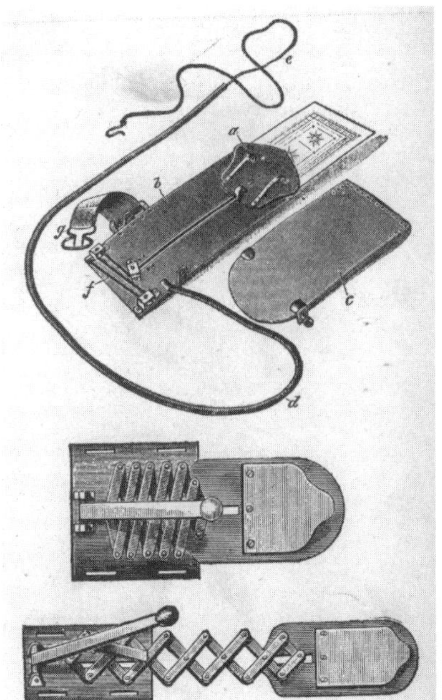

Gamblers sometimes used various mechanical devices to manipulate cards.

Prostitution

"Houses" were everywhere. Don't think for a second they were only in the "sinful big cities." And they didn't disappear 50 years ago. The girls and houses are still with us today. In seems every week or so a newspaper carries an "expose" of a local enterprise. For example, the Waukesha, Wisconsin Freeman of October 26, 2006 carried a story about a local madam being "busted" for operating a "house." Remember, this is in Waukesha, Wisconsin, not Chicago or New York. Houses are indeed everywhere.

Port Huron, Michigan at the bottom of Lake Huron had a number of establishments each with a covey of "soiled doves." As long as the boats sailed the St. Clair River, trains ran on rails and men sought female company, the Port Huron girls were ready, willing and able to service all comers.

The sleeping little town of East Tawas, Michigan had the old Bluewater Bar, a popular hitching post for lumber schooner crews as well as men from steamers. When the boats were in town, the "hoot'n and holler'n" could be heard for miles as well as the "squeal'n and giggl'n."

When the Air Force Base was in operation outside Oscoda, Michigan a house was just out the front gate. "Everyone" knew it was there but it was in the woods and off the road so it was easy to say it wasn't there. Never the less for lonely airmen stuck deep in the desolate north woods of Nowhere, Michigan it was a place of solace and companionship… for a price.[vi]

Buffalo was one of the greatest red light cities on the Lakes.

During the turn of the Century many young girls came into the field via the big department stores and mail order houses like Marshall Fields, Sears or Montgomery Ward in Chicago and Hudson's in Detroit among others. Young women flocked to the cities looking for adventure, opportunity and romance. Anything was better than being stuck on the farm in the middle of Iowa, or Indiana, or Wisconsin, or Illinois! If they hung around home long enough they would likely end up married to some nearby dirt farmer! All they could look forward to was a life of constant drudgery and hard work broken only by a weekly rant by a preacher on Sunday. There had to be a better life! The bright lights of the cities beckoned and the girls came in droves. Can you blame them?

A party girl at work.

In most cases the best job the girls could get was clerking in a big department store and the stores paid very poorly. It was barely a living wage. When the true situation became clear to the girls, the stores often pointed out

Oswego isn't the old hell roaring city it used to be in it's hey day, but careful research still shows evidence of it's rich history.

they had the perfect job to earn more money by finding outside "clients" willing to "compensate" them for their company and services. Many of the customers after all were rich men and if a girl couldn't snare one in marriage at least he could provide temporary company. For lecherous men cruising the department stores became a good way to snare a fresh young "date." Around the turn of the Century an undercover reporter estimated a third of the girls were "working" on the side.

The girls weren't just preyed on by customers. Floorwalkers, men hired to see that the clerks were properly dressed, on time and being properly deferential to the customers, lorded over them in a thousand petty ways. A fine could be levied for any transgression, real or imagined. The floorwalkers' word was beyond challenge. It wasn't uncommon of a girl to "work off" her offense to the floorwalker's satisfaction.[vii]

A "woman of the night" with a customer.

This old woodcut shows a real "hoot'n and holler'n" time on the waterfront.

Panel House Capers

The infamous "panel house" scam had several variations. In it's most simple form a prostitute brought her client into her bedroom and the pair "went at it." At the height of passion a panel on the wall noiselessly slid open and a confederate slips in and lifts the customers wallet. After pocketing the money the thief sneaks out as silently as he came. Only later does the customer discover his missing money. This variation was usually used in the vice districts proper and then only in the most disreputable houses. A good brothel wanted return business and stealing from customers was counterproductive.

The upscale version was more complicated and involved considerably greater skill. The rewards were also greater.

A house is rented in a better part of town but within an easy walk of the main street, train station and other public gathering places. The bedrooms must be so arranged that a panel can be cut through the wall and constructed to noiselessly open and shut. A small hole is drilled in the wall to allow the male accomplice to peer inside the room as well as hear. A front and back entrance to the house is also needed. One or two men will run the house while at least three but usually more women act as the bait. The women can't appear to be prostitutes but must dress and act as normal housewives although they need to be attractive but not stunning.

He can't carry her home to mother.

Even being a little bit plump is OK. Several women will be on the street but only one can use the house at the same time. Normally the women receive a third of the take as a "commission."

When all is in readiness the women start "trolling" in the main streets, train station and "good" hotels. When she finds a man who appears to be well to do and from out of town she presents the bait. She never speaks to him, but gives him a "coquettish" look and tries to entice him to follow her. If he does she leads him on down the street, looking back occasionally to encourage his pursuit. At some point he will catch her and in conversation she lets it be known she is married but her husband is out of town and she is lonely. No one is home and she has this great big house all to herself. If he will be discreet, she will take him home and they can "talk." Once he accepts, the hook is set.

The pair returns to the house. When she leads him to the bedroom a male accomplice is waiting and listening in the next room. Inside the bedroom the woman slowly disrobes, all the while talking of her reluctance and how she "never did this kind of thing before." The man also disrobes and soon the bedsprings are creak'n and the man is otherwise "distracted." At this point the accomplice comes in through the panel and lifts the man's bankroll taking care to only take part of the money, leaving enough that a casual inspection will not reveal a theft. He quietly vanishes back through the panel.

Now the real action starts. The accomplice or a second one comes stomping in the front door yelling for his wife, he's home early and where is she? The woman panics, telling her lover "Good Lord, It's my husband! I'll distract him while you go out the back door." Both quickly dress and she runs out to meet her husband. The terrified man dashes out the back door and away from the house. Score one for the crooks.

A further variation is to have the husband burst into the room with a gun and threatening the man with death, causing him to immediately

Illustration of panel house downtown.

flee in a state of absolute terror. The house is never used for long, perhaps a month or so, before the crooks move on. The women will also travel to another city to run the same scam, being replaced with a new set of fisherwomen. If the same bait is used too long, the fish catch on.

Most victims would never report the crime since they didn't want their names in the published police report in the newspaper. That said, at one point the police were still recording up to 100 complaints nightly. It was claimed there were upwards of 200 panel houses operating in the vice districts in the 1890s so such numbers are not unrealistic. The panel houses were especially effective on the hordes of tourists coming in for the 1893 Columbia Exposition.

Blackmail

There is even a more refined version of the scheme. A pretty young woman goes fishing for a middle aged married businessman of some value whose family is out of town. The crooks must do their homework to identify the right victim, a man with considerable money and social position and a family. By using her female charms she entices him to either a bedroom or sitting room. It must be a private room. Whether they "do" anything or not is immaterial. The point is the man was in the room and for the scam to work that is vital.

After a day or so a well-dressed man calls at the businessman's office and is shown in. After exchanging pleasantries the stranger produces a large envelope and pulls out a photograph of the man and the young woman in a very compromising position. The man claims the woman is his wife and he is outraged but for a substantial payment his feelings can be soothed. If he is not paid, a copy of the photograph will be given to the businessman's wife. Invariably the blackmail is successful.

In the early days, say 1900 or so, it was impossible to take an "instant" photograph. Exposure time was long and producing one inside without a powerful explosion of flash power impossible. Clearly the photographs used were doctored to show the condition of "delicate" embrace. Even if the victim realizes this, the photograph was graphic enough he couldn't explain it away to his wife so he paid the demand. The explanation of photographic trickery wouldn't convince a hysterical wife presented with irrefutable evidence of her husband's infidelity.

In later years as photography improved the same scam was worked with holes in the walls or one-way mirrors. In some instances a photographer burst into the room to catch the pair in bed. The blackmail was the same.

The scheme also worked on the wives of wealthy businessmen too. Again, good research was key. Typically during the summer season the husband stayed in the city to tend to business and his wife headed out to the stylish resorts in the east or north. A woman blackmailer follows along, keeping close tabs on her intended victim. She will pay attention to every move the wife makes, who she meets and where she goes. Often she will commit at least one "indiscretion," perhaps several. The blackmailer carefully records all of the details. When the season ends, the wife returns to her husband and the blackmailer to her male accomplice.

The male accomplice studies the details and commits them to memory then manages to meet the wife as if by chance in a public place such as an exclusive retail shop. He greets her in surprise and as a friend. When she acts as if she doesn't know him, he responds by using the name of a man she met at the resort, recalling who introduced them and where the meeting occurred. Faced with such an overwhelming amount of detail and a bit confused, she greets him as a friend. In the end he will wheedle an invitation to her home and will call when her husband is out. He may in fact return several times before springing the trap and threatening to reveal all of her "indiscretions" to her husband unless paid off. She may have done nothing at all, but will of course pay him to keep the merest hint of scandal from her door.

A Classic Shakedown

Bogus detectives sometime preyed on men with a hidden past. If they knew he had committed a crime in his youth or perhaps served a stretch in the state pen, it was a weakness to be exploited. Pay me and I will keep your terrible secret. Crooked cops were sometimes in on the same shakedown.[viii]

A Goon's Palace

If only the walls could talk. What stories of murder and mayhem would be told! How many mysteries would be solved and questions answered?

Not all crimes are prosecuted. Sometimes political influence and money prevents the administration of justice and surely this was true for Harry Bennett, Henry Ford's chief goon. In the 1930s and 40s he headed Ford's infamous "Ford Service Department" which was a fancy term for keeping the Ford plants from unionizing. Bennett made certain his crew of toughs were just the kind needed to intimidate labor, hiring criminals well experienced in bashing heads, breaking bones and perhaps fitting concrete overshoes as needed. Some folks claimed Bennett also embezzled huge amounts of money from Ford too. A crook like Bennett certainly had no scruples over a little thievery given his primary job of cracking heads and enforcing labor policy! He worked for the Company until 1945 when Henry Ford II finally managed to fire him.

While on the Ford payroll Bennett built a couple of very unusual homes. One was on Grosse Ile just north of Detroit and the other in Ann Arbor, 40 miles to the west. After obtaining the property on Grosse Ile from Henry Ford in 1939 Bennett constructed a 6,570 square foot "fortress" on it. Sitting on steel pilings in the Trenton Channel on the east side of the island and fronting the Detroit River, it resembles a bizarre cross between a Chinese pagoda and concrete pillbox. A surrounding verandah is said to have small slots cut for machine guns at each corner. While some folks deny it, given Bennett's legion of enemies, cutting well located firing holes makes perfect sense for a fellow like Bennett.

Inside the house is supposed to be a whole set of tricks, including hidden passages, stairways and slides, all manner of escape artist gimmicks. Certainly Bennett was a man who planned for every contingency. When the house was unoccupied in the 1960s several people managed to gain entrance to explore its secrets. One reported finding a slide running alongside a set of stairs enabling someone to quickly glide down unseen and unheard. A secret door in a bedroom led to the boathouse where a fast speedboat presumably was kept in readiness. An underground passage also ran from the house under West River Road surfacing in an old shed. A hidden pit in the passage was located to be unseen by a pursuer. Bennett, knowing where it was could easily jump it but anyone chasing him would not, and likely fall into it. The pit is reminiscent of an old Indiana Jones movie. The Ann Arbor house claimed to be similar in design and purpose. A third secret camp was near Clare, Michigan.

Bennett died in 1979 never having been brought to justice for his terrible deeds. Clearly he was protected by Ford influence and money.[ix]

Killer Burke

One of the most infamous inmates in Marquette Branch Prison was Frederick R. (Killer) Burke, a key gunman from the nefarious St. Valentine's Day massacre. By all accounts his time in the prison was without incident. He was content to live out his days.

Burke's real name was Thomas Camp and he was born in 1893 in Mapleton, Kansas. He had eight brothers and sisters. Considered very intelligent, he attended school and church regularly.

Somehow he "went bad" entering a life of crime. In June 1925 St. Louis Police arrested Fred and two companions with a cache of weapons consisting of a Smith and Wesson revolver, two .45 caliber automatics and a Waffenbrak Mauser .30 caliber machine gun!

Burke made his living as a traveling hit man and bank robber, a gun for hire. If the "price was right" he was the right man for the job. He also knocked over a couple of banks in Ohio with a partner. Both dressed in police uniforms, similar to the trick used in Chicago. When he wasn't on the job his friends remembered him as a friendly guy worth having a beer or two with.

After the St. Valentine's Day massacre Burke's life changed forever. Now he was on the run and tried to lay low for a while but fate intervened. While driving through St. Joseph, Michigan in December 1929 his car was hit by a Ford sedan driven by a local farmer. The two men got into an argument over the accident and when a police officer approached, Burke quickly drove off. The officer jumped on to the farmer's running board and told him "chase that car." It was scene right out a good Hollywood "B" movie. The two autos careening over country dirt roads until Burke pulled his revolver and plugged the officer. Shooting back at the officer while looking backwards over his shoulder from a speeding car was a real trick. To hit the officer with a revolver was either the mark of an expert shot or a very lucky shot. Burke was known to be very, very good so perhaps it was more skill than fortune. The policeman later died on the operating table. Clearly Burke was a better shooter than driver since he later crashed his car into a ditch and fled on foot.

When the country sheriff found the abandoned car and searched the glove box he discovered it was registered to a Fred Dane with a residence listed near town. When the sheriff raided the house Fred was long gone and his "wife" claimed to know nothing of his whereabouts. It later turned out the innocent wife was a girlfriend with a long record including a charge for murder. Although they didn't find Fred when they searched the house they found the next best thing; two Thompson submachine guns and several drums filled with ammunition. As a bonus they also found a high-powered rifle, two sawed off shotguns, several pistols, a couple of bullet proof vests and over $300,000 in stolen bank bonds. Laundry marks showed "FRB." There was no longer any doubt who they were after. The Thompsons were later traced to several murders including the St. Valentine's Day massacre.

Killer Burke stayed at large for another year as rewards climbed to $100,000. Police finally nabbed him in March 1931 in Green City, Indiana. He married a woman who had no idea who he was and lived under the alias Richard F. White. The critical tip to the police came from an amateur detective who noticed his picture in a True Detective magazine and compared it to White. Extradited to Michigan for the St. Joseph police killing he pled guilty and was sentenced to Marquette Branch Prison. He died at Marquette on July 10, 1940, never being charged with the brutal St. Valentine's massacre.[x]

END NOTES

Murder

[i]Edward Burns, *Tales of Great Lakes Lighthouses, Guiding Lights, Tragic Shadows* (Thunder Bay Press: Holt, Michigan, 2005), pp. 168-171; Andrea Gutsche and Cindy Bisaillon, *Mysterious Islands, Forgotten Tales of the Great Lakes* (Toronto: Lynx Images, 1999), pp. 162-183; Stonehouse Collection-Clapperton Island.

[ii]*Detroit Free Press*, September 10, 1871.

[iii]Marie Caroline Watson Hamlin, *Legends of Le Detroit* (Detroit: Throndike Nourse, 1884), pp. 40- 47.

[iv]William M. Morgan and the Masons; The Morgan Affair, *The Short Talk Bulletin* - Vol. XI, March, 1933 No. 3; the Morgan Affair

[v]John Tanner's Narrative and the Anishinaabeg in a Time of Change; Dave Dempsey, *On the Brink, the Great Lakes in the 21st Century* (East Lansing; Michigan State University Press, 2002) p. 40; Michigan Pioneer and Historical Collections, 22:246-254; Lansing, Michigan: Michigan Pioneer and Historical Society, 1899.

[vi]Dempsey, *On the Brink* pp. 156-159; *Detroit Free Press*, August-October 1938; *Marquette Mining Journal*, August-October 1938; Lost Cite.

[vii]Erick Larson, *The Devil in the White City* (New York: Crown, 2003); The Murder Castle of H.H. Holmes; Holmes, Sweet Holmes; Franke, David, *The Torture Doctor* (New York: Hawthorne Books, 1975).

[viii]The more proper term "interned" is too good for a bum like Dillinger.

[ix]Praire Ghosts.com, http://www.praireghosts.com/dillinger.html; Robert Cromie and Joe Pinkston, *Dillinger: a Short Violent Life*, (Chicago: Chicago Historical Bookworks, 1990); G. Russell Girardin and William J. Helmer, *Dillinger: The Untold Story*, (Evanston: Indiana University Press, 1994).

[x]*The Great Chicago Theater Disaster: The Complete Story Told by the Survivors* by Marshall Everett (1904). *Publishers Union of America Almanac*, Chicago Daily News (1905,1906); The Iroquois Theater Fire, http://www.infi-cad.com/~ksup/iroquois.html; *Chicago (Ill.). Fire Marshall. Annual Report*, 1903; Cook County (Ill.) Coroner. *Iroquois Theater Fire*, Chicago.

[xi]*Detroit Free Press*, July-August 1960; *Marquette Mining Journal*, July-August 1960.

Lynching

[i]This is intended as a joke. The NYT is certainly one of the most biased rags ever published. Of late NYT staff reporters have been caught "making up" stories! A quick "google" search will reveal a host of instances of appallingly bad journalism.

[ii]The word Sioux means "snake" or "snakelike enemy." It came from the Ojibwe, their traditional enemy. While Sioux is still in common use, it isn't a name the Dakota people use or recognize. Dakota means "friends" or "allies," and is preferable. The term "Dakota Sioux" is also incorrect. Further west, the name is Lakota or Nakota.

[iii]Death Penalty News-Michigan; Lynchings, State by State 1882-1962; Lynching at Corunna Michigan; Wisconsin Local History and Biography Articles; Minnesota Public Radio; Duluth Lynching Online; Tragedies and Triumphs in Black History; Sioux Uprising; Lost Cite; Capital Punishment in Indiana; The History of Lynching; Desperadas.Com; CattleKate-Mystery of a Lynching; Old West Female Outlaws; Justice in Colonial Upper Canada 1790-1934; Frank W. Anderson, *A Concise History of Capital Punishment in Canada* (Toronto, 1974), pp. 11-12,16, 24, 31.

The Reno Gang and the First Big Train Robbery "http://www.legendsofamerica.com/WE-RenoGang2.html"

Wisconsin State Journal, August 6, 1922; *Oconto County Reporter*, October 8, 1881; *Green Bay Advocate*, October 1, 1881; *Mankato Daily Free Press*, June 17, 1920; *Minneapolis Journal*, June 17, 1920; William Renwick Riddell, *Michigan Under British Rule, Law and Law Courts 1760-1796* (Michigan Historical Commission, 1926), pp. 28-31, 49-50, 414.: Michael Fedo, *The Lynchings in Duluth* (St. Paul, Minnesota, Minnesota Historical Society, 2000), pp. vii, 4-6, 60-61, 171-172. *Ely Miner*, June 25, 1920.

Piracy And Other Desperate Acts

[i]Kohl, Cris, *Shipwreck Tales of the Great Lakes* (West Chicago: Seawolf Communications, 2004), pp. 89-100; Walton Collection, University of Michigan; *Detroit Free Press,* August-September 1882; *Canadian Observer* (Sarnia), August-September 1882; *Port Huron Daily Times*, August-September 1882.

[ii] Johnson File – unknown; *Watertown Daily Times*, October 26, 1870.

[iii]*Oswego Palladium*, May 5, 1847.

[iv]Libby Hill, *The Chicago River: A Natural and Unnatural History* (Lake Claremont Press: Chicago, 2000), pp. 76-77.

Smuggling, An Old And Honored Activity

[i]Ralph M. Faust, *The Story of Oswego* (Ralph M. Faust: Oswego, n.d.). p. 59.

[ii]Boatnerd. http://www.boatnerd.com/news/archives/8-98.htm

[iii]*Inland Seas*, Fall 2005, p. 73.

[iv]Royal Canadian Mounted Police

[v]Mackinac Center for Public Policy – Smoke and Terrors, *Washington Post*, June 8, 2004; Mackinac Center for Public Policy, Cigarette Smuggling – Financing

[vi]*Inland Seas*, Fall 2005, p. 73.

Detroit And Environs

[i]Bootleg booze was typically cut 3-1 to begin with, a $5 bottle morphing into $15 of booze. Cutting it yet again meant not only was the customer getting damn little alcoholic kick, but also assured he would never buy from the same source again. It was strictly a desperation ploy.

[ii]Lost Cite; *Detroit Free Press*, February 1, 2006; W. Hawkins Ferry, *The buildings of Detroit: a History* (Detroit: Wayne State University Press, 1968.)

[iii]Lost Cite; Gambling Magazine Mob Stories; Court TV Crime Library, Bootleggers Paradise; *The Detroit News*, The Rearview Mirror.

[iv]*The Chronicle*, Algonac-Clay Township Historical Society, Summer 1996 - Volume 1 – Issue; Robert B. Coulter, *A Kid on the Flats* (Robert B. Coulter, 1993), pp. 46-47; Michael M. Dixon, *When Detroit Rode the Waves* (Mervue Publications, nd) pp. 133-134; The road to Catholic sainthood: one miracle at a time; Michigan's Harsens Island; Lost Cite; Harsens Island; *River Scene*, October 2005.

Chicago, Gotham Of Crime

[i]Organized Crime and Political Corruption; Encyclopedia of Chicago History, Vice Districts; Homicide in Chicago, Capital Punishment; A History of the Fair; Lost Cite; Encylopedia of Chicago History, Chicago in the Middle Ground; Chicago; Notorious Chicago; Chi-Town Spooks; Lost Cite; Weird and Haunted Chicago, St. Valentine's Day Massacre; "http://www.prairieghosts.com/valentine.html"; Find a Grave "http://www.findagrave.com/php/famous.php?page=pr&FSctf=109"; Lost Cite; Crime Magazine, The Brothers Capone; John H. Lyle, *The Dry and Lawless Years*, (Englewood Cliffs, N.J.: Prentice Hill, 1960).

Perry R. Duis, *The Saloon, Public Drinking in Chicago and Boston 1880-1920*, (Chicago: University of Illinois Press, 1993). 52-55, 63, 68-69, 232-243, 248-248, 264; Richard Lindberg, *Chicago by Gaslight, A History of Chicago's Netherworld*, 1880-1920, (Chicago: Academy Publishers, 1996), pp. 21, 111-112, 117, 130-131, 147, 168-170; The Mind of James Donahue; Frederick Lewis Allen, *It Was Only Yesterday*, (New York: Bantam Books, 1931), pp. 174-177; Homicide In Chicago, Mayor James Carter Harrison; Roe, Clifford G., *Panders and Their White Slaves*, (Chicago: Fleming H. Revell Company, 1910), pp. 29-32, 74-75, 57; Bohemian National Cemetery; Encyclopedia of Chicago; Homicide in Chicago, 1879-1930; Kenneth Allsop, *The Bootleggers and Their Era* (New York: Doubleday and Company, 1961), pp. 27, 33-36, 209-211, 228-229, 258, 272-279, 294, 303-304; Libby Hill, *The Chicago River: A Natural and Unnatural History* (Lake Claremont Press: Chicago, 2000), pp. 78-81; Robert Hendrickson, *The Grand Emporiums, the Illustrated History of America's Great Department Stores* (Stein and Day, New York, 1979), pp. 306-311, 319; Axel Madsen, *The Marshall Fields* (John Wiley and Sons, New York 2002), pp. 154-158, 171-173; William Thomas Stead; Lost Cite; The Grave Robbing Business; Dana L. Thomas, *The Money Crowd* (G.P. Putnam's Sons: New York, 1972), pp. 33-36.

[ii]Biography for Sally Rand; Encyclopedia Britannica Online; San Francisco Museum – Sally Rand; http://www.geocities.com/~limlowe/sally/sallydex.html; Sex Kitten.Net - Sally Rand; Lost Cite.

Prohibition

[i]Lyle, pp, (Englewood, N.J.: Prentice Hall, 1960) 38-45; Perry R. Duis, *The Saloon*, p. 223; John Gurda, *Making of Milwaukee,* (Milwaukee: Milwaukee County Historical Society, 1994), p. 238; Lost Cite, http://library.thinkquest.org/04Oct/0042/index.htm; Edward Dean Sullivan, *Chicago Surrenders*, (New York: Vanguard Press, 1930), pp. 40-49, 138:

Kenneth Allsop, *The Bootleggers and Their Era* (New York: Doubleday and Company), p. 317

[ii]Interview, anonymous, October 1, 2005,

[iii]Interview, former U.S. Customs agent, May 21, 2005

[iv]Shipwrecked Brew Pub, Restaurant and Inn, http://www.shipwreckedmicro-brew.com/brewery.html

[v]Wisconsin Hotels and Inns, http://www.ghosttraveller.com/wisconsin.html; Nelsen's Hall, http://www.washingtonisland.com/nelsens

[vi]Historic Orange Blossom Inn, http://www.oakmanagement.com/blossomheath-innpage.html; *Detroit Free Press*, June 12, 1986.

[vii]The Times Magazine, http://walkervilletimes.com/33/roadhouses.html, International Metropolis, RIP Chappell House, http://internationalmetropolis.com/?p=145; *Cass City Chronicle*, January 14, 1921; Meeting of the Windsor Historical Society, June 14, 2006; Fire Fighting News.Com http://www.firefightingnews.com/article.cfm?articleID=10751

The Roaring Twenties

[i]Major General J.I.H. Owen, O.B.E., *Brassey's Infantry Weapons of the World 1950-1975*. (New York: Bonanza Books, 1975), pp. 43-44.

[ii]The Sight, M1911A1; Beretta 92; http://en.wikipedia.org/wiki/Beretta_92S-1

[iii]Texas State Rifle Association; Owen, *Brassey's; pp. 73-74*

[iv]Women, Feminism and Sex in Progressive America; Peaches Browning; *Putnam County News and Recorder*, Cold Spring, Edward and Frances; 1927 Timeline

[v]Powell, Adam Clayton Jr. *Adam by Adam, the Autobiography of Clayton Powell Jr.* (New York: Kensington Books, 1971), p. 171.

Bits And Pieces Of This And That

[i]Lost Cite.

[ii]Lager Beer Riot, Encyclopedia of Chicago; John J. Flinn, *History of the Chicago Police* (Montclair, NJ: Patterson Smith, 1884).

[iii]Bernard C. Peters, "A Duel Leaves a Name on Michigan's Lake Superior Shoreline," Michigan Historical Review, (Spring 1991), 83-85.

[iv]Dictionary of Wisconsin History?; Metis Culture, 1805-1808.

[v]Bill Van Kosky, *Harlow's Wooden Man*, Fall 2005; The Iron Men, The Cuyahoga, George Merk, "The Legacy of Peter White", *Michigan History*, May-June 1999.

[vi]Interview, April 9, 2005, author with anonymous; *The Freeman,* October 26, 2006; Sullivan Woman Convicted of Running Prositution Ring; http://www.gmtoday.com/news/local_stories/2006/Oct_06/10262006_03.asp

[vii]Robert Hendrickson, *The Grand Emporiums, the Illustrated History of America's Great Department Stores* (Stein and Day, New York, 1979), pp. 244, 324-325.

[viii]Bartonville State Hospital; Clifton R. Wooldridge, *Twenty Years a Detective In the Wickedest City in the World* (Clifton R. Wooldridge, 1908), pp. 90-92, 121 -127, 256, 273-277, 349-355, 358-378;

[ix]*Detroit Free Press*, January 6, 2005; Harry Bennett

[x]Lost Cite; Ike Woods, *One Hundred Years at Hard Labor*.

BIBLIOGRAPHY

Books

Allen, Frederick Lewis. *It Was Only Yesterday*, New York: Bantam Books, 1931.

Allsop, Kenneth. *The Bootleggers and Their Era*, New York: Doubleday and Company, 1961.

Ashbury, Herbert. *Gem of the Prairie*, Dekalb, Illinois: Northern Illinois University Press, 1986.

Anderson, Frank W. *A Concise History of Capital Punishment in Canada*, Toronto, 1974.

Burns, Edward. *Tales of Great Lakes Lighthouses, Guiding Lights, Tragic Shadows*, Thunder Bay Press: Holt, Michigan, 2005.

Byrnes, Thomas. *Rouge's Gallery, 247 Professional Criminals of 19th Century America*, 1886.

Chardavoyne, David G. *A Hanging in Detroit*, Detroit: Wayne State University Press, 2003.

Coulter, Robert B. *A Kid on the Flats,* Robert B. Coulter, 1993.

Cromie, Robert and Pinkston, Joe. *Dillinger: a Short Violent Life*, Chicago: Chicago Historical Bookworks, 1990.

Dempsey, Dave. *On the Brink, The Great Lakes in the 21st Century*, East Lansing: Michigan State University Press, 2002.

Dixon, Michael M. *When Detroit Rode the Waves*, Mervue Publications, nd.

Duis, Perry R. *The Saloon, Public Drinking in Chicago and Boston 1880-1920*, Chicago: University of Illinois Press, 1993.

Engel, Howard. *Lord High Executioner, An Unashamed Look at Hangman, Herdsmen and Their Kind*, London: Robson Books, 1997.

Faust, Ralph M. *The Story of Oswego*, Ralph M. Faust: Oswego, n.d.

Ferry, W. Hawkins. *The Buildings of Detroit: a History*, Detroit: Wayne State University Press, 1968.

Flinn, John J. *History of the Chicago Police*, Montclair, NJ: Patterson Smith, 1884.

Girardin, G. Russell and Helmer, William J. *Dillinger; The Untold Story*, Evanston: Indiana University Press, 1994.

Gurda, John. *The Making of Milwaukee*, Milwaukee: Milwaukee County Historical Society, 1994.

Gutsche, Andrea and Bisaillon, Cindy. *Mysterious Islands, Forgotten Tales of the Great Lakes*, Toronto: Lynx Images, 1999.

Halliday, Hugh A. *Murder Among Gentlemen: A History of Dueling in Canada*, Toronto: Robin Bass Studio, 1999.

Hamlin, Marie Caroline Watson. *Legends of Le Detroit*, Detroit: Throndike Nourse, 1884.

Hendrickson, Robert. *The Grand Emporiums, the Illustrated History of America's Great Department Stores*, Stein and Day, New York, 1979.

Hill, Libby. *The Chicago River: A Natural and Unnatural History*, Lake Claremont Press: Chicago, 2000.

Kohl, Cris. *Shipwreck Tales of the Great Lakes*, West Chicago: Seawolf Communications, 2004.

Larson, Erick. *The Devil in the White City*, New York: Crown, 2003.

Lindberg, Richard. *Chicago by Gaslight, A History of Chicago's Netherworld, 1880-1920*, Chicago: Academy Publishers, 1996.

John H. Lyle, *The Dry and Lawless Years*, Englewood Cliffs, N.J.: Prentice Hill, 1960.

Madsen, Axel. *The Marshall Fields*, John Wiley and Sons: New York, 2002.

Mansfield, John. *History of the Great Lakes, Volume II*, Chicago: J.H. Beers and Company, 1899.

Medium, A. *Revelations of a Spirit Medium*, New York, 1871.

Owen, Major General J.I.H., O.B.E., *Brassey's Infantry Weapons of the World 1950-1975*, New York: Bonanza Books, 1975.

Pfeifer, Michael J. *Rough Justice: Lynching and American Society, 1874-1947*, Urbana: University of Illinois, 2004.

Powell Jr., Adam Clayton. *Adam by Adam, the Autobiography of Clayton Powell Jr.,* New York: Kensington Books, 1971.

Publishers Union of America Almanac, Chicago Daily News (1905,1906).

Riddell, William Renwick. *Michigan Under British Rule, Law and Law Courts 1760-1796*, Michigan Historical Commission, 1926.

Roe, Clifford G. *Panders and Their White Slaves*, (Chicago: Fleming H. Revell Company, 1910.

Steffens, Lincoln. *The Shame of the Cities*, New York: Hill and Wang, 1904.

Sullivan, Edward Dean. *Chicago Surrenders*, New York: Vanguard Press, 1930.

The Great Chicago Theater Disaster: The Complete Story Told by the Survivors, by Marshall Everett. 1904.

Thomas, Dana L. *The Money Crowd*, G.P. Putnam's Sons: New York, 1972.

Wooldridge, Clifton R. *Twenty Years a Detective in the Wickedest City in the World*, Clifton R. Wooldridge, 1908.

Wood, Ike. *One Hundred Years at Hard Labor, A History of Marquette Prison*, Marquette, 1985.

Newspapers

Cass City Chronicle, January 14, 1921

Canadian Observer (Sarnia), August-September 1882

Detroit Free Press, September 10, 1871

Detroit Free Press, August-September 1882

Detroit Free Press, August-October 1938

Detroit Free Press, July-August 1960

Detroit Free Press, June 12, 1986.

Detroit Free Press, January 6, 2005

Detroit Free Press, February 1, 2006

Ely Miner, June 25,1920

Green Bay Advocate, October 1, 1881

Mankato Daily Free Press, June 17, 1920

Marquette Mining Journal, August-October 1938

Marquette Mining Journal, July-August 1960

Milwaukee Sentinel, July 2, 1922

Minneapolis Journal, June 17, 1920

Oconto County Reporter, October 8, 1881

Oswego Palladium, May 5, 1847.

Port Huron Daily Times, August-September 1882

The Freeman, October 26, 2006

Washington Post, June 8, 2004

Watertown Daily Times, October 26, 1870.

Wisconsin State Journal, August 6, 1922

Collections

Stonehouse Collection - Clapperton Island.

Stonehouse Collection - Johnson File

Walton Collection, Bentley Historical Library, University of Michigan

Reports

Chicago (Ill.). Fire Marshall. Annual Report, 1903.

Cook County (Ill.). Coroner. *Iroquois Theater Fire*, Chicago.

Journals

Chronicle, Algonac-Clay Township Historical Society, Summer 1996, Volume 1-Issue.

Inland Seas, Fall 2005.

Peters, Bernard C. "A Duel Leaves a Name on Michigan's Lake Superior Shoreline," *Michigan Historical Review*, Spring 1991.

River Scene, October 2005.

The Lynchings in Duluth. St. Paul, Minnesota, Minnesota Historical Society, 2000.

Michigan Pioneer and Historical Collections, 22:246-254, Lansing, Michigan: Michigan Pioneer and Historical Society, 1899.

The Morgan Affair, *The Short Talk Bulletin* - Vol. XI, March, 1933 No. 3.

Van Kosky, Bill. *Harlow's Wooden Man*, Fall 2005.

Internet

1927 Timeline, "http://din-timelines.com/1927_timeline.shtml#jan"

Bartonville State Hospital "http://www.rootsweb.com/~asylums/bartonville_il/index.html"

Bellesiles, Michael. Lethal Imagination: *Violence and Brutality in American History*. New York: New York University Press, 1999.

Biography for Sally Rand "http://www.imdb.com/name/nm0709491/bio"

Boatnerd. http://www.boatnerd.com/news/archives/8-98.htm

Bohemian National Cemetery "http://www.graveyards.com/IL/Cook/bohemian/cermak.html"

Beretta 92 http://en.wikipedia.org/wiki/Beretta_92S-1

Capital Punishment in Indiana "http://www2.indystar.com/library/factfiles/crime/capital_punishment/deathrow.html"

Cattle Kate – Mystery of a Lynching "http://www.legendsofamerica.com/WE-CattleKate.html"

Chicago http://www.yourhometown.org/page15.html"

Chi-Town Spooks "http://www.wormwoodchronicles.com/lab/spooks/spooks.html"

Court TV Crime Library, Bootleggers Paradise "http://www.crimelibrary.com/gangsters_outlaws/gang/purple/1.html"

Crime Magazine, *The Brothers Capone* "http://crimemagazine.com/brothers_capone.htm"

Detroit News, The Rearview Mirror http://info.detnews.com/history/story/index.cfm?id=157&category=life"

Death Penalty News–Michigan "http://venus.soci.niu.edu/~archives/ABOLISH/rick-halperin/apr00/0180.html"

Desperadas.Com http://www.desperadas.com/index.html"

Dictionary of Wisconsin History "http://www.wisconsinhistory.org/dictionary/index.asp"

Duluth Lynching Online Resource "http://collections.mnhs.org/duluthlynchings/"

Encyclopedia of Chicago History, Homicide in Chicago 1870-1930 "http://homicide.northwestern.edu/"

Encyclopedia of Chicago History, Vice Districts "http://www.encyclopedia.chicagohistory.org/pages/1304.html"

Encylopedia of Chicago History, Chicago in the Middle Ground "http://www.encyclopedia.chicagohistory.org/pages/254.html"

Encyclopedia of Chicago http://www.encyclopedia.chicagohistory.org"

Encyclopedia Britannica Online "http://www.britannica.com/eb/article-9062649"

Find a Grave "http://www.findagrave.com/php/famous.php?page=pr&FSctf=109"

Fire Fighting News.Com "http://www.firefightingnews.com/article.cfm?articleID=10751"

Franke, David, *The Torture Doctor*, New York: Hawthorne Books, 1975.

Gambling Magazine Mob Stories "http://www.gamblingmagazine.com/articles/53/53-66.htm"

George Merk, "The Legacy of Peter White", *Michigan History*, May-June 1999 "http://www.michiganhistorymagazine.com/extra/up/pdfs/white.pdf"

Harry Bennett, "http://en.wikipedia.org/wiki/Harry_Bennett"

Harsens Island.Com "http://www.harsensisland.com"

Harsens Island "http://en.wikipedia.org/wiki/Harsens_Island"

Historic Orange Blossom Inn "http://www.oakmanagement.com/blossomheathinnpage.html"

Homicide in Chicago, Capital Punishment "http://homicide.northwestern.edu/context/legal/capital1"

Homicide In Chicago, Mayor James Carter Harrison, "http://homicide.northwestern.edu/crimes/carter/"

History of the Fair, "http://xroads.virginia.edu/~MA96/WCE/history.html"

Holmes, Sweet Holmes, "http://www.philadelphiaweekly.com/view.php?id=6365"

International Metropolis, RIP Chappell House "http://internationalmetropolis.com/?p=145"

John Tanner's Narrative and the Anishinaabeg in a Time of Change, "http://www.archives.gov/nhprc/annotation/june-2002/john-tanner-narrative.html"

Justice in Colonial Upper Canada 1790-1934, "http://www.russianbooks.org/crime/cph2.htm"

Lager Beer Riot, Encyclopedia of Chicago, "http://www.encyclopedia.chicagohistory.org/pages/703.html"

Lost Cite, "http://www.alpenacvb/fall.htm"

Lost Cite, "http://www.undelete.org/woa/woa01-02.html"

Lost Cite, "http://www.detnews.com/history/river300/0529a/o529a.htm"

Lost Cite, "http://travel.discovery.com/convergence/hauntedtravels/interactive/chicago/html"

Lost Cite, "http://members.fortunecity.com/moran9/id91.htm"

Lost Cite, "http://www.galafilm.com/1812/events/ftdearborn.html"

Lost Cite, "http://gambio.com/bio/alcapone.htm"

Lost Cite, "http://www.channel4.com/history/microsites/V/victorians/battersley_t.html"

Lost Cite "http://www.nhc.rtp.nc.us:8080/ideasv41/halttun4.htm"

Lost Cite, "http://www.mysteriesofcanada.com/Ontario/dodge.htim"

Lost Cite, "http://library.thinkquest.org/04Oct/0042/index.htm"

Lost Cite, "http://www.themediadrone.com/content/articles/history_articles/purple_gang.htm"

Lost Cite, "http://www.bartleby.com/69/HO1511.html"

Lost Cite, "http://algonac-clay-history.org/VOLIISS2.htm"

Lost Cite, "http://www.algonac-clay-history.org/VOLIISS1.htim"

Lynching at Corunna Michigan, "http://www.shiawasseehistory.com/lynch.html"

Lynchings, State by State 1882-1962, "http://www.nathanielturner.com/lynchingbystateandrace.htm"

Mackinac Center for Public Policy–Smoke and Terrors, "http://www.mackinac.org/print.asp?ID=7151"

Mackinac Center for Public Policy, Cigarette Smuggling–Financing Terrorism, "http://www.mackinac.org/print.asp?ID=4461"

Metis Culture 1805-1808, "http://www.agt.net/public/dgarneau/metis34.htm"

Meeting of the Windsor Historical Society, June 14, 2006, "http://www.citywindsor.ca/DisplayAttach.asp?AttachID=4952"

Michigan's Harsens Island, "http://www.rootsweb.com/~miharsen/"

Minnesota Public Radio, "http://news.minnesota.publicradio.org"

Nelsen's Hall, "http://www.washingtonisland.com/nelsens"

Notorious Chicago, "http://chicagology.com/notorious-chicago/"

Old West Female Outlaws, "http://www.suite101.com/lesson.cfm/19285/2824/4"

Organized Crime and Political Corruption, "http://www.ipsn.org"

Peaches Browning, "http://en.wikipedia.org/wiki/Peaches_Browning"

Praire Ghosts.com, "http://www.praireghosts.com/dillinger.html"

Putnam County News and Recorder, Cold Spring, Edward and Frances, "http://www.pcnr.com/News/Column/03-21-01_1.html;n"

Reconciliation Park, " http://www.snowbizz.com/Diogenes/NotEndora02/herewerehanged.htm"

Royal Canadian Mounted Police, "http://www.rcmpgrc.gc.ca/on/press/2004/2004_june_07_e.htm"

San Francisco Museum–Sally Rand, http://www.sfmuseum.org/bio/rand.htim

Sex Kitten.Net - Sally Rand, "http://www.sex-kitten.net/2453268105606.html"

Shipwrecked Brew Pub, Restaurant and Inn, "http://www.shipwreckedmicrobrew.com/brewery.html"

Shiawassee County Lynching, "http://www.shiwasseehistory.com/lynch.html"

Sioux Uprising, "http://en.wikipedia.org/wiki/Sioux_Uprising"

Sullivan Woman Convicted of Running Prostitution Ring, "http://www.gmtoday.com/news/local_stories/2006/Oct_06/10262006_03.asp"

Texas State Rifle Association, "http://www.tsra.com/TommyGun.htm"

The Grave Robbing Business, "http://www.crimelibrary.com/serial_killers/weird/burke/index_1.html"

The History of Lynching, "http://www.crimelibrary.com/classics2/carnival/2.htm"

The Iron Men, The Cuyahoga, "http://www.clevelandmemory.org/ellis/chap19.html"

The Iroquois Theater Fire, "http://www.inficad.com/~ksup/iroquois.html"

The Mind of James Donahue, "http://perdurabo10.tripod.com/id747.html"

The Morgan Affair, "http://freemasonry.bcy.ca/texts/morgan_affair.html"

The Murder Castle of H.H. Holmes, "http://www.prairieghosts.com/holmes.html"

The Reno Gang and the First Big Train Robbery, "http://www.legendsofamerica.com/WE-RenoGang2.html"

The road to Catholic sainthood: one miracle at a time, "http://www.cbc.ca/news/background/catholicism/sainthood.html"

The Sight, M1911A1, "http://www.sightm1911.com/Care/45acp.htm"

The Times Magazine, "http://walkervilletimes.com/33/roadhouses.html"

Tragedies and Triumphs in Black History, "http://whchurch.org/content/page_282.htm"

Weird and Haunted Chicago, St. Valentine's Day Massacre, "http://www.prairieghosts.com/valentine.html"

William Thomas Stead, "http://en.wikipeida.org/wiki/William_Thomas_Snead"

William M. Morgan and the Masons, "http://en.wikipdia.org/wiki/William_M._Morgan"

Wisconsin Hotels and Inns, "http://www.ghosttraveller.com/wisconsin.htm#hotels"

Wisconsin Local History and Biography Articles, "http://www.wisconsinhistory.org/wlhba/articleView.asp?pg=2&order"

Women, Feminism and Sex in Progressive America, "http://polyglot.lss.wisc.edu/hist102/lectur14/lectur14.html"

Interviews

Interview, anonymous April 9, 2005.

Interview, anonymous, October 1, 2005.

Interview, former U.S. Customs agent, May 21, 2005.

ABOUT THE AUTHOR

Frederick Stonehouse holds a Master of Arts Degree in History from Northern Michigan University, Marquette, Michigan, and has authored many books on Great Lakes maritime history and is the 2006 recipient of the Association for Great Lakes Maritime History Award for Historic Interpretation. *Steel On The Bottom, Great Lakes Shipwrecks, Great Lakes Crime, Murder, Mayhem, Booze & Broads, Lake Superior's "Shipwreck Coast," Dangerous Coast: Pictured Rocks Shipwrecks, The Wreck Of The Edmund Fitzgerald, Great Lakes Lighthouse Tales, Women And The Lakes, Untold Great Lakes Maritime Tales, Women And The Lakes II, More Untold Great Lakes Maritime Tales, Final Passage, True Shipwreck Adventures, My Summer At The Lighthouse, A Boy's Journal* and *Cooking Lighthouse Style, Favorite Recipes From Coast To Coast* are all published by Avery Color Studios, Inc.

He has also been a consultant for both the U.S. National Park Service and Parks Canada, and an "on air" expert for National Geographic Explorer and the History Channel as well as many regional media productions. He has taught Great Lakes Maritime History at Northern Michigan University and is an active consultant for numerous Great Lakes oriented projects and programs. Check www.frederickstonehouse.com for more details.

His articles have been published in numerous publications including *Skin Diver, Great Lakes Cruiser Magazine* and *Lake Superior Magazine*. He is a member of the Board of Directors of the Marquette Maritime Museum and a member of the Board of Directors of the United States Life Saving Service Heritage Association.

Stonehouse resides in Marquette, Michigan.